INTERNATIONAL DEVELOPMENT IN FOCUS

Rising from the Depths

Water Security and Fragility in South Sudan

EDOARDO BORGOMEO, CLAIRE CHASE, NICOLAS SALAZAR GODOY,
AND VICTOR OSEI KWADWO

WORLD BANK GROUP

Contents

Maps

Tables

Acknowledgments

This publication received the support of the Global Water Security and Sanitation Partnership (GWSP). GWSP is a multidonor trust fund administered by the World Bank's Water Global Practice and supported by Australia's Department of Foreign Affairs and Trade, Austria's Federal Ministry of Finance, the Bill & Melinda Gates Foundation, Denmark's Ministry of Foreign Affairs, the Netherlands' Ministry of Foreign Affairs, Spain's Ministry of Economic Affairs and Digital Transformation, the Swedish International Development Cooperation Agency, Switzerland's State Secretariat for Economic Affairs, the Swiss Agency for Development and Cooperation, and the U.S. Agency for International Development.

The report is the result of close cooperation between the government of South Sudan and the World Bank.

The team would like to express its sincere appreciation to the late Minister of Water Resources and Irrigation, Hon. Manawa Peter Gatkuoth.

The contributions and guidance of the Hon. Minister of Water Resources and Irrigation, Pal Mai Deng; the Hon. Undersecretary of the Ministry of Water Resources and Irrigation (MWRI), Emmanuel Parmenas; the Hon. Managing Director of the South Sudan Urban Water Corporation (SSUWC), Yar Paul Kuol; the Hon. Undersecretary of the Ministry of Environment and Forestry, Joseph Africano Bartel; the Hon. Deputy Governor, Nyok Kucha; the Hon. State Adviser and Chairperson for the Jonglei State Disaster Management Committee, Diing Akol; and the Hon. Minister for Physical Infrastructure, Elijah Mabior, are gratefully acknowledged.

The report was commissioned by Ousmane Dione, World Bank Country Director for Ethiopia, Eritrea, Sudan, and South Sudan, whose guidance is gratefully acknowledged. Firas Raad (Country Manager), Maria Angelica Sotomayor (Practice Manager), Soma Ghosh Moulik (Practice Manager), and David Malcolm Lord (Sector Leader) provided support and guidance throughout preparation of the report. Early guidance from Erwin De Nys (Practice Manager) is gratefully acknowledged.

The support and guidance of directors at the MWRI and SSUWC are gratefully acknowledged: Thomas Jang Kan (Director, water resources management, MWRI), Andrew Yunda (Director, programs and planning, MWRI), Peter Mahal Dhieu Akat (Director, rural water supply and sanitation, MWRI), Koboji Charles

Yakata (Acting Director, hydrology and survey, MWRI), Makuac Ador (Director, MWRI), Robert Zakayo (Hydrologist, MWRI), Simon K. Kuay (Director General, administration and finance, SSUWC), Osama Mahdi (Director General, planning, SSUWC), and Jacob Kuot Daniel (Area Manager, SSUWC).

The report benefited from guidance provided by peer reviewers Anders Jagerskog, Xiaokai Li, Lukas Loeschner, and Melissa Williams.

The following World Bank colleagues provided feedback and advice: Daniel Balke, Eileen Burke, Dominick de Waal, Zewditu Banteyehun Haile, Tracy Hart, Droma Bank Dominic Kat, Stephen Ling, Eric Nimungu, Juvenal Nzambimana, Diego Rodriguez, Antonio Rodriguez Serrano, Susanna Smets, Habab Taifour, Yukio Tanaka, Pieter Waalewijn, Makiko Watanabe, and Ximing Zhang. The report also benefited from the support provided by Joyce Gamba and Florence Poni.

During the consultations for the study, invaluable contributions were received from a range of international organizations and partners: Richard Aludra (Embassy of the Kingdom of the Netherlands to South Sudan), Ekarem Bassey (United Nations Office for Project Services [UNOPS]), Mitu David (South Sudan Red Cross), Julius Egbeyemi (Embassy of Canada), Johan Gély (Swiss Agency for Development and Cooperation), Younes Hassib (German Agency for International Cooperation GmbH [GIZ]), Dara Johnston (United Nations Children's Fund), Amuda Joseph (United States Agency for International Development), James Kai (GIZ), Maria Kiani (United Nations High Commissioner for Refugees), Aleksandra Krajczynska (World Food Programme [WFP]), Brimo Majok (Norwegian Refugee Council), Tafadzwa Makata (WFP), Harald Mannhardt (WFP), Leslie Mhara (UNOPS), William Muchira (UNOPS), Peter Mutoredzanwa (UNOPS), William Nall (WFP), Nick Rowe (International Committee of the Red Cross), Johannes Rumohr (GIZ), Taban Sabir (South Sudan Red Cross), Michiel Smet (Embassy of the Kingdom of the Netherlands to South Sudan), Papa Moussa Tall (International Federation of Red Cross and Red Crescent Societies), David Thomas (WFP), Muhammad Asar Ul Haq (International Organization for Migration), and Thiago Xavier (WFP).

The report draws from three commissioned background papers:

- Rift Valley Institute. 2022. "Fragility and Water Security in South Sudan." Study conducted for the World Bank by the Rift Valley Institute in collaboration with the Centre for Humanitarian Change. Background paper prepared for this report. Rift Valley Institute, Juba.
- Salazar Godoy, Nicolas. 2022. "Forced Displacement and Water Security in South Sudan." Unpublished background paper prepared for this report. World Bank, Washington, DC.
- Osei Kwadwo, Victor. 2022. "South Sudan: Policies, Institutions and Regulations in the Water Sector." Unpublished background paper prepared for this report. World Bank, Washington, DC.

The team gratefully acknowledges input from Amjad Muhammad Khan (Economist, World Bank), who contributed to the empirical analysis of drought and conflict; Mansoor Leh and Petra Schmitter of the International Water Management Institute, who contributed to the solar irrigation potential analysis; and Ahmad Shah Durrani, who contributed to the section on gender.

The work was led by Edoardo Borgomeo and Claire Chase, with Nicolas Salazar Godoy, Jacob Manyuon Deng, Gabriel Levin, Andres Fernando Chamorro Elizondo, Victor Osei Kwadwo, Stephen Shisoka Okiya, and Benny Istanto. The Rift Valley Institute team was led by Nancy Balfour and comprised Machot Amuom, Emmanuel Luga, Anna Rowett, and Anna Sebet.

The report was copyedited by Sherrie M. Brown and maps were redrawn by Marlee Beers.

Main Messages

WATER IN SOUTH SUDAN: MENACE WITH HOPE

South Sudan is the world's most vulnerable country to climate change and also the one most lacking in coping capacity.[1] Most of the harm from climate change will come in the form of water: increased frequency of droughts and floods, changes in flow patterns in rivers, lower water quality, and impacts on groundwater availability. The South Sudanese have long dealt with these water-related risks, but today's situation is different for two reasons. First, decades of conflict and insecurity have undermined communities' ability to cope with water-related risks. Second, climate change is tremendously increasing the destructive potential of these risks. If unmanaged, these risks will lead to worsening impacts on food security; the movement of people; and the security of communities, ecosystems, and the economy. But therein lies opportunity: through improvements in water management, South Sudan can improve the lives and livelihoods of communities and better prepare for climate change.

This overview summarizes *Rising from the Depths: Water Security and Fragility in South Sudan*, a World Bank report exploring opportunities and trade-offs for aligning South Sudan's water investments and policies with its commitment to peace and stability. The report elevates water security as an issue critical for national development and stability, not just a humanitarian need. Focusing on water security for people, production, and protection, it shows that water insecurity is indeed an existential threat to South Sudan. South Sudan is a global hotspot for flood risk: it ranks seventh in the world for share of total country population exposed to river floods. The dramatic flood events of 2019, 2020, 2021, and 2022 are stark reminders of this extremely high exposure to flood hazards. Floods in 2021 affected between 800,000 and 1.2 million people, displaced more than 300,000 people, and caused economic damage of at least US$671 million.[2]

Although flood risks are capturing headlines, they are just one of the many threats from water insecurity. Lack of access to safe water supply and sanitation is a core concern for the dignity and well-being of millions of South Sudanese, with more than 60 percent of the population (about 6.6 million people) using unimproved sources, such as surface water and unprotected wells, and 75 percent

(8.2 million people) practicing open defecation. South Sudan also experiences frequent droughts, especially in the southeast and northeast, which affect the mobility of pastoralists and farmers who rely on natural resources for their livelihoods. Moreover, lack of reliable irrigation and drainage, along with human-induced soil erosion, contribute to low agricultural productivity. Women and girls tend to be disproportionately affected by these water-related threats.

However, the story of water in South Sudan is also a story of opportunity. The report shows that South Sudan can harness the ubiquity of water as a tool for advancing national development and stability. Seasonal flooding sustains the livelihoods of at least 6 million people who live along the Nile and Sobat Rivers and the wide eastern and western floodplains. In the country's agricultural areas, especially in the Equatoria region, increased water availability during the main crop-growing seasons through irrigation and improved land and water management can enhance yields and bolster food production. Interventions in water supply and sanitation reduce public health risks and the incidence of neglected tropical diseases and improve the personal safety of women and girls, thereby promoting school attendance, among other benefits.

FIVE PRIORITIES FOR HARNESSING WATER FOR PEACE AND DEVELOPMENT

How can South Sudan harness water's potential to sustain development and stability? Five priorities include the following:

1. *Strengthen nascent policy and institutional frameworks to guide water sector investments and ensure their sustainability.* This task includes empowering and building the capacity of the sector's human resources, undertaking technical consultations to revise and update the 2013 Water Bill and achieve its ratification, and developing a water resources master plan.

2. *Address the water supply and sanitation crisis.* It will be necessary to strengthen service delivery models for rural households, sustainable use and management of groundwater resources, and promotion of climate-resilient solutions. Continued collaboration with international partners will be essential to delivering much-needed water services.

3. *Advance disaster risk preparedness and early warning.* Responding to floods and droughts is a matter not just of building infrastructure but also of preventing populations from moving into harm's way and of devising information systems and institutional arrangements to increase preparedness and early warning. In the short term, the expansion of hydrometeorological services, the development of early warning systems, and the delineation of flood-prone areas are key to reducing losses from floods and droughts.

4. *Harness water's productive potential and ecosystem services.* This priority area includes enhancing flood-based livelihoods with investments supporting domestic fish production, wetland restoration, and flood-recession agriculture.

5. *Use a portfolio of infrastructure options to manage water resources.* Although large-scale river engineering might contribute to improving water security, the absence of sector frameworks, required feasibility assessments, and

capacity for strategic planning and infrastructure management means that these projects are unlikely to deliver the expected outcomes and could have unintended consequences. Hence, in the short term, policy makers should prefer community-level water storage and flood control alternatives that can be built over shorter time horizons and with less harmful environmental and social externalities.

THE WAY AHEAD

In the long term, a more ambitious program of policies and investments is required, including strategic investments in urban water systems and water storage. The identification, design, and implementation of these investments should be guided by comprehensive feasibility assessments that take into account their impact on the rich biodiversity and complex social and conflict dynamics of South Sudan. Although infrastructure will be needed, it will not be sufficient. Water security is achieved not solely by trying to control water and diverting its flow but also by focusing on (a) increasing community preparedness and delineating areas for water, leaving "room for the river," and (b) making productive use of the water for household consumption, livelihoods, and development. This approach is followed across the world in flood-prone areas such as Bangladesh, Japan, and the Netherlands, where planners work with—rather than against—the floodwaters and complement every investment with institutional measures to involve all levels of government: national, provincial, and local.

Finally, policies and investments needed to achieve water security involve uncertainty, making commitment to an iterative planning approach crucial. Countries that successfully manage water risks do so by implementing water policies, carefully monitoring their impacts and results, and learning from their successes and failures. A water-secure future—one that harnesses the productive potential of water while managing its destructive force—can be achieved by putting in place the levers and tools needed to adapt this complex system to a dynamically changing world.

NOTES

1. International Monetary Fund Climate-driven INFORM Risk, 2022 (https://climatedata .imf.org/pages/fi-indicators).
2. GRADE Note on May–October 2021 South Sudan Floods (unpublished World Bank report).

Executive Summary

OVERVIEW

Extreme floods in 2020, 2021, and 2022 are a stark reminder of South Sudan's vulnerability to the destructive force of water. These disasters compounded an already challenging situation characterized by a protracted humanitarian and forced displacement crisis, unprecedented levels of food insecurity, widespread violence, and fragile institutions. Although water's destructive force can compound existing fragilities, its productive potential can also enable stability and development. As South Sudan works to consolidate peace and to stabilize the economy, water management and policy are key instruments with which to support the country's efforts toward recovery and to strengthen community resilience.

This report identifies constraints and opportunities to leverage water sector interventions to strengthen resilience to conflict, climate, and disease shocks. It seeks to elevate water security as an issue critical for national development and stability, not just a humanitarian need. Through geospatial and econometric methods; policy, institutional, and regulatory assessments; expert interviews; and focus group discussions, the report describes the importance of water security for sustaining livelihoods and ecosystems and for advancing human development and inclusion in South Sudan. The report considers key challenges and opportunities relating to water security in three dimensions: people, production, and protection (table ES.1). The first two dimensions relate to water management for harnessing water's productive potential for human well-being, livelihoods, and ecosystems; the third aspect relates to management of water to protect societies, economies, and ecosystems from the destructive impacts of water such as water-borne disease, floods, and droughts. The report also analyzes the relationship between these three core dimensions of water security and broader human and social development outcomes for communities and society. In particular, the report focuses on the intersection of water security with four outcome areas: health and nutrition, forced displacement, gender, and conflict.

TABLE ES.1 **Key water security aspects and related facts for South Sudan**

WATER SECURITY ASPECT	FACTS
Water security for people	• Nationally, just 10 percent of households have access to sanitation and 75 percent practice open defecation. • Close to 15 percent of households without improved drinking water in the dry season travel more than two hours roundtrip to access water. • An estimated 33 percent of schools have no drinking water service and 21 percent have no sanitation.
Water security for production	• Seasonal flooding sustains livelihoods for about 6 million people who live along the Nile and Sobat Rivers and the wider eastern and western floodplains. • Out of a total agricultural land area of about 28.5 million hectares, as much as 24 million hectares are suitable for irrigated agriculture. • South Sudan has some of Sub-Saharan Africa's highest solar irrigation adoption potential: the suitable area for solar-based irrigation is about 6–10 million hectares using groundwater and 1–3 million hectares using surface water.
Water security for protection	• South Sudan is a global hotspot for flood risk: it ranks seventh in the world for share of total country population exposed to river floods. • One in two South Sudanese—about 5.4 million people—live in areas exposed to moderate flood hazard (areas where water depths of a 1-in-100-year flood event reach or exceed 0.15 meters). • One in four South Sudanese—about 2.7 million people—live in areas exposed to high and potentially deadly flood hazard (areas where water depths of a 1-in-100-year flood event reach or exceed 0.5 meters). • Droughts are very frequent in the south and northeast; under climate change, droughts are projected to become 60–100 percent more frequent by the end of the century compared with the 2020s.

Source: World Bank.

WATER SECURITY FOR PEOPLE, PRODUCTION, AND PROTECTION

Water security for people

Access to drinking water supply is a core challenge, with more than 60 percent of South Sudan's population using unimproved sources, such as unprotected wells and river water. Even at these levels, access to basic water supply further declines during the rainy season because floodwaters submerge water sources and make water points inaccessible. Access to drinking water supply and sanitation services is characterized by a large urban-rural divide, with the bulk of improvements reported for urban areas failing to reach most South Sudanese since 2011. In urban areas, access to at least basic drinking water sources has improved in the past decade, increasing from 52 percent in 2011 to 70 percent in 2020, while in rural areas, access to at least basic drinking water supplies declined by 5 percentage points, from 38 percent in 2011 to 33 percent in 2020.

Nationally, just 10 percent of households have access to sanitation and 75 percent practice open defecation. Although recent data suggest that modest improvements were made on increasing access to basic drinking water in urban areas, fewer households have access to sanitation than before the conflict that started in 2013. In South Sudan, the rates of open defecation are substantially higher and access to at least basic sanitation is substantially lower than in other countries in Sub-Saharan Africa.

Water security for production

Availability and variability of water resources play a key role supporting productive and resilient livelihoods and ecosystems in South Sudan. Seasonal flooding sustains livelihoods for about 6 million people who live along the Nile and Sobat Rivers and the wide eastern and western floodplains. These populations and their livelihoods depend heavily on the country's natural capital, notably the iconic Sudd wetland, whose economic value for livelihoods alone has been estimated to be more than US$250 million (NBI 2020). The total economic value of the multiple services from the wetland is estimated to be at least US$3.2 billion (NBI 2020). Although new and emerging livelihoods—such as artisanal mining, charcoal production, and brickmaking—support income generation, they also contribute to deforestation and land degradation, undermining natural capital and exacerbating vulnerability to droughts and floods.

The potential for water infrastructure to support livelihoods remains unexploited. There are no large dams or reservoirs in South Sudan with storage capacity greater than 0.1 cubic kilometers, and most water storage structures are community based. Water storage is limited to roadside dugout pits, rock catchments, water barriers, and *haffir* (pond in Arabic). Many of the most recently constructed haffir are reported to be nonfunctional because of inadequate site selection, design, and maintenance. South Sudan's irrigation potential remains largely untapped: irrigated agriculture currently makes up less than 5 percent of the total area under cultivation. Although innovations in irrigation service provision—including farmer-led irrigation development and small-scale solar-powered irrigation systems—offer potential opportunity, careful assessments and strategies are required to prioritize rehabilitation and expansion.

Water security for protection

Droughts and floods are the most obvious manifestations of South Sudan's highly variable and unpredictable freshwater resources. Their frequency and intensity are influenced by interactions between climate patterns occurring at local and global scales and that are intensifying under climate change. South Sudan is a global hotspot for flood risk: it ranks seventh in the world for share of total country population exposed to river floods. The dramatic flood events of 2019, 2020, and 2021 are stark reminders of this extremely high exposure to flood hazards. South Sudan faces flood hazards from both fluvial and pluvial sources. Fluvial sources dominate in the central and eastern parts of the country, where the largest rivers are located. These floods are directly linked to rainfall patterns in the African Great Lakes region, where the Bahr el Jebel (White Nile) originates, and in the Ethiopian highlands, where the Sobat River originates. Pluvial sources dominate in the southwest, where the steeper topography and the lack of large water bodies mean that most surface water floods occur after heavy rainfall events rather than from the overflow of water bodies.

Hydrological variability also means that South Sudan is at risk from droughts. The southeastern and northeastern parts of the country experience more frequent droughts compared with other parts of the country. In these areas, droughts can affect the mobility options of pastoralists and others who rely on natural resources for their livelihoods, bringing them into competition with neighboring communities and increasing the risk of cattle raids. As temperatures increase because of climate change, the frequency and intensity of droughts are projected to increase. These increasing temperatures will amplify the impact of drought, given that warming typically leads to increased evaporation and further reductions in the availability of water.

LINKS WITH HUMAN DEVELOPMENT AND STABILITY

To examine the far-reaching implications of water insecurity in South Sudan, the report illustrates links with key human development, inclusion, and fragility features. Given the country context, characterized by dire human development needs and fragile sociopolitical systems, this intersection analysis sheds light on the links with four key aspects: health and nutrition, forced displacement, gender, and conflict.

Health and nutrition

Low levels of access to water supply, sanitation, and hygiene (WASH) severely undermine health and nutrition outcomes in South Sudan. WASH-related neglected tropical diseases are widespread across the country, and the persistence of the underlying factors that intensified successive cholera outbreaks in South Sudan between 2014 and 2017 puts the country at high risk for a resurgence of the disease. In addition, lower respiratory tract infections and diarrheal disease are the second- and third-largest causes of death in South Sudan, with poor WASH being the second leading risk factor for all death and disability combined. Conflict dynamics, population movement, and climate change all influence the emergence and dispersal of many infectious disease pathogens, and the risks are exacerbated by lack of access to water supply and sanitation services, and poor-quality health services.

Forced displacement

South Sudan is the dominant source of refugees in Sub-Saharan Africa and hosts one of the world's largest internally displaced populations. Floods trigger temporary or more permanent population displacement, with forcibly displaced populations often having to settle in flood-prone areas because of insecurity. Forcibly displaced populations face heightened water challenges, with forcibly displaced women and girls experiencing distinctive WASH-linked needs and risks at different phases of the displacement cycle. If unattended, such needs and risks can increase their vulnerability to gender-based and intimate partner violence and contribute to deepening gender inequalities. The provision of clean drinking water in areas of return or local integration is one of the Six Priority Areas under the 2021 South Sudan Durable Solutions Strategy. Without water and water services, durable solutions cannot materialize.

Gender

South Sudan is one of the most unequal societies in the world along gender lines, which affects women's and girls' ability to cope with and adapt to water insecurity. Although women take part in water management committees, their active participation is low, and key decisions about siting water points and allocation of water resources are made by men. There are also large differentials between women and men with regard to access to water and ability to cope with natural disasters. Women and girls often walk long distances to access water, which increases the risk of sexual and gender-based violence, especially when water points are constructed without their prior involvement and consultation. Women play a predominant role in farming, providing 80 percent of farm labor in the country, making them more vulnerable to floods and droughts than men, who have control and access to "movable" livestock assets. Finally, the relationship between water and gender is influenced by social norms and belief systems. Personal stories collected as part of focus group discussions show that women carry much of the responsibility for ensuring households' water supplies but are excluded from decision-making. Because of social norms, water-related decisions are the responsibility of men: they "own" households' productive assets (livestock), which grants them the authority to make decisions with respect to water.

Conflict

Quantitative and qualitative assessments demonstrate important interactions between water availability and the occurrence of violence. The report's empirical analysis of drought and conflict data suggests that more severe drought is associated with higher levels of violence. This evidence can be explained by considering drought's potential to disrupt two key components of South Sudanese livelihoods: cattle and mobility. Drought disrupts livestock grazing activities by limiting land and water resources available for rearing. In turn, this disruption can induce tensions as herders try to access limited supplies of these resources. In addition, drought impacts mobility patterns. Pastoralist routes adapt to the changing availability of water and groups move closer together in areas with remaining water and pasture. By moving away from customary mobility routes, pastoralists are more likely to end up closer to groups from other areas, with which they might lack shared customary institutions and mechanisms for settling disputes. Too much water can also be associated with violence. When water is overly abundant, pastoralists may not always follow negotiated access and customary institutions for accessing water resources and land. In turn, this means that they might move closer to other groups, inciting competition over shared resources or making them more vulnerable to cattle raiding. Despite these links between water and conflict, it is important to emphasize that droughts or floods rarely if ever explain the occurrence of conflict and violence. Community vulnerability to water-conflict issues differs widely and is mediated by political and social factors, including (a) small arms proliferation among civilians, (b) government interventions restricting mobility, and (c) elite exploitation of local grievances and tensions over water to inflict damage on opponents. Beyond influencing violence and conflict dynamics, water is often a weapon and casualty of conflict in South Sudan: warring parties systematically destroyed or stole pumps used by communities, depriving them of access to water.

THE NEED FOR STRONGER INSTITUTIONS IN THE TRANSITION FROM HUMANITARIAN MODALITIES OF WATER MANAGEMENT TO A LONG-TERM AND GOVERNMENT-LED DEVELOPMENT APPROACH

This report identifies five key priorities and related recommendations to improve water security and gradually make the transition to a government-led and long-term approach to water management. Three priorities are linked to the three dimensions of water security examined in the report (people, production, and protection), while two are cross-cutting priorities and related recommendations aimed at advancing water security across multiple dimensions. Action on some of the recommendations should begin immediately because of the urgency of the challenges they address and because of their low to moderate technical, social, and environmental complexity. More complex recommendations should be pursued in the medium to long term once core water institutions infrastructure have been put in place (figure ES 1). Chapter 5 provides a more detailed breakdown of recommendations under each priority area, including a mapping of relevant stakeholders and potential sites.

Priority 1: Water security for people

Low coverage of water supply and sanitation services contributes to low levels of human capital attainment through its effects on nutrition, health, and educational outcomes. Access to water supply and sanitation is a daily struggle for millions of South Sudanese. Although the coverage of drinking water supply services in urban areas has improved, service levels in rural areas have declined since 2013. Overall, fewer households have access to sanitation than before the conflict

FIGURE ES.1

Sequencing priorities for water policy and investment in South Sudan

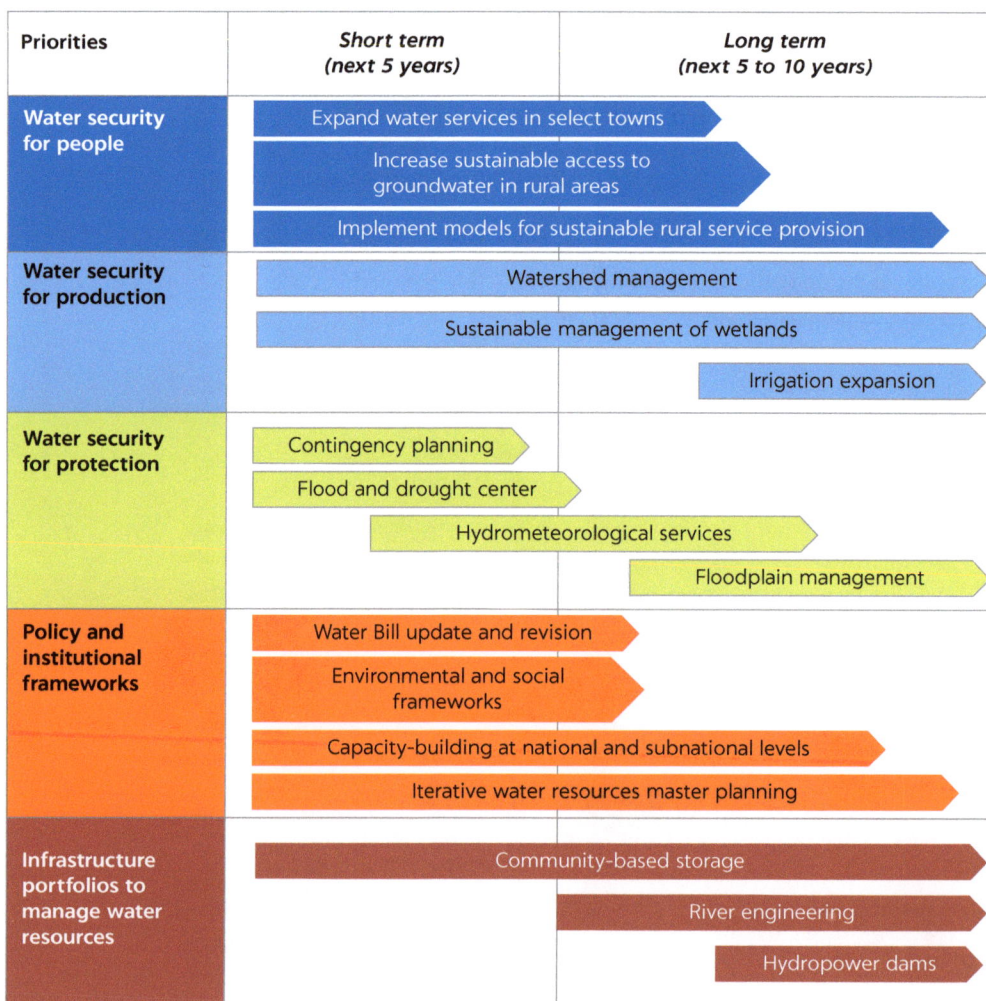

Source: World Bank.

period. To address the water supply and sanitation crisis in the short term, the government needs to continue working with international partners to deliver much-needed water services, including the following recommendations:

- Recommendation (R) 1.1 Increase central coordination and oversight of water supply and sanitation interventions.
- R 1.2 Increase sustainable access and management of groundwater resources in small towns and rural areas.
- R 1.3 Expand coverage of water supply and sanitation services in rural areas.
- R 1.4 Design any urban and rural services (infrastructure design and operating and maintenance practices) around preferences and priorities of water users (in particular, women and girls) and consolidate lessons into revised WASH guidelines to incorporate climate resilience and social inclusion considerations.
- R 1.5 Define institutional accountability and mandates for water service provision across urban and rural areas.
- R 1.6 Increase capacity, extend distribution networks, and improve service delivery performance of water and sanitation infrastructure in selected cities.

Priority 2: Water security for production

Although water resources engender significant risks, they also provide benefits for people and the economy. Receding and rising floodwaters are a key enabler of livelihoods in South Sudan, and water is highly valued in pastoralist communities. The country's natural capital provides a range of ecosystem services, supporting livelihoods, regulating water flows, and providing habitats for biodiversity. Furthermore, the potential for irrigation to bolster food production remains untapped. To harness water's productive potential for food and ecosystems, the report identifies these recommendations:

- R 2.1 Sustain flood-based livelihoods with investments supporting domestic fish production and preservation, rice production, and flood-recession agriculture.
- R 2.2 Update the irrigation master plan to include identification of areas suitable for farmer-led irrigation initiatives.
- R 2.3 Rehabilitate and expand irrigation and drainage infrastructure.
- R 2.4 Promote watershed management activities.

Priority 3: Water security for protection

Coping with droughts and floods presents a profound challenge to climate adaptation and development in South Sudan; however, the country's disaster risk preparedness and early warning systems remain largely inadequate. Responding to floods and droughts is not just a matter of building infrastructure, but also of preventing populations from moving into harm's way and of devising information systems and institutional arrangements to increase preparedness and early warning. Floodplain management, including delineation of flood-prone areas, and managed retreat away from areas that are frequently affected by floods are alternatives to structural protection that also have to be pursued to prepare for water-related disasters. Responding to floods and droughts is also a matter of transboundary cooperation: the regional nature of floods and droughts requires coordinated efforts in forecasting and early warning and in infrastructure

xx | RISING FROM THE DEPTHS

planning and operation. Specific recommendations under this priority area include the following:

- R 3.1 Repair and upgrade existing hydrometric stations.
- R 3.2 Build national and subnational capacity to prepare for and respond to floods and droughts.
- R 3.3 Expand hydrometric network and establish a hydrometeorological telemetry system, including for water quality and groundwater monitoring.
- R 3.4 Build knowledge base to advance flood risk management, including constructing topographic maps and defining technical standards for flood protection infrastructure.
- R 3.5 Develop minimum standards and principles to evaluate options for a contextualized, conflict-sensitive approach when resettling populations currently living in highly flood-prone areas.
- R 3.6 Develop a hydrological assessment of the Sudd wetland.
- R 3.7 Strengthen information exchange with Nile riparians on floods and droughts.

Priority 4: Policy and institutional frameworks

Water governance is weak and institutional mandates are overlapping. Policy intentions from the first Southern Sudan Water Policy of 2007 have yet to be translated into legislation, and the 2013 Water Bill has not been ratified. Addressing these constraints is essential so that the transition from humanitarian to government-led water management can begin, and involves the following recommendations:

- R 4.1 Undertake technical consultations to revise and update the 2013 Water Bill and achieve its ratification, including through engagement of subnational entities and humanitarian and development partners.
- R 4.2 Develop a capacity-building plan with targets for professionals and staff at national and subnational levels; enhance technical and professional education and training.
- R 4.3 Undertake technical consultations to lay the groundwork for the development of an environmental and social framework for water sector interventions.
- R 4.4 Develop a water resources master plan, comprising (a) formulation of a nationwide investment plan to enhance water's contribution to economic growth and employment and (b) a monitoring plan to track impacts and results and adaptively update the plan.

Priority 5: Infrastructure portfolios to manage water resources

In his PhD thesis, Dr. John Garang de Mabior identified the economic potential of investments to manage the country's water resources and natural capital (Garang de Mabior, 1981). However, he also raised concerns about the potential for such large activities to engender a range of unintended consequences, including social inequality and tensions, if not properly planned and implemented. As proposals for large river engineering works return to South Sudan, policy makers are advised to prefer more agile and easy to implement infrastructure options over the short term while they identify the large-scale investments needed to provide long-term responses to the country's water insecurity. Over the long term, more significant investments in water storage are likely to be required, and should be guided by comprehensive feasibility assessments, including of their impact on social and conflict dynamics. The following recommendations apply:

- R 5.1 Conduct an inventory of existing flood embankments and related status.
- R 5.2 Conduct an inventory of existing water storage structures (haffir) and related status.
- R 5.3 Rehabilitate and reinforce selected existing embankments.
- R 5.4 Rehabilitate and expand community-based water storage structures.
- R 5.5 Construct flood control and water storage structures integrating green and gray solutions.

THE WAY AHEAD: SEQUENCING AND MONITORING WATER POLICY AND INVESTMENT

Over the long term, an ambitious program of policies and investments is required, including strategic investments in urban water systems and water storage. The identification, design, and implementation of these investments should be guided by comprehensive feasibility assessments that include their impact on the rich biodiversity and complex social and conflict dynamics of South Sudan. Although infrastructure will be needed, it will not be enough. Water security is achieved not by trying solely to control water and diverting its flow, but by also focusing on (a) increasing community preparedness and delineating areas for water, leaving "room for the river," and (b) making productive use of the water for household consumption, livelihoods, and development. This approach is followed across the world in flood-prone areas such as Bangladesh, Japan, and the Netherlands, where planners work with—rather than against—the floodwaters and complement every investment with institutional measures that involve all levels of government: national, provincial, and local.

This ambitious water policy and investment program will involve uncertainty, making a commitment to an iterative planning approach crucial. Uncertainty arises from political developments, insecurity, and climate change, among other factors. Careful monitoring and evaluation are needed to detect and manage expected and unexpected negative effects arising from these uncertainties and to adjust policies over time. To successfully manage water risks, South Sudan should implement water policies, carefully monitor their impacts and results, and learn from their successes and failures. A water secure future, one that harnesses the productive potential of water while managing its destructive force, can be achieved by putting in place the levers and tools needed to adapt this complex system to a changing world.

REFERENCES

Garang de Mabior, J. 1981. "Identifying, Selecting, and Implementing Rural Development Strategies for Socio-Economic Development in the Jonglei Projects Area, Southern Region, Sudan." PhD thesis, Iowa State University, Ames, IA.

NBI (Nile Basin Initiative). 2020. "Sudd Wetland Economic Valuation of Biodiversity and Ecosystem Services for Green Infrastructure Planning and Development." Nile Basin Initiative, Entebbe, Uganda.

Abbreviations

AA	Administrative Area
CPA	Comprehensive Peace Agreement
GBV	gender-based violence
IDPs	internally displaced persons
IPV	intimate partner violence
JMP	UNICEF/WHO Joint Monitoring Programme
MICS	Multiple Indicator Cluster Survey
MWRI	Ministry of Water Resources and Irrigation
NTDs	neglected tropical diseases
PoC	Protection of Civilian
R-ARCSS	Revitalized Agreement on the Resolution of Conflict in the Republic of South Sudan
R-NDS	Revised National Development Strategy
RVI	Rift Valley Institute
SGBV	sexual and gender-based violence
SPEI	Standardized Precipitation-Evapotranspiration Index
SPI	Standardized Precipitation Index
UN	United Nations
WASH	water supply, sanitation, and hygiene
WHO	World Health Organization
WRM	water resources management

1 Introduction

OVERVIEW

South Sudan faces hard times ahead. For decades prior to independence, the country experienced conflict, marginalization, and underdevelopment, which led to a protracted humanitarian crisis and prevented the development of human and natural capital. Since independence in 2011, South Sudan has experienced generalized chronic instability and a protracted civil war resulting in hundreds of thousands of fatalities and displacement of at least 4 million people, with more than 2 million fleeing to neighboring countries, and at least 2 million internally displaced. Now, as the country grapples with unprecedented levels of food insecurity caused by conflict, political interference, climate shocks, COVID-19 (coronavirus), and rising global food prices, millions are in need of humanitarian assistance and at risk of famine. Populations continue to be displaced by violence, insecurity, and natural hazards. Weak governance, low levels of government transparency, and the isolation of key leaders and ethno-political groups from power-sharing arrangements are some of the risks to the country's fragile institutions and transition toward stability. As populations grow and geopolitical conditions change, the country's vast and unique natural assets are once again gaining increasing attention from regional and global powers. What is water's role in these dynamics? Can water sector investments support South Sudan's efforts to recover from decades of conflict and strengthen the resilience of its communities?

This report addresses these questions and shows that water, if successfully managed, can bolster South Sudan's economic recovery and stability prospects. On the other hand, water's destructive force also means that it can cause loss of lives and livelihoods and hinder the transition toward economic and political stability. Water sector policies and institutional frameworks to harness water's productive potential date to the era before independence, but implementation has been limited because of the eruption of civil war and prolonged conflict. Following the Revitalized Agreement on the Resolution of the Conflict in the Republic of South Sudan, the country now has an opportunity to embark on a reform and investment program to address structural water challenges and move beyond the emergency humanitarian aid response that has steered water sector interventions for the past decade. A comprehensive and long-term development approach to water sector challenges in South Sudan—aligned with the 2021–2024 Revised National Development Strategy (Government of South Sudan and United Nations Development Programme 2021)—is urgently needed to adapt to a changing climate and provide sustainable services. To facilitate growth and livelihoods, South Sudan needs to act decisively on water.

PURPOSE AND STRUCTURE OF THE REPORT

This report builds on novel data and analysis to assess water security and its potential to contribute to human development and resilient livelihoods in South Sudan. The report highlights the complex interactions between water and selected key outcomes in the human, social, and political spheres. In doing so, it does not aim to provide a comprehensive picture of all the water-related impacts in South Sudan, but rather to highlight key areas where water-related risks and opportunities intersect with human development, social inclusion, and community resilience. The report seeks to elevate water security as an issue critical for national development and stability, and not just a humanitarian need as it has been considered in the past decade.

The report follows existing frameworks to analyze water security and adapts them to the context of South Sudan (Sadoff et al. 2015; Sadoff, Borgomeo, and de Waal 2017). Water security can be thought of as the goal of water management, and definitions of water security typically recognize the need for water management to (a) harness water's productive potential for human well-being, livelihoods, and ecosystems; and (b) protect societies, economies, and ecosystems from the destructive impacts of water such as water-borne diseases, floods, and droughts (Grey and Sadoff 2007; UN Water 2013). Building on this understanding of water security, this report examines South Sudan's status in three key areas: water security for people, water security for production, and water security for protection.

The report then analyzes how these three core areas of water security relate to broader water risks and impacts for communities and society. In particular, the report focuses on the influence of water security on human development (health and nutrition), conflict, gender, and forced displacement (figure 1.1). Although these aspects clearly cover only a part of the complex interactions between the water sector and the country's economic, social, and environmental challenges, they were selected given their relevance to the country's fragile context and alignment with the focus of South Sudan's Revised National Development Strategy 2021–2024 on consolidating peace and stabilizing the economy. Broader links with macro-economic performance, trade, transport, and energy policy are not considered because of lack of data and because of the report's focus on human well-being and community resilience.

The report is structured as follows:

- Chapter 1 provides an overview of South Sudan's water sector and serves as an introduction to the topics that are explored in more detail in the following chapters.
- Chapter 2 examines South Sudan's key water security challenges, grouping them into three main areas: water security for people, water security for production, and water security for protection.

FIGURE 1.1
Framework for the study

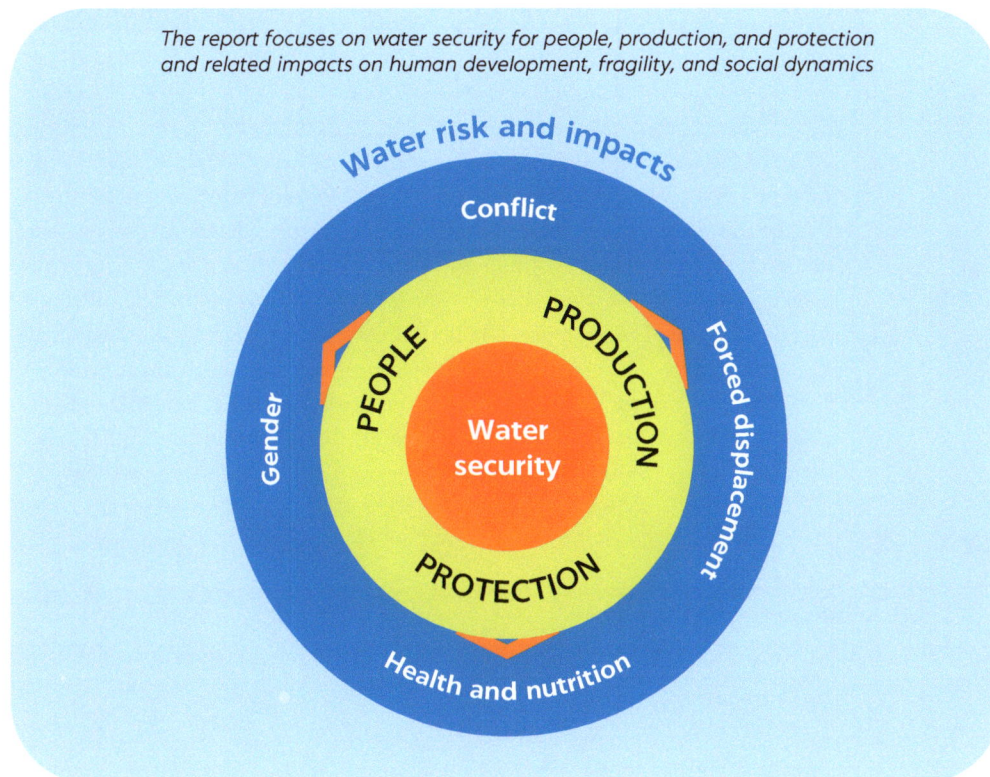

Source: World Bank.

- Chapter 3 examines the far-reaching implications of these challenges on South Sudan, focusing on four key water risks and impacts: human health and nutrition, forced displacement, gender, and conflict.
- Chapter 4 positions the findings from the previous chapters in the context of the sector's institutional architecture and some of the related constraints.
- Chapter 5 puts forward priority areas for water sector investments and the transition from humanitarian modalities of addressing water challenges to a government-led, long-term water resources management approach.
- Appendix A provides a description of the data and methods used in this report, and appendix B provides water security profiles for each of the country's 13 states and administrative areas.

SOUTH SUDAN'S WATER RESOURCES ENDOWMENT

South Sudan's water endowment is profoundly intertwined with the Nile River basin, one of most complex riverine systems in the world. The majority of the country's surface and groundwater resources are in this basin, whose variable flows therefore influence the country's water availability and the occurrence of droughts and floods. The country can be divided into three main hydrological units (surface water systems) (Sutcliffe and Parks 1999): (a) the Bahr el Jebel receiving the outflow from the East African lakes, (b) the Baro-Akobo-Sobat system flowing along the east from Ethiopia, and (c) the Bahr el Ghazal, formed by streams arising along the Nile-Congo divide in the northwest of the country (map 1.1). These major subbasins converge into the White Nile in the northeast of the country, creating the Upper Nile subbasin as shown in map 1.1. As a result of spills from the river channels into the wide floodplains, it is estimated that about half of the inflow from the East African lakes into the Bahr el Jebel evaporates and is recycled back into the system in the form of moisture and rainfall.

The confluence of the Bahr el Ghazal and the Bahr el Jebel forms a vast area of marshes and wetlands (permanent and temporary) located mainly in Jonglei, Warrap, Unity, and Northern Bahr el Ghazal states, known as the Sudd wetland. The Sudd is one of the largest wetlands in the world, and is designated a Ramsar site, which confers it globally recognized importance for containing representative, rare, or unique wetland types and for conserving biodiversity (see chapter 2). Estimates of its size differ (table 1.1), demonstrating the high levels of intra- and interannual hydrological variability and the overall lack of

MAP 1.1

Main hydrological units of South Sudan within the Nile basin

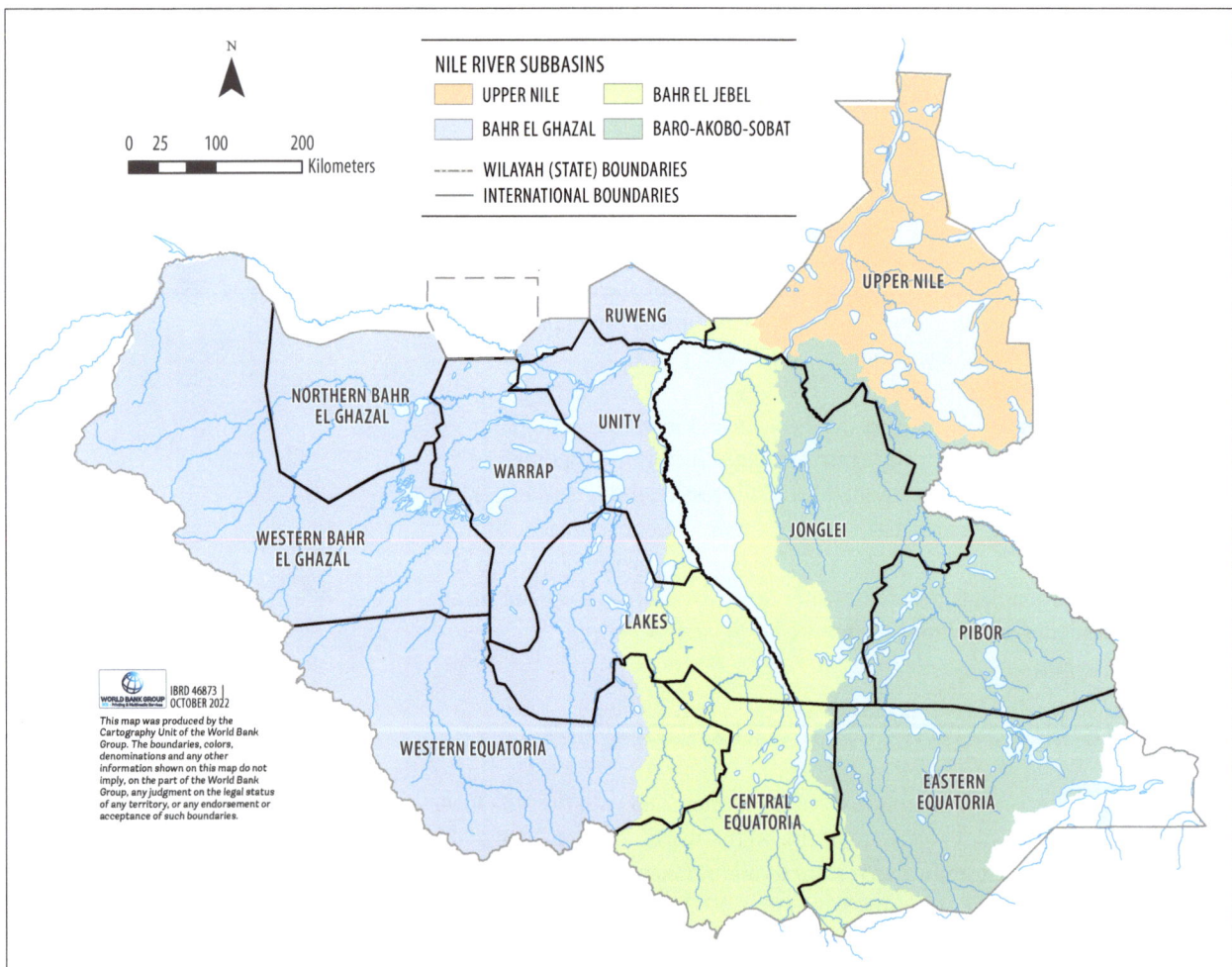

Source: World Bank.

TABLE 1.1 **Select estimates of the size of the Sudd wetland**

SUDD AREA ESTIMATE (KM²)	MEASUREMENT METHOD	SOURCE
More than 100,000	Not specified	UNEP 2018
57,000, varying from 90,000 to 42,000	Not specified	UNESCO 2017
30,000, of which 14,000 is seasonal and 16,000 permanent	Not specified	World Bank 2013
30,000–40,000	Based on various estimates	Mohamed et al. 2005
8,300	Water balance and aerial surveys	Hurst and Phillips 1938
22,000	Water balance model	Sutcliffe and Parks 1999
28,000–48,000	Remote sensing	Travaglia, Kapetsky, and Righini 1995
8,000–40,000	Remote sensing	Mason et al. 1992, cited in Mohamed, Bastiaanssen, and Savenije 2004
38,300	Remote sensing	Mohamed, Bastiaanssen, and Savenije 2004
14,000–24,000	Remote sensing	Di Vittorio and Georgakakos 2021

Source: World Bank.

standardized and long-term monitoring data on the extent of water bodies, which can be increasingly addressed through satellite products (Pekel et al. 2016). Overall, estimates suggest that wetlands cover 7 percent of the total area of South Sudan, with the Sudd alone accounting for at least 5 percent (AfDB 2013).

Although South Sudan is well endowed with groundwater resources, very limited information is available with which to support its sustainable management and development. Three major aquifer types have been identified in the country (Lasagna et al. 2020). The Umm Ruwaba sedimentary formation, comprising unconsolidated superficial sediments (sands, gravels, clays) with little stratification, has traditionally been identified as a key groundwater source in the country (Garang de Mabior 1981; World Bank 2013). This unconsolidated formation underlies a large part of the central and eastern areas of the country (Greater Upper Nile region and parts of Eastern Equatoria and Lakes states) and is contained within the larger Sudd basin transboundary aquifer (map 1.2). The Precambrian basement underlying the east of the country has been identified as having low productivity, with groundwater occurring in fractures, and is associated with the regional Karoo-Carbonate system (Upton, Ó Dochartaigh, and Bellwood-Howard 2018). In the northwest of the country, the Baggara aquifer, part of the regional Nubian Sandstone formation, might contain major groundwater reserves; however, no detailed hydrogeological assessments exist (Upton, Ó Dochartaigh, and Bellwood-Howard 2018). Although hydrogeological maps have been developed and provide a starting point for groundwater management, more detailed studies are required to determine the hydrogeological characteristics of aquifers, their water quality, sustainable groundwater yields, and interaction with surface water.

Existing evidence suggests that water quality issues further influence groundwater potential in the country. Areas with groundwater quality issues include Eastern Equatoria, Lakes, and oil-producing regions in the north (Goes 2022). In Eastern Equatoria, groundwater was found not to meet World Health Organization drinking water quality standards for some chemical elements,

MAP 1.2

Main aquifer types and productivity in South Sudan and related transboundary aquifers

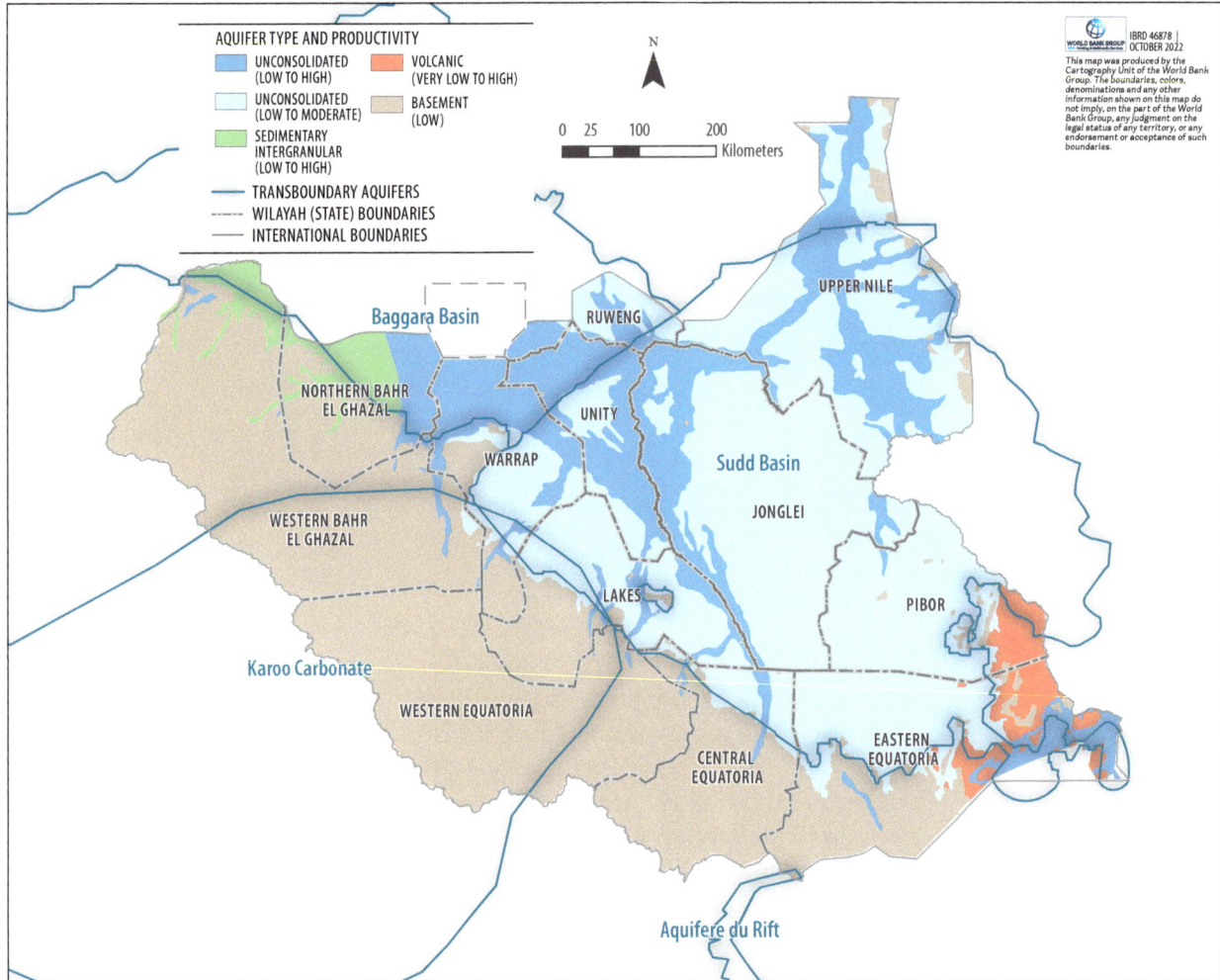

Source: World Bank using data from the International Groundwater Resources Assessment Centre and Upton, Ó Dochartaigh, and Bellwood-Howard (2018).

likely because of natural causes (rock-water interactions) (Kut et al. 2019). Saline and brackish groundwater bodies have been identified in part of Lakes state and in the northeastern part of the Sudd basin (Upper Nile state), though further mapping is required to understand the occurrence and depth of salinity in groundwater across South Sudan (Goes 2022). In the oil-producing regions in the north, oil spills lead to contamination of shallow aquifers and surface waters (Löw, Stieglitz, and Diemar 2021); however, no comprehensive assessment of the scale of pollution exists.

Water consumption is not directly measured and hence difficult to assess. Of the water withdrawn from the environment, an estimated 30 percent goes to municipal uses and 34 percent to industrial uses. About 36 percent is withdrawn for agriculture (figure 1.2). Much of this water flows back into the water system, typically with a lower quality. In absolute terms, average annual water withdrawals are currently 658 million cubic meters per year. In per capita terms, this is 59.95 cubic meters per person, compared with about 787.4 for the Arab

FIGURE 1.2

Freshwater withdrawals by sector as a share of total withdrawals, South Sudan and Sub-Saharan Africa, 2018

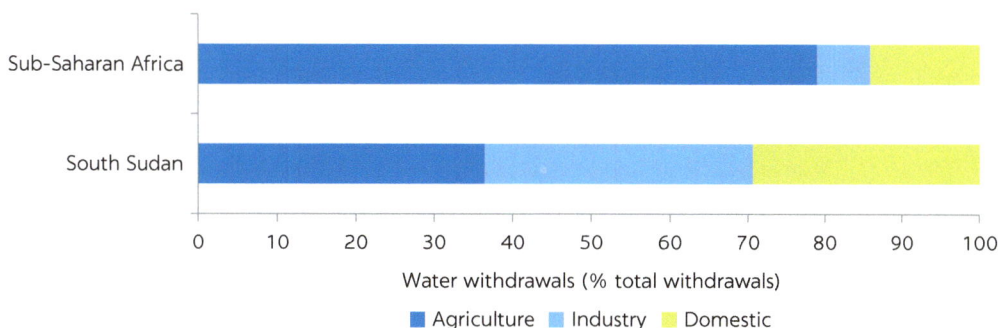

Water withdrawals (% total withdrawals)

■ Agriculture   ■ Industry   ■ Domestic

Source: FAO AQUASTAT.

Republic of Egypt, 644.4 for Sudan, and 96.57 for Ethiopia. For South Sudan, this value is only indicative given the lack of accurate information on water resource availability and the considerable year-to-year variability. It should also be emphasized that these per capita figures do not correspond to the amount of water that people are able to access, which is considerably lower and determined by access to infrastructure and institutions (see chapter 2).

INSTITUTIONS

South Sudan's protracted armed conflicts have stalled institutional development, especially in the water sector. The sector's institutional landscape is fraught with human and financial resource constraints, overlapping institutional responsibilities between ministries and across stakeholders, and fragile planning, monitoring, and management systems. The dominance of humanitarian partners involved in the sector has effectively sidelined the government and slowed national institutional development since the outbreak of conflict (Mosello, Mason, and Aludra 2016).

The Ministry of Water Resources and Irrigation (MWRI) has overall responsibility for water policy and management. Within MWRI, water-related functions are housed under four technical directorates: Water Resources Management, Rural Water Supply and Sanitation, Hydrology and Survey, and Irrigation and Drainage. Although MWRI is an umbrella ministry for the water sector, several other line ministries and actors at the state and county level are involved in water resources management and service delivery, including the Ministry of Lands, Housing and Urban Development; the Ministry of Energy and Dams; the Ministry of Environment and Forestry; and the Ministry of Humanitarian Affairs and Disaster Management. Under the Local Government Act of 2009, local government has a mandate to provide basic services, including rural water and sanitation and urban sanitation as well as responsibility for managing water resources, but local governments lack the institutional capacity and sufficient funding to carry out this mandate. Actors at the county level include the Department of Water and Sanitation, which is responsible for service delivery management, and the Department of Public Works, which is responsible for managing service infrastructure. The organization, staffing, and capacity for water services vary greatly among state and local governments. Chapter 4 presents a more detailed assessment of the sector's policies, institutions, and regulations.

Water supply services in urban areas fall under the remit of the South Sudan Urban Water Corporation. The corporation is run by a managing director and has a board of directors chaired by the minister of MWRI. The Directorate of Urban Sanitation under the Ministry of Land, Housing and Urban Development is mandated to provide sanitation services in Juba and other major towns, including provision of suitable schemes for sewerage disposal and treatment in housing and urban areas. Rural water supply and sanitation services are delegated to county governments under the Department of Water and Sanitation. Delivery of water supply and sanitation services in urban and especially in rural areas relies for its funding and capacity almost entirely on the support of nongovernmental organizations, donors, and humanitarian organizations.

Policy and institutional frameworks to guide water sector investments and ensure their sustainability are available, but implementation is lagging. In 2007, following the Comprehensive Peace Agreement of 2005, MWRI published the first water policy for South Sudan covering water resources management, rural water supply and sanitation, and urban water supply and sanitation. The policy outlined the country's vision and established basic principles, objectives, and priorities for the water sector. It recognized the need for active participation of water users and stakeholders at the lowest appropriate administrative level and called for the development of institutions with clear functions for efficient resource management and service delivery. In 2011, the water, sanitation, and hygiene (WASH) Sector Strategic Framework was formulated to systematically implement the 2007 Water Policy; attract investment; move from ad hoc emergency relief interventions to holistic, government-led planning and implementation of well-targeted development programs; and initiate inclusive sectorwide governance and development. Although referred to as a WASH framework, it went beyond the traditional boundaries to incorporate water resource management for livelihoods.

A draft Water Bill was formulated in 2013 to operationalize the recommendations of the preceding water policies. Though yet to be enacted, the bill covers procedures to manage water allocation for different uses, conservation, water quality, water-related disasters, and intersectoral coordination. MWRI has initiated a review and consultation process to revise the bill and aims to submit it for review across all federal government ministries in accordance with the Comprehensive Peace Agreement and subsequently to parliament for ratification.

INFRASTRUCTURE AND INFORMATION

South Sudan's hydrometric monitoring network is extremely weak. Hydrometric monitoring networks are defined as observation networks composed of gauging stations that measure stream flow–related parameters (primarily river and lake water levels and river discharge). Of the seven stations currently in South Sudan, only five are operational (table 1.2). These stations are manually operated and lack any automatic data transmission mechanisms (telemetry). The country lacks capability for surface water quality monitoring, sediment sampling, and groundwater quantity and quality measurement. No systematic data management tool is used to store and harmonize data.

TABLE 1.2 Hydrometric stations in South Sudan as of April 2022

LOCATION OF STATION	RIVER	STATUS
Hillet Dolieb	Sobat	Nonoperational
Mongalla	Bahr el Jebel	Operational
Bor	Bahr el Jebel	Nonoperational
Wau	Bahr el Ghazal	Operational
Malakal	White Nile	Operational
Juba	Bahr el Ghazal	Operational
Nimule	Bahr el Ghazal	Operational

Source: Nile Basin Initiative and Ministry of Water Resources and Irrigation.

South Sudan lags behind the rest of Sub-Saharan Africa in coverage of key gray water infrastructure; however, it contains some of the continent's most extensive green water infrastructure. Gray infrastructure refers to built structures and mechanical equipment to manage water resources, such as dams, canals, embankments, and pumps. Green infrastructure refers to natural systems such as forests, floodplains, and riparian areas that are intentionally and strategically preserved to provide water services. Many of the country's water facilities were damaged or destroyed during the civil war. Existing flood protection structures are poorly maintained, and there is no information on the location or technical details of existing structures to help identify investments in need of rehabilitation. A large part of South Sudan is covered by wetlands, which constitute a key nature-based component of the country's water infrastructure assets. Chapter 2 provides more details on South Sudan's water infrastructure system and its links with water access and livelihoods.

REFERENCES

AfDB (African Development Bank). 2013. *Infrastructure Action Plan in South Sudan: A Program for Sustained Strong Economic Growth*. Tunis, Tunisia: AfDB.

Di Vittorio, C. A., and A. P. Georgakakos. 2021. "Hydrologic Modeling of the Sudd Wetland Using Satellite-Based Data." *Journal of Hydrology: Regional Studies* 37: 100922.

Garang de Mabior, J. 1981. "Identifying, Selecting, and Implementing Rural Development Strategies for Socio-Economic Development in the Jonglei Projects Area, Southern Region, Sudan." PhD thesis, Iowa State University, Ames, IA.

Goes, B. J. M. 2022. "Assessment of the Aquifers in South Sudan with a Focus on Lakes State." *Hydrogeology Journal* 30: 1035–53.

Government of South Sudan and United Nations Development Programme. 2021. *Revised National Development Strategy 2021–2024: Consolidate Peace and Stabilize the Economy*. Juba: Government of South Sudan and United Nations Development Programme.

Grey, D., and C. W. Sadoff. 2007. "Sink or Swim? Water Security for Growth and Development." *Water Policy* 9 (6): 545–71.

Hurst, H. E., and P. Phillips. 1938. "The Hydrology of the Lake Plateau and Bahr el Jebel." In *The Nile Basin*, Vol. 5, edited by H. E. Hurst and P. Phillips. Cairo: Schindler's Press.

Kut, K. M. K., A. Sarswat, J. Bundschuh, and D. Mohan. 2019. "Water as Key to the Sustainable Development Goals of South Sudan: A Water Quality Assessment of Eastern Equatoria State." *Groundwater for Sustainable Development* 8 (April): 255–70.

Lasagna, M., S. M. R. Bonetto, L. Debernardi, D. A. De Luca, C. Semita, and C. Caselle. 2020. "Groundwater Resources Assessment for Sustainable Development in South Sudan." *Sustainability* 12 (14): 5580.

Löw, F., K. Stieglitz, and O. Diemar. 2021. "Terrestrial Oil Spill Mapping Using Satellite Earth Observation and Machine Learning: A Case Study in South Sudan." *Journal of Environmental Management* 298: 113424.

Mason, I. M., A. R. Harris, J. N. Moody, C. M. Birkett, W. Cudlip, and D. Vlachogiannis. 1992. "Monitoring Wetland Hydrology by Remote Sensing: A Case Study of the Sudd Using Infra-Red Imagery and Radar Altimetry." *Proceedings of the Central Symposium of the International Space Year*, Munich, ESA SP-341, 79–84.

Mohamed, Y. A., B. J. J. M. Van den Hurk, H. H. G. Savenije, and W. G. M. Bastiaanssen. 2005. "Impact of the Sudd Wetland on the Nile Hydroclimatology." *Water Resources Research* 41 (8).

Mohamed, Y. A., W. G. M. Bastiaanssen, and H. H. G. Savenije. 2004. "Spatial Variability of Evaporation and Moisture Storage in the Swamps of the Upper Nile Studied by Remote Sensing Techniques." *Journal of Hydrology* 289: 145–64.

Mosello, B., N. Mason, and R. Aludra. 2016. "Improving WASH Service Delivery in Protracted Crises." Overseas Development Institute, London.

Pekel, J. F., A. Cottam, N. Gorelick, and A. S. Belward. 2016. "High-Resolution Mapping of Global Surface Water and Its Long-Term Changes." *Nature* 540 (7633): 418–22.

Sadoff, C. W., E. Borgomeo, and D. De Waal. 2017. "Turbulent Waters: Pursuing Water Security in Fragile Contexts." World Bank, Washington, DC.

Sadoff, C. W., J. W. Hall, D. Grey, J. C. J. H. Aerts, M. Ait-Kadi, C. Brown, A. Cox, et al. 2015. *Securing Water, Sustaining Growth*. Report of the GWP/OECD Task Force on Water Security and Sustainable Growth. Oxford, U.K.: University of Oxford.

Sutcliffe, J. V., and Y. Parks. 1999. *The Hydrology of the Nile*. IAHS Special Publication No. 5. Oxfordshire, U.K.: IAHS Press, Institute of Hydrology.

Travaglia, C., J. Kapetsky, and G. Righini. 1995. "Monitoring Wetlands for Fisheries by NOAA AVHRR LAC Thermal Data." FAO/SDRN, Rome.

UNEP (United Nations Environment Programme). 2018. *South Sudan: First State of Environment and Outlook Report*. Nairobi: UNEP.

UNESCO. 2017. "Sudd Wetland." UNESCO World Heritage Convention. https://whc.unesco.org/en/tentativelists/6276/#:~:text=Description,freshwater%20ecosystems%20in%20the%20world.

UN Water. 2013. "What Is Water Security? Infographic." May 8. https://www.unwater.org/publications/what-water-security-infographic.

Upton, K., B. É. Ó Dochartaigh, and I. Bellwood-Howard. 2018. "Africa Groundwater Atlas: Hydrogeology of South Sudan." British Geological Survey. https://earthwise.bgs.ac.uk/index.php/Hydrogeology_of_South_Sudan.

World Bank. 2013. "Republic of South Sudan: The Rapid Water Sector Needs Assessment and a Way Forward." World Bank, Washington, DC.

2 Water Security in South Sudan

WATER SECURITY FOR PEOPLE

Key points

- Water supply and sanitation improvements since South Sudan's independence in 2011 have failed to reach most South Sudanese, and although recent data suggest that modest improvements were made on access to basic drinking water, fewer households have access to sanitation than before the conflict period.
- Seasonal water access varies sharply at subnational levels, with most states and administrative areas having lower access to basic water supply during the rainy season.
- Close to 15 percent of households without improved drinking water in the dry season travel more than two hours roundtrip to access water.
- Nationally, just 10 percent of households have access to sanitation and 75 percent practice open defecation.

Overview

Water security entails the capacity of a population to safeguard sustainable access to adequate quantities of acceptable quality water for human well-being. Under the notion of *water security for people*, this section captures this important aspect of water security and assesses South Sudan's status with regard to access to safely managed water supply, sanitation, and hygiene (WASH) services. These are an essential part of improving human health and dignity, and also reducing the risk of infectious disease outbreaks, notably, cholera. However, the benefits of water security for people do not just include improved health outcomes; they also result in important quality-of-life benefits, such as reduced vulnerability to violence and assault, especially for women; time savings; and environmental quality.

This section uses data from the UNICEF/WHO Joint Monitoring Programme (JMP) and the 2020 South Sudan Household Health Survey to assess water security for people. JMP publishes global indicators on access to WASH by service level, indicating quality and availability (see box 2.1). JMP reports safely

BOX 2.1

Measuring access: Sustainable development goal indicators

In 2015, the 2030 Agenda for Sustainable Development replaced the Millennium Development Goals with a more ambitious blueprint for achieving universal prosperity by 2030, underpinned by the Sustainable Development Goals (SDGs). The objective of SDG 6 Clean Water and Sanitation is to ensure the availability and sustainable management of water and sanitation for all. With the SDGs came the expansion of the "service ladder" used to measure the quality of access to water, sanitation, and hygiene, including an aspiration for "safely managed" levels of service that include provisions for quality and availability

(table B2.1.1). The new UNICEF/WHO JMP service ladders go beyond measuring access to water supply and sanitation to include safely managed services for all, as well as incorporating key indicators on access to hygiene. Target 6.1 of the SDGs reads, "by 2030, achieve universal and equitable access to safe and affordable drinking water for all," and Target 6.2 reads, "by 2030, achieve access to adequate and equitable sanitation and hygiene for all and end open defecation, paying special attention to the needs of women and girls and those in vulnerable situations."

TABLE B2.1.1 **Joint Monitoring Programme service ladders for measuring achievement of the Sustainable Development Goal targets for drinking water supply, sanitation, and hygiene**

SERVICE LEVEL	DEFINITION
Drinking water	
Safely managed	Drinking water from an **improved water source** that is located on premises, available when needed, and free from fecal and priority chemical contamination
Basic	Drinking water from an **improved source**, provided collection time is not more than 30 minutes for a roundtrip including queuing
Limited	Drinking water from an **improved source** for which collection time exceeds 30 minutes for a roundtrip including queuing
Unimproved	Drinking water from an unprotected dug well or unprotected spring
Surface water	Drinking water directly from a river, dam, lake, pond, stream, canal, or irrigation canal
Sanitation	
Safely managed	Use of **improved facilities** that are not shared with other households and where excreta are safely disposed of in situ or transported and treated off-site
Basic	Use of **improved facilities** that are not shared with other households
Limited	Use of **improved facilities** shared between two or more households
Unimproved	Use of pit latrines without a slab or platform, hanging latrines, or bucket latrines
Open defecation	Disposal of human feces in fields, forests, bushes, open bodies of water, beaches, and other open spaces or with solid waste
Hygiene	
Basic	Availability of a handwashing facility on premises with soap and water
Limited	Availability of a handwashing facility on premises without soap and water
No facility	No handwashing facility on premises

Source: WHO/UNICEF 2017.

managed drinking water only when information on drinking water quality and either accessibility or availability is available for at least 50 percent of the population. Likewise, estimates for safely managed sanitation require comprehensive data on excreta disposal and management. South Sudan lacks sufficient data for estimates on safely managed access to be made. Therefore, the highest level of access to drinking water and sanitation for which JMP estimates are available are for "at least basic." Hygiene data are not available in sufficient detail or for a large enough share of the population for JMP to make estimates for South Sudan.

Water supply and sanitation improvements since 2011 have not reached most South Sudanese

Although substantial efforts were made following independence in 2011 to operationalize a governance structure for water supply and sanitation, along with significant donor investment to expand rural access to improved drinking water supply, develop small-scale water distribution systems, and improve access to safe drinking water and sanitation in urban areas, the bulk of these efforts were eroded in the subsequent conflicts. Civil war not only destroyed water infrastructure but also made it obsolete because of population displacement or lack of management. Moreover, the emphasis during the period following independence was almost exclusively on building infrastructure, with less attention to sustainable operation and maintenance of the completed schemes or financial viability of utilities (World Bank 2013). As a result, access to at least basic drinking water has stagnated in South Sudan since estimates from JMP began in 2011 (figure 2.1). A larger share of the population has gained access to limited service

FIGURE 2.1

Population with access to drinking water services, 2011 and 2020

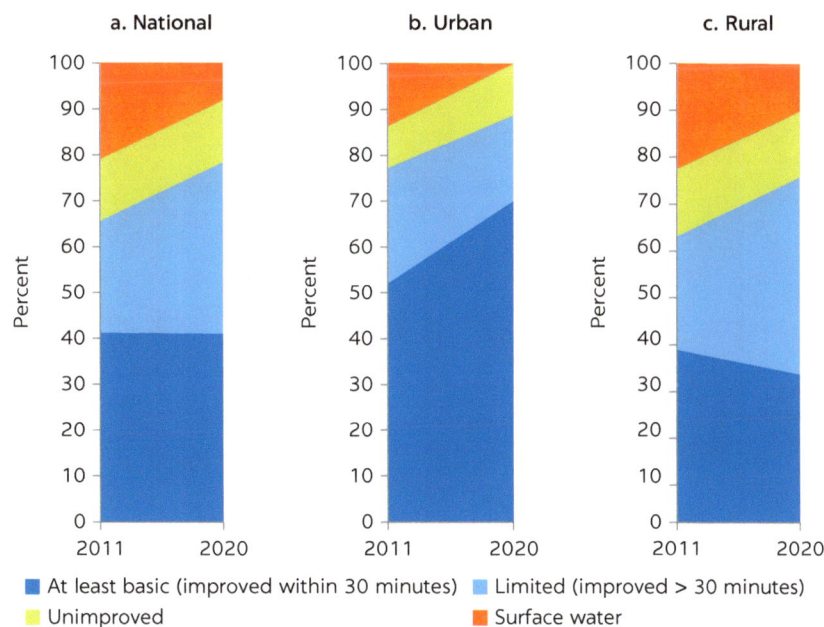

Source: WHO/UNICEF 2021a.

(improved with collection time exceeding 30 minutes roundtrip), with an increase from 24.4 percent in 2011 to 37.4 percent in 2020. The share of the population that relies on surface water declined from 20.9 percent in 2011 to 8.1 percent in 2020, with the population mostly shifting to limited sources in rural areas (for example, an improved source such as a borehole or a protected spring for which collection time exceeds 30 minutes roundtrip) and at least basic sources in urban areas.

There is a large urban-rural divide in access to drinking water supply services. In urban areas, access to at least basic drinking water sources has improved in the past decade, increasing from 52.1 percent in 2011 to 70 percent in 2020. In rural areas, access declined by 5.2 percentage points, from 38.8 in 2011 to 33.6 percent in 2020. Furthermore, whereas urban areas were successful in eliminating surface water dependency, 10 percent of the population in rural areas still relies on surface water. Since four out of five people live in rural areas of South Sudan, these figures indicate that water supply improvements between 2011 and 2020 have failed to reach most South Sudanese. The divergence of trends for urban and rural populations suggests that a large share of the rural population is being left behind.

Sanitation figures also clearly illustrate large disparities between urban and rural populations. Nationally, just 9 percent of people living in rural areas have access to sanitation and 73 percent practice open defecation. Open defecation only declined 10 percentage points over the nine-year period of the JMP estimates, with most of the declines occurring among urban populations (figure 2.2). According to JMP data, an estimated 60 percent of the population still defecates in the open.

FIGURE 2.2

Population with access to sanitation services, 2011 and 2020

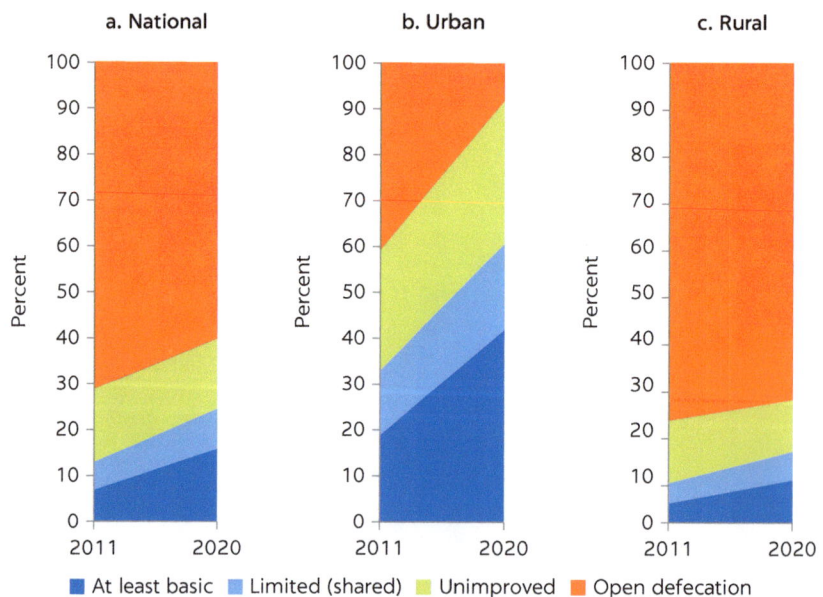

Source: WHO/UNICEF 2021a.

FIGURE 2.3

Population with access to drinking water and sanitation in South Sudan and Sub-Saharan Africa, 2020

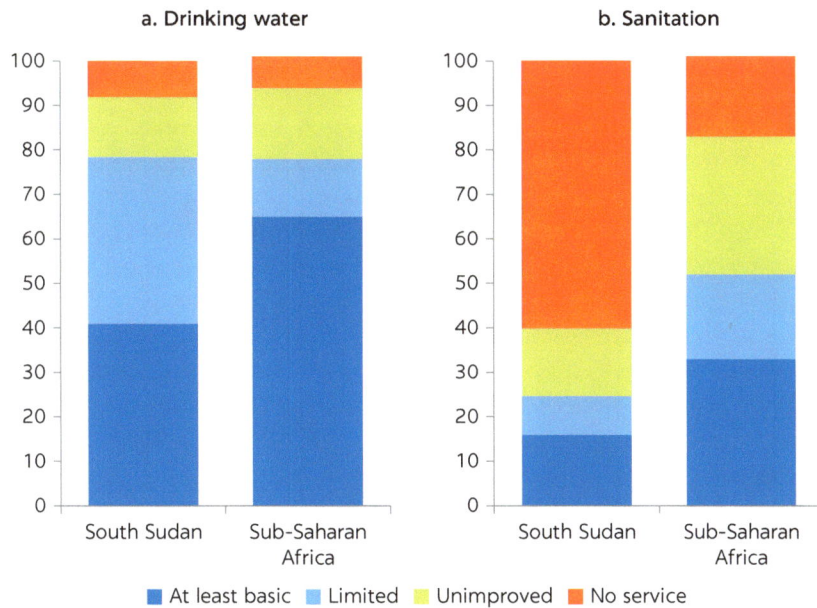

Source: WHO/UNICEF 2021a.
Note: "No service" refers to surface water use for drinking water (panel a) and open defecation for sanitation (panel b).

South Sudan lags behind the rest of Sub-Saharan Africa in access to drinking water supply and sanitation services. Figure 2.3 (panel a) compares national access statistics in South Sudan with averages for Sub-Saharan Africa. Although South Sudan performs better than the average of countries in Sub-Saharan Africa on access to at least basic water supply, it is important to note that lack of data on safely managed access for South Sudan prevents a full comparison on service standards. South Sudan is substantially behind the average of countries in Sub-Saharan Africa on levels of open defecation (no service) and access to at least basic sanitation (see figure 2.3, panel b).

Access to WASH services in schools is also very low, affecting children's right to quality education. In 2021, an estimated 33 percent of schools in South Sudan had no drinking water service and 21 percent had no sanitation. An estimated 80 percent of schools have no hygiene services. For health facilities, 36 percent lack drinking water service and 8 percent lack sanitation. In one out of five schools, students and staff spend more than 30 minutes per roundtrip to collect water from sources located off premises, representing an enormous opportunity cost (WHO/UNICEF 2021b).

Seasonal water access varies sharply at subnational levels, with most states and administrative areas having lower access to basic water supply during the rainy season

To further explore trends and variability in water security for people, this section uses the most recent data available on access to WASH in South Sudan. These data were collected as part of the 2020 South Sudan Household Health Survey, with representative estimates for the 10 states and three administrative areas.

There are important differences in the methodology used for estimates across these two sources, with the main difference being that JMP sources data from multiple nationally representative surveys to estimate coverage using a simple linear regression model, whereas the household survey draws estimates directly from the survey responses.[1] The health survey provides information on seasonal access and use of drinking water as well as estimates of access to handwashing facilities with soap and water. This section first presents estimates from this survey in comparison with JMP estimates, followed by figures on trends in access to WASH at state and administrative area levels.

In 2020, year-round access to at least basic drinking water is estimated to be 41.0 percent, with a slightly higher share of households having access to basic drinking water during the dry season (44.4 percent).[2] Access to improved sanitation is 10 percent (compared with 24.6 percent in JMP), while 75 percent of households report defecating in the open (compared with 60.1 percent in JMP) nationally. Findings from the 2020 health survey are consistent with JMP for access to drinking water but indicate that households are worse off for access to sanitation.

National estimates of WASH access and estimates for urban and rural populations separately can hide important subnational variation. Figure 2.4 presents WASH statistics by state and administrative area. The estimates show that

FIGURE 2.4

Household access to drinking water supply, sanitation, and hygiene in states and administrative areas of South Sudan, 2020

(percent)

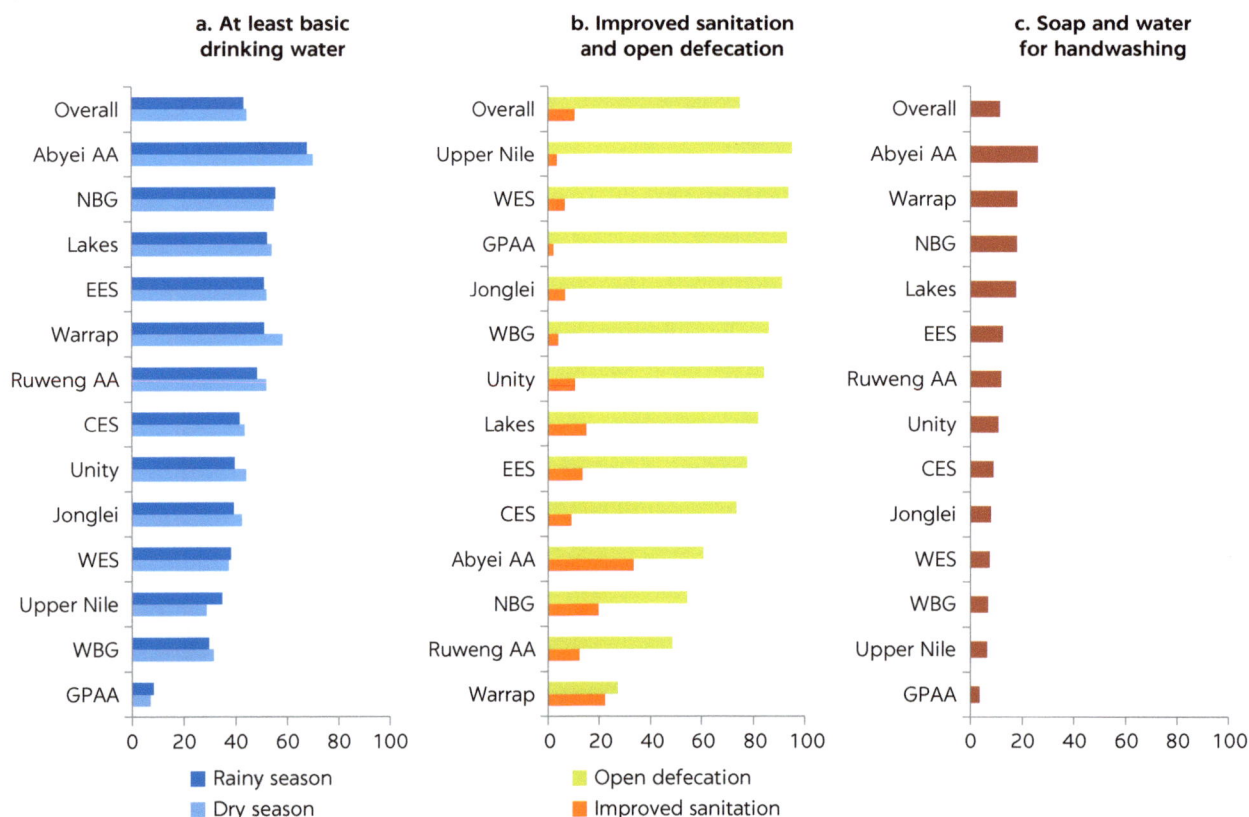

Source: World Bank using National Household Health Survey (2020).
Note: AA = Administrative Area; CES = Central Equatoria; EES = Eastern Equatoria; GPAA = Greater Pibor Administrative Area; NBG = Northern Bahr el Ghazal; WBG = Western Bahr el Ghazal; WES = Western Equatoria.

open defecation is highest in Upper Nile (95.0 percent), Western Equatoria (93.6 percent), and Greater Pibor Administrative Area (AA) (93.1 percent), and lowest in Warrap (27.2 percent), followed by Ruweng AA (48.4 percent) and Northern Bahr el Ghazal (54.4 percent). Access to improved sanitation is highest in Abyei AA (33.3 percent), Warrap (22.3 percent), and Northern Bahr el Ghazal (19.8 percent), compared with the national average of 10.3 percent. States with higher levels of improved sanitation are also more likely to have higher coverage of handwashing facilities and lower levels of open defecation, suggesting better hygiene practices overall.

Year-round access to at least basic drinking water is highest in Abyei AA (67.8 percent) and Eastern Equatoria (51.0 percent), and lowest in Greater Pibor AA (5.8 percent), compared with the national average of 41.0 percent. Drinking water access differs between the dry and rainy seasons in all geographic areas of South Sudan, although the differences are minor. The dominant trend is greater access to at least basic drinking water in the dry season, with only Northern Bahr el Ghazal, Upper Nile, Western Equatoria, and Greater Pibor AA having greater access during the rainy season.

Map 2.1 illustrates the extent of the change in access to basic drinking water from the dry to the rainy season. Households living in states shown in lightest blue are less likely to have access to basic drinking water during the rainy season compared with the dry season. There are numerous accounts of water sources being submerged by floodwaters during the rainy season, forcing households to seek out other sources of water that may require them to walk longer distances or the water will be of lower quality. United Nations reports highlight the severe impacts of floods in 2019, 2020, and 2021 on access to

MAP 2.1

Percentage-point change in access to basic drinking water between rainy and dry season, by state and administrative area

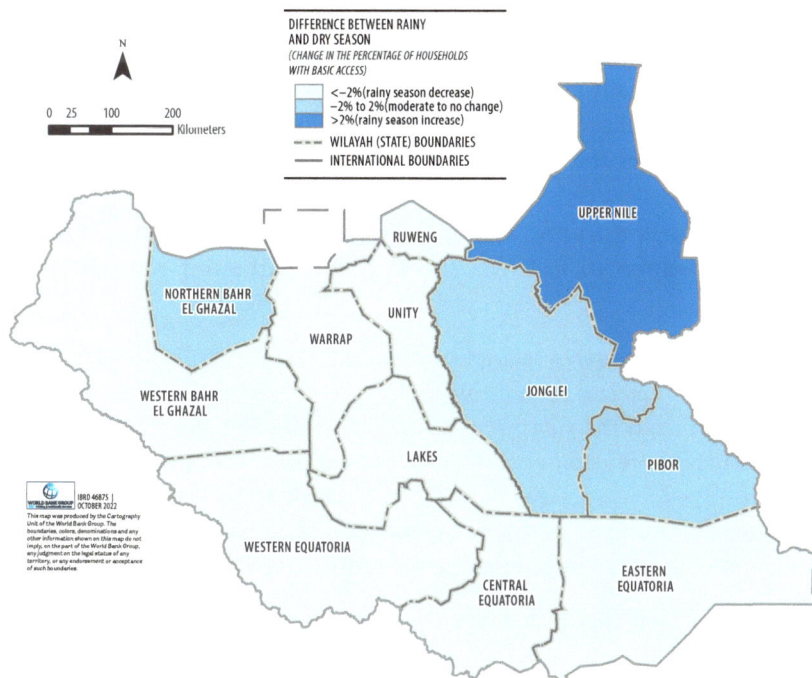

Source: World Bank using National Household Health Survey (2020).

MAP 2.2

Change in surface water use between rainy and dry seasons, by state and administrative area

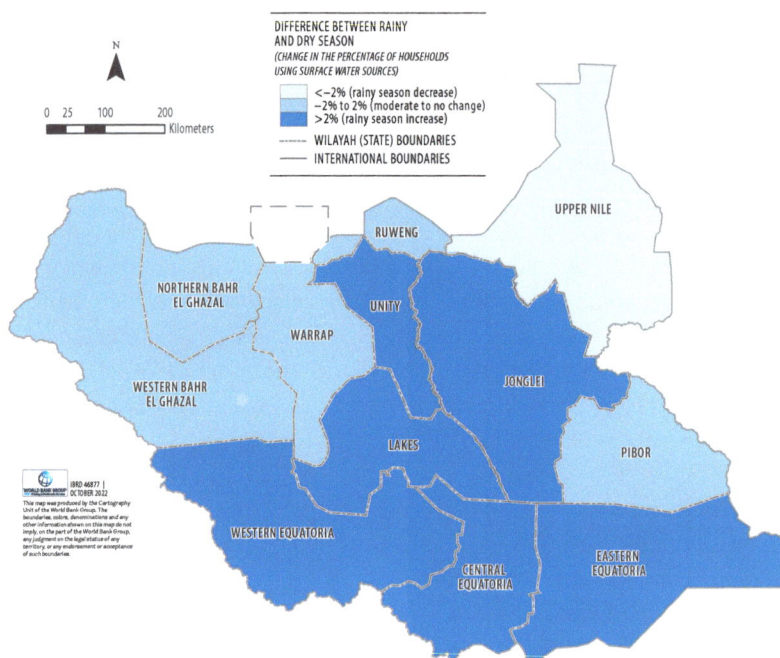

Source: World Bank using National Household Health Survey (2020).

drinking water supply (OCHA 2021); however, no countrywide estimate of the impacts of these events on access levels exists.

Surface water dependence increases especially for Jonglei and Unity states during the rainy season, with the southern states also reporting increases in the use of surface water during the rainy season (map 2.2). These trends largely explain the decline in access to basic drinking water during the rainy season. In addition to the possibility that water sources are affected by flooding, these trends may also be due to convenience factors (surface water sources are more readily available during rainy season), low awareness of the risks of using unimproved sources of water, and taste preferences.

Access to basic drinking water increased in 5 out of 10 states, while open defecation increased in most states between 2010 and 2020

The following analysis uses Multiple Indicator Cluster Survey (MICS) data from 2010 to analyze changes in access up to the most recent household survey data in 2020. Although the surveys use different methodologies, they are both designed to be representative at the state and administrative area level, making comparison possible. Because the MICS 2010 questionnaire does not differentiate seasonal access to water supply, the analysis generates the following categories for 2020 data to allow comparison with 2010 MICS data:

- *Improved* = Household has access to improved (or basic) drinking water year-round in 2020
- *Unimproved* = Household has access to only unimproved water year-round in 2020

- *Surface* = Household uses only surface water year-round in 2020
- *At least unimproved year-round* = Household has access to improved (or basic) in one season but unimproved in another in 2020
- *Surface reliant* = Household has access to improved (or basic) or unimproved in one season but uses surface water in another in 2020

Using these categories, figure 2.5 presents two estimates for 2020. The first bar for 2020 shows estimates for the 2020 dry season and the second shows the year-round access categories. Access to improved water supply decreased in 5 out of 10 states (Jonglei, Western Bahr el Ghazal, Lakes, Central Equatoria, and Eastern Equatoria), while the greatest increases were in Warrap and Northern Bahr el Ghazal states (22 percent and 23 percent, respectively). The highest share of "surface reliant" households, that is, households that use surface water for part of the year, is observed in Unity (13 percent) and Western Equatoria (11 percent).

Trends for access to sanitation are more readily comparable across the two data sources (figure 2.6). The comparisons suggest that all but two states (Western Bahr el Ghazal and Central Equatoria) have had large increases in rates of open defecation, with the largest increases in Lakes and Unity states. Access to improved sanitation increased slightly in Jonglei, Warrap, and Northern and Western Bahr el Ghazal.

WASH quality standards in emergencies are not being met or barely met

According to data published by the United Nations High Commissioner for Refugees (UNHCR), WASH service provision is not always meeting targets, and the quality of WASH services in refugee settings in South Sudan is generally low (UNHCR 2022). The World Health Organization's recommended amount of at least 20 liters of water per capita per day to meet basic hygiene needs and ensure basic food hygiene is not being met in many refugee camps. Data show that post-emergency water supply and sanitation quality standards in many refugee camps are not being met or are barely met. For example, only 42 percent of households in the camps have access to a latrine, and the ratio of persons to a functioning water point exceeds 2,500 (table 2.1).

Accessibility, quality, and affordability challenges further constrain access to drinking water

The highest level of service for drinking water and sanitation is defined by JMP as "safely managed." To meet these criteria, drinking water must be from an improved water source that is located on premises, available when needed, and free from fecal and priority chemical contamination. For sanitation, the definition includes use of improved facilities that are not shared with other households and where excreta are safely disposed of in situ or transported and treated off-site. Most of the data required to estimate access to safely managed services are not available in South Sudan; however, this section presents evidence on indicators of accessibility, water quality, and affordability.

Water accessibility
Nearly 15 percent of households without dry season access to an improved drinking water source report walking more than 4 kilometers (approximately

FIGURE 2.5

Trends in access to drinking water supply, 2010 and 2020, by state

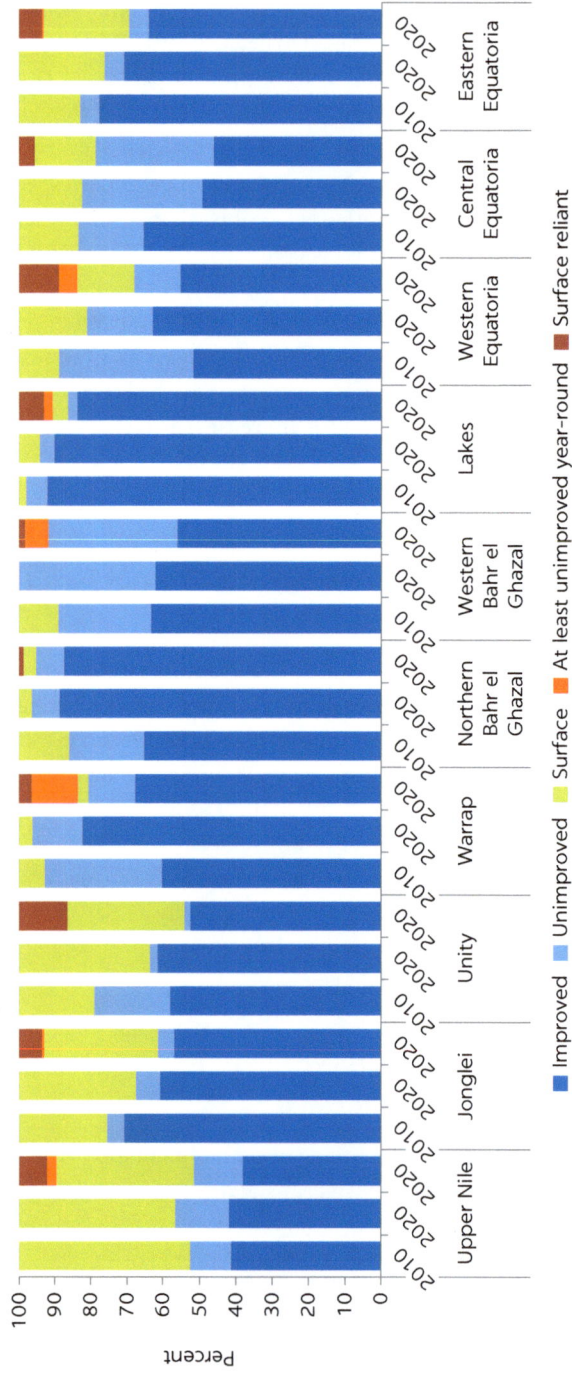

Source: World Bank using MICS (2010) and National Household Health Survey (2020).
Note: For the 2020 data, the first bar shows estimates for the dry season and the second bar shows year-round access.

FIGURE 2.6

Trends in access to sanitation, 2010 and 2020, by state

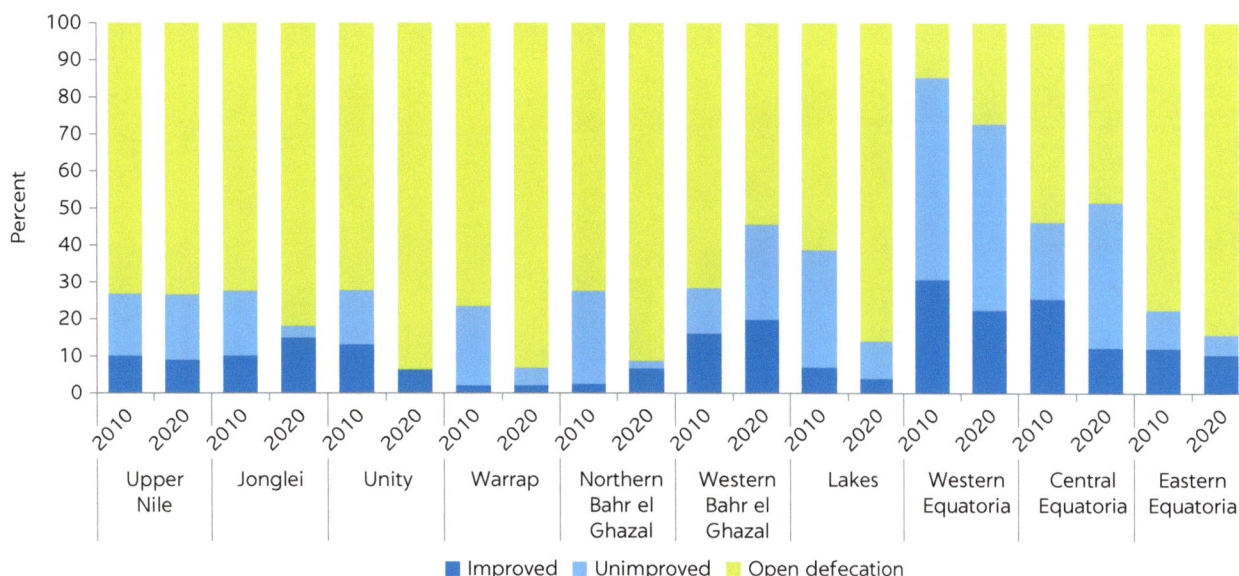

Source: World Bank using MICS (2010) and National Household Health Survey (2020).

TABLE 2.1 WASH indicators for selected refugee camps in South Sudan

WASH INDICATOR	COVERAGE	TARGET
Share (%) of households with household toilet or latrine (monthly)	42	≥ 85
Share (%) of water quality tests at chlorinated collection locations with FRC in the range 0.2–2mg/L and turbidity <5 NTU	97	≥ 95
Share (%) water quality tests at nonchlorinated water collection locations with 0 CFU/100ml	56	≥ 95
Average number of liters of potable water available per person per day	17	≥ 20
Number of persons per bath shelter or shower	364	≤ 20
Number of persons per hygiene promoter	1,092	≤ 1,000
Number of persons per toilet or latrine	13	≤ 20
Number of persons per usable hand pump, well, or spring	2,666	≤ 200
Number of persons per usable water tap	102	≤ 100

Source: UNHCR 2022.
Note: Based on data for Ajoung Thok, Doro, Gendrassa, Kaya, Pamir, and Yusuf Batil camps.
CFU = colony forming units; FRC = free residual chlorine; NTU = nephelometric turbidity unit; WASH = water supply, sanitation, and hygiene.

2 hours roundtrip) for water. Survey data suggest that households without access to improved drinking water travel longer distances to access the water source compared with those that do have access (figure 2.7). Assuming a walking speed of 4 kilometers per hour, water at a distance less than 1 kilometer (approximately 15 minutes one way) would meet the criteria of less than 30 minutes roundtrip.[3] An estimated 66.9 percent of households with access to an improved source in the dry season can access it in less than 30 minutes, compared with 58.3 percent of households without dry season access to an improved source.

Map 2.3 shows the share of population by county living more than 30 minutes roundtrip from a water point, using the Water Information Management

FIGURE 2.7

Distance to water source in dry season for households with and without access to improved drinking water supply

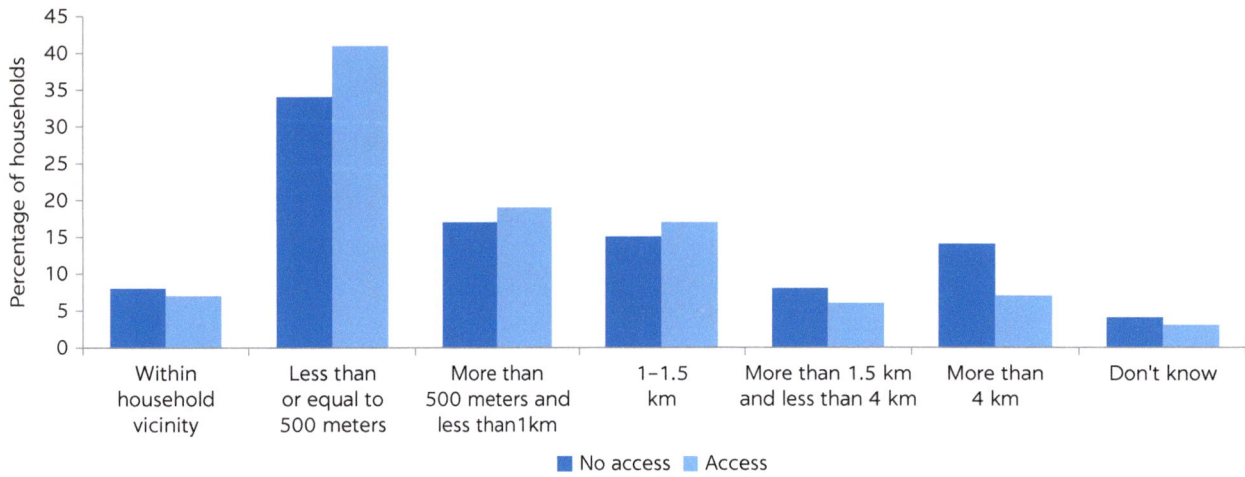

Source: World Bank using National Household Health Survey (2020).

MAP 2.3

Percentage of population living more than 30 minutes roundtrip from water point

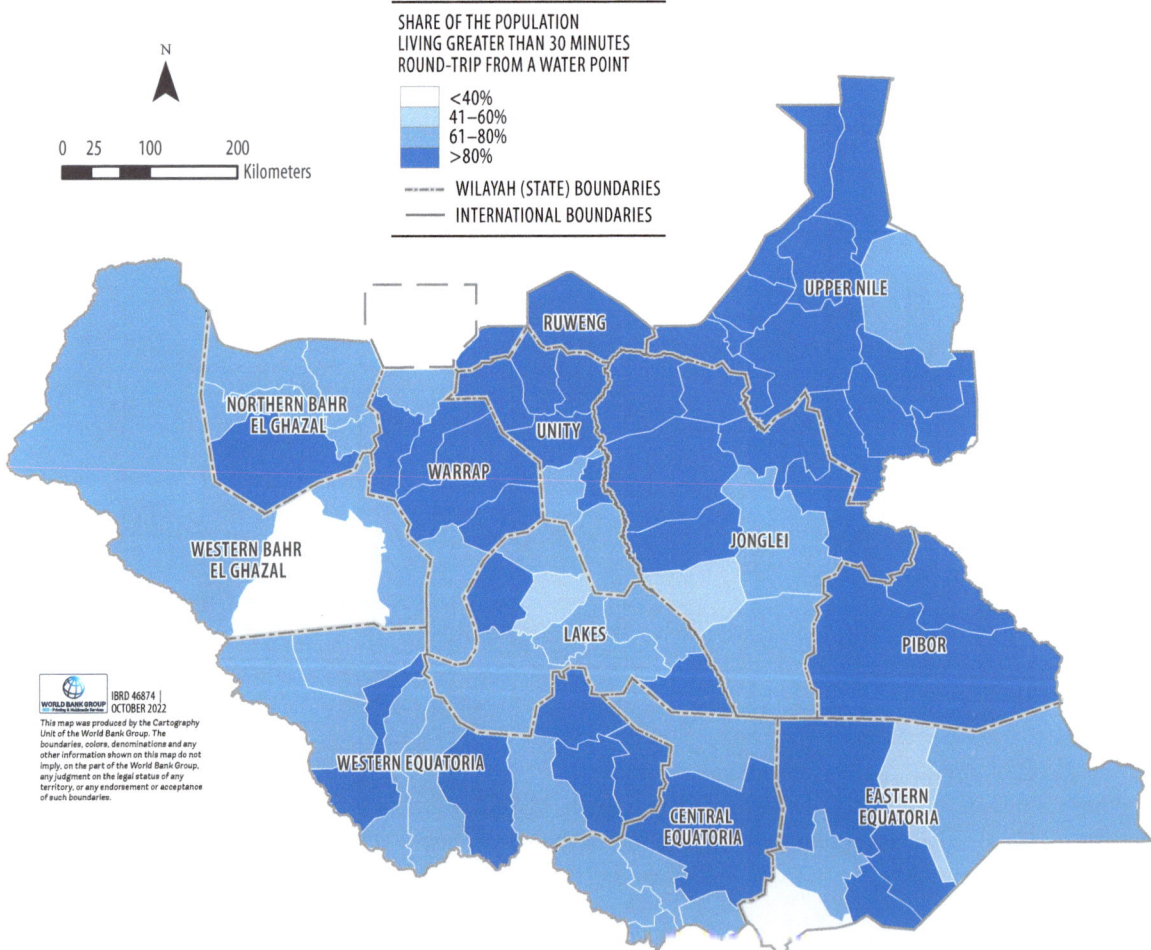

Source: World Bank using Water Information Management System, Ministry of Water Resources and Irrigation (2012).

System of the MWRI. Although these data were last updated in 2012, the findings are indicative of population proximity to water points identified by the government of South Sudan, regardless of whether they are functional.[4] The analysis shows 32 counties where more than 90 percent of the population is located more than 30 minutes roundtrip from the closest water point, the majority of these located in the northern states.

Water quality

Despite 2020 estimates showing 41 percent of households with year-round access to at least basic drinking water, there is a high likelihood that these water sources—most of which are nonnetworked—are contaminated. Furthermore, evidence indicates that water treatment practices are very low in South Sudan. Water Information Management System data from 2012 indicate that 89 percent of households reported that they did nothing to treat their drinking water.

Although guidelines on drinking water quality were developed in 2008 (UNICEF 2008), there appears to be no routine water quality monitoring or enforcement of the standards in South Sudan. A department of Water Quality Monitoring is housed in the Water Resources Management Directorate of MWRI; its role is to supervise, oversee, and manage water quality issues; quality monitoring; water quality assessment; and pollution control (and a small water quality laboratory housed in MWRI) (AfDB 2013). However, there is no evidence that these activities are funded or implemented. Currently, the Ministry of Health is mandated to manage water treatment and enforce drinking water quality standards. The draft Water Bill foresees the mandate for setting and monitoring compliance with potable water quality standards to be assigned to the proposed Safe Water Supply and Sanitation Services Regulator.

Systematic data on water quality are not available for South Sudan. However, a few ad hoc surveys have been conducted, which are reported here. For example, a study conducted in Juba collected samples from three water distribution points: Juba Bridge, Konyokonyo, and Gumbo Water Treatment Plant. The study reports that both Juba Bridge and Konyokonyo water collection points are used by water tankers licensed by Juba City Council to collect and to distribute water to the city. Water quality tests showed bacterial growth in Konyokonyo samples, while for Juba Bridge the tests showed 55 colony forming units (CFUs) per 100 milliliter sample. Only Gumbo Water Treatment Plant met the WHO standard of zero CFU, making it safe for human consumption (Health of Mother Earth Foundation 2019).

Water expenditure and affordability

Affordability is enshrined in the definition of Sustainable Development Goal (SDG) targets 6.1 and 6.2 on drinking water and sanitation; however, this indicator has not been part of SDG monitoring to date because of lack of agreement on how to measure affordability. Recommendations point to the use of nationally representative income and expenditure surveys and imputation of time costs based on distance to drinking water source and place of defecation (WHO/UNICEF 2021c).

Data from the High Frequency South Sudan Survey (2012–16) indicate that, on average, 39 percent of household respondents reported water among

FIGURE 2.8

Priorities for household expenditure, based on 14 focus group discussions in Juba, Kapoeta, and Rumbek counties, 2022

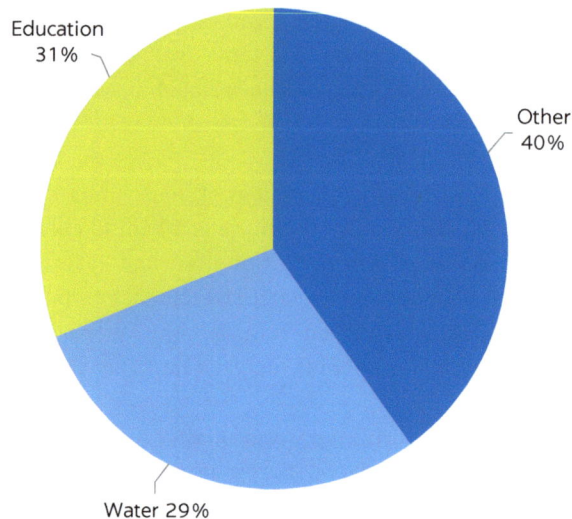

Source: RVI 2022.
Note: Figure shows percentage of focus groups (n = 14) that ranked water, education, or other as their first priority for household expenditure.

the household's top three expenditures (Pape and Parisotto 2019). Qualitative data from focus group discussions conducted as part of this work in Juba, Kapoeta, and Rumbek counties indicate a high priority given to water payments over other household expenditure (RVI 2022). A participatory exercise was used to indicate the relative importance of water payments in overall household expenditure (see appendix A for details). Whereas most focus groups gave highest priority to education spending, water was second in priority, followed by other categories of livestock, health, and food (figure 2.8).

Reliance on water trucks in urban areas further compounds affordability challenges. Although there are no official estimates for the price of tanker water, existing reports suggest that the price of water depends on the distance and the tank used. A large drum of water costs between 500 and 1,000 South Sudanese pounds (US$1.13–US$2.27), and a jerry can costs 100 pounds ($0.77) (Magot 2021).

WATER SECURITY FOR PRODUCTION

Key points

- Variability of water resources in time and space influences all livelihood systems in South Sudan and the combination of activities pursued by populations for sustenance and income generation.
- Seasonal flooding sustains livelihoods for about 6 million people living along the Nile and Sobat Rivers and the wider eastern and western floodplains.
- South Sudan has some of Sub-Saharan Africa's highest solar adoption potential, with a suitable area for solar-based irrigation using groundwater

and surface water of about 6–10 million and 1–3 million hectares, respectively.

- Although new emerging livelihoods, such as artisanal mining, charcoal production, and brickmaking, support income generation, they also contribute to deforestation and land degradation, exacerbating vulnerability to droughts and pluvial flooding.

Overview

Water's productive potential sustains livelihoods and ecosystem services across South Sudan. Through the term *water security for production*, this section recognizes two fundamental dimensions linking water security to production. First, water security inherently speaks to the provision of water as an input to production, that is, an input to the creation and sustenance of human-made capital assets and livelihoods. Because of the country context and because of the broad range of activities and assets that South Sudanese leverage to support themselves, generate income, and meet their food security needs, the section focuses specifically on water as an input to livelihoods. Second, water security also speaks to water resources as an input to sustaining natural assets of social, economic, and environmental value, such as freshwater ecosystems (including wetlands). Building upon this understanding of water security for production, this section describes the potential for water to sustain productive livelihoods and ecosystems. The section then examines the potential for water sector investments to moderate the effects of hydrological variability on livelihoods.

Livelihoods are highly dependent on water resources and water-related ecosystems

Most South Sudanese derive their livelihoods from activities that are highly dependent on water availability and variability. About 78 percent of households rely on subsistence agriculture and pastoralism as the primary source of income (AfDB 2013). Although the relative contribution of agriculture and pastoralism to the economy is low—accounting for about 10 percent of GDP—these activities play a crucial role for food security and well-being (World Bank 2021b). In addition, approximately 12–15 percent of the population relies on freshwater fisheries as their primary source of livelihood (AfDB 2013). Agriculture, pastoralism, and freshwater fisheries are highly dependent on water resources, and therefore vulnerable to changes in its quantity and quality. To assess the link between these sources of livelihoods and water resources, the report combines data on livelihood zones with information on population distribution and water availability.

The most recent Livelihood Zone Classification for South Sudan (map 2.4) identifies 12 different livelihood zones, which can be aggregated into 6 major livelihood systems following classifications developed by SSCCSE (2011) and UNEP (2018). The correspondence between the 12 livelihood zones and the broader livelihood systems is shown in table 2.2. Overall, this classification suggests that livelihood systems are a combination of five activities: cattle grazing, crop production, wild food collection, fishing and hunting, and trade.

MAP 2.4

Livelihood zones of South Sudan

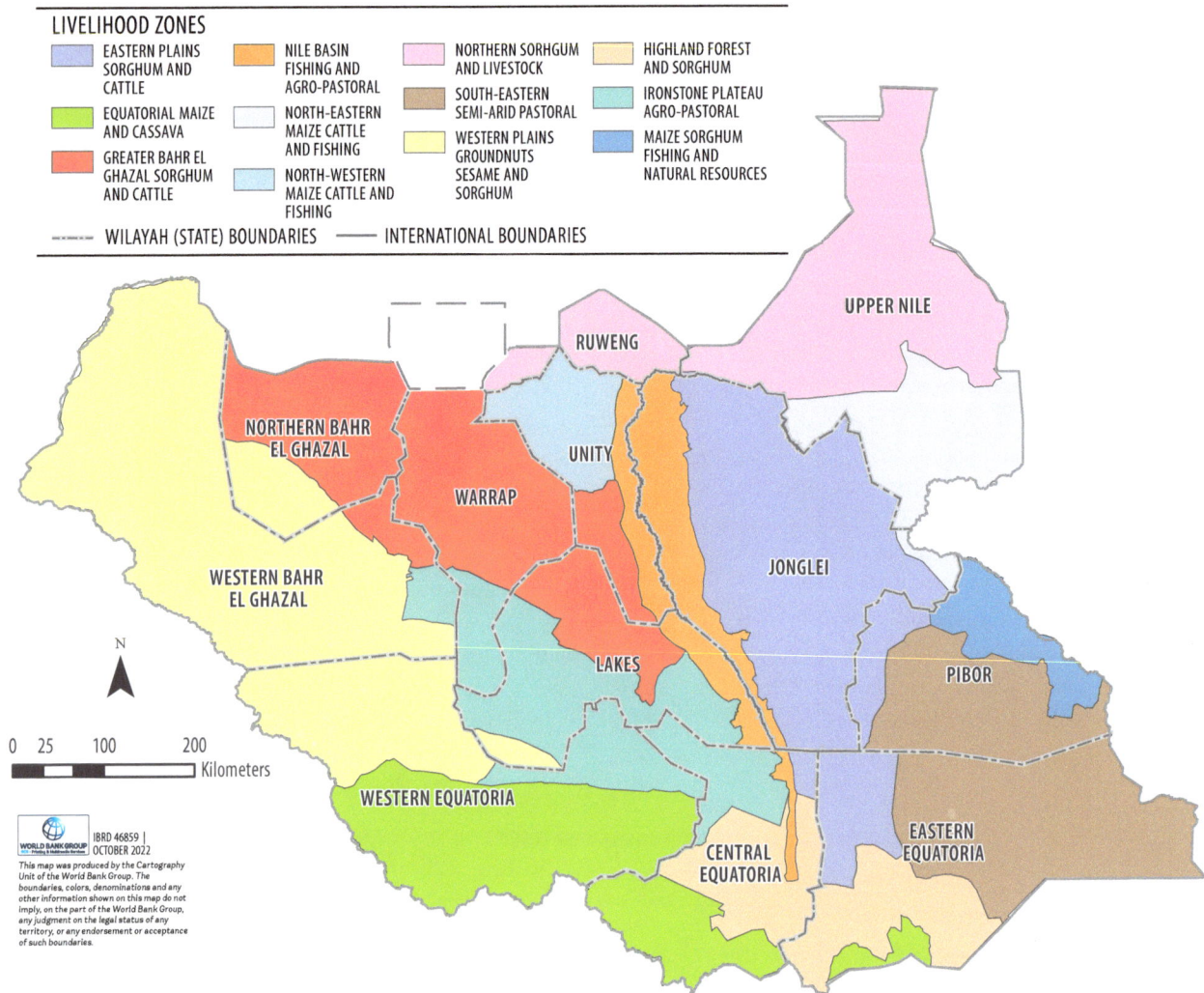

LIVELIHOOD ZONES

- EASTERN PLAINS SORGHUM AND CATTLE
- EQUATORIAL MAIZE AND CASSAVA
- GREATER BAHR EL GHAZAL SORGHUM AND CATTLE
- NILE BASIN FISHING AND AGRO-PASTORAL
- NORTH-EASTERN MAIZE CATTLE AND FISHING
- NORTH-WESTERN MAIZE CATTLE AND FISHING
- NORTHERN SORHGUM AND LIVESTOCK
- SOUTH-EASTERN SEMI-ARID PASTORAL
- WESTERN PLAINS GROUNDNUTS SESAME AND SORGHUM
- HIGHLAND FOREST AND SORGHUM
- IRONSTONE PLATEAU AGRO-PASTORAL
- MAIZE SORGHUM FISHING AND NATURAL RESOURCES

- - - - WILAYAH (STATE) BOUNDARIES ——— INTERNATIONAL BOUNDARIES

IBRD 46859 | OCTOBER 2022

This map was produced by the Cartography Unit of the World Bank Group. The boundaries, colors, denominations and any other information shown on this map do not imply, on the part of the World Bank Group, any judgment on the legal status of any territory, or any endorsement or acceptance of such boundaries.

Source: World Bank, based on data from SSCCSE (2011) and UNEP (2018).

Variability of water resources in time and space influences each of these livelihood systems and the combination of activities pursued by populations. More specifically, this variability engenders water-related risks and opportunities, which tend to vary in each of the livelihood systems (table 2.2). Although table 2.2 describes livelihood systems based on different activities and water-related risks and opportunities, it is important to emphasize a few features that are common across livelihood zones. First, cattle are central to most livelihoods in South Sudan, except in the southwest, and their importance extends well beyond food production (milk and meat). Cattle signify—and to some extent determine—wealth and status, form the foundations for social networks, and are an important part of the dowry (bride price). Second, mobility is a key feature of most livelihood systems. Mobility allows people to take advantage of seasonal food opportunities in different areas, such as fish and wild foods; it is also crucial for the survival of livestock, which depend on

TABLE 2.2 Main livelihood systems, related water risks and opportunities, and livelihood zone names

LIVELIHOOD SYSTEM	WATER-RELATED RISKS	WATER-RELATED OPPORTUNITIES	LIVELIHOOD ZONE NAME (MAP CODES)	POPULATION (MILLION)
Ironstone Plateau	• Multiyear drought • Seasonal water shortage in the dry season due to the low water retention capacity of soils	Improved access to water for agriculture through targeted expansion of water storage and irrigation infrastructure	• Ironstone Plateau: agro-pastoral • Western plains: groundnuts, sesame, and sorghum	1.40
Semiarid	• High vulnerability to drought • Overgrazing and gully erosion • Artisanal mining activity threatening water quality	Integrated catchment management and water storage to reduce drought vulnerability and soil erosion risk	Eastern: semiarid pastoral	0.62
Floodplains	Catastrophic flood events result in heavy crop and livestock losses	• Harness benefits of seasonal flooding • Support local governance systems and agreements between groups over access to seasonal water and grazing areas for livestock	• Eastern plains: sorghum and cattle • Greater Bahr el Ghazal: sorghum and cattle • Northwestern Nile basin: cattle and maize • Northern: sorghum and livestock	5.03
Nile and Sobat corridors	Catastrophic flood events	• Maximize opportunities provided by the Nile basin, including domestic fish production and preservation, water lily farming and production, rice production, flood-recession agriculture, and navigation • Protection of water resources from pollution	• Northeastern: maize, cattle, and fishing • Nile basin: fishing and agro-pastoral	0.98
Hills and mountains	• Drought and timing of seasonal rains • Land use change and erosion	Integrated catchment management to reduce drought vulnerability and soil erosion risk	• Maize, sorghum, fishing, and natural resources • Highland forest and sorghum	1.01
Greenbelt	Pluvial flooding and crop losses due to poor drainage and infrastructure	High water availability and bimodal rainfall pattern offer opportunities to strengthen rainfed agriculture and generate food surplus	Equatorial: maize and cassava	1.47

Source: World Bank based on SSCCSE (2011), UNEP (2018), and WorldPop data.

regular migrations between dry and wet season grazing areas (Martell 2019). As described more in chapter 3, when floods or conflict restrict mobility, livelihoods are more likely to be disrupted.

Water is highly valued in pastoralist communities—among pastoralists "water is food." This means that water is not just about drinking but can also be a source of food, prestige, and influence in the community. As one elder explained in the focus groups, "If you have 20 cows, 30 goats, and 50 sheep you pay 30,000 South Sudanese pounds [about US$60] a month for water, which is a large amount for a poor pastoralist" (RVI 2022).

Seasonal flooding sustains floodplain livelihoods for millions of people living along the Nile and Sobat Rivers and in the eastern and western floodplain zones. An estimated 6 million people live in these areas where livelihoods depend on changing water levels, with the highest share of the population relying on flood-based livelihoods found in the Upper Nile and parts of Unity, Jonglei, Warrap, Northern Bahr el Ghazal, and Lakes. This includes about 1 million people living in the Nile and Sobat River corridors, whose livelihoods and food security rely heavily on freshwater fisheries. The water resources of the two rivers have enabled communities to withstand the impact of the protracted conflict better than other zones (SSCCSE 2011). Seasonal flooding between July and September increases yields of fish and wild foods. In some areas where receding floods leave sufficient soil moisture, more than one maize or sorghum crop can be grown in a year. For poor groups, a combination of fish and wild foods commonly contributes about 40 percent of annual household food requirements in the floodplain zones (SSCCSE 2011). When catastrophic flooding occurs, such as the 2020 and 2021 events, access to wild foods (fish and water lilies) tends to decline, and the incidence of crop pests and livestock disease increase, severely disrupting livelihoods along the river corridors (UNEP 2018).

Receding and rising floodwaters are also key drivers of agro-pastoralism. Pastoralists follow the receding flow, with grazing land becoming available as the flood waters retreat to the main river channel (Catley 2018). When crop or livestock production fails, agro-pastoralists rely on riverine environments for fish, wild foods, and alternative pasture. Hence, riverine environments become important safety nets for agro-pastoralists during food shortfall years. The productivity of these flood-based livelihood systems can be further enhanced by improved maintenance of small-scale water control structures, such as community dikes, that can allow for better control of water, protection of livestock routes and fishing zones, and reduced erosion and waterlogging, and also by enhancements to field water management and agronomic practices.

The unique Sudd wetland is the principal basis of livelihoods for millions

A large part of South Sudan is covered by wetlands, which are a cornerstone for livelihoods, especially in the floodplains. Wetlands cover 7 percent of the total area of South Sudan, with the Sudd covering at least 5 percent (AfDB 2013). As described in chapter 1, the Sudd is Africa's largest wetland and one of the largest tropical wetlands in the world. The Sudd is a Ramsar site, which confers it globally recognized importance for containing representative, rare, or unique types of wetland and for conserving biodiversity. The Sudd-Sahelian Flooded Grasslands and Savannas eco-region, of which the Sudd is a part, is a key unrepresented ecological system globally (UNESCO 2017).

The economic value of the Sudd wetland for livelihoods alone has been estimated to be more than US$250 million (NBI 2020). However, it is important to note that the ecosystem services that the Sudd wetland provides go well beyond supporting livelihoods and include water regulation, biodiversity, and cultural services. Among the services provided by the wetland are the regulation of microclimate, flood control, and water regulation. Microclimate regulation takes place as a result of the high proportion of water that evaporates from wetlands. The evaporated water is not lost from the system given that it is partly recycled in the form of rain and it contributes to an increase of the air moisture index, which results in a reduction of evaporation in the dry season (Mohamed et al. 2005). The Nile Basin Initiative estimates the total economic value of the multiple services, all underpinned by water, from the wetland to be at least US$3.2 billion (NBI 2020).

Global analysis confirms the importance of natural assets, and of the water resources that sustain them, for societal well-being. A vast majority of South Sudanese (about 75 percent of the country's population) directly depend on nature for their food, clean water, and energy through subsistence uses (Fedele et al. 2021). This positions South Sudan among the top 10 countries in the tropics for the total number of people who directly depend on natural capital for their well-being and basic needs. This strong, direct dependence on nature contributes to increased climate vulnerability and is also typically associated with lower levels of human development.

The potential of water resources to sustain and enhance livelihoods and food security remains unexploited

Different types of gray water infrastructure are key enablers of sustainable livelihoods, particularly in the drier areas of the country. There are no large dams or reservoirs in South Sudan with storage capacity greater than 0.1 cubic kilometer, and most water storage structures are community based. Water is commonly stored in community ponds, roadside dugout pits, rock catchments, water barriers, and *haffir* (Arabic word for pond). These water storage structures have been constructed by communities, the government, and international partners, and no inventory of them exists. They typically serve multiple purposes, including human consumption and livestock water needs.

Many of the more recently constructed haffir are reported to be nonfunctional because of inadequate site selection, design, and maintenance (FAO 2015b). In some cases, these water storage structures have been promoted as a means of reducing tensions over access to water, particularly for livestock. Guidelines for improved technical designs have been developed (FAO 2015a) and can form the basis for a countrywide needs assessment of haffir.

South Sudan's irrigation potential remains largely untapped. According to the MWRI, irrigated agriculture currently accounts for less than 5 percent of the total area under cultivation (South Sudan MWRI 2021). The irrigated land is distributed across the country, with about 12,700 hectares in Upper Nile state, and other irrigated areas in Jonglei and Western Equatoria (AfDB 2013). The overall suitability of South Sudan for irrigated agriculture is very high, with the Nile Basin Initiative setting it at 24 million hectares based on physical characteristics and accessibility (NBI 2012) out of total agricultural land of about 28.5 million hectares. In the short to medium term, the African Development Bank estimates that 1.5 million hectares could be developed in the floodplain, greenbelt, and Nile and Sobat zones (AfDB 2013). The 2015 Irrigation Development Master Plan recognizes the potential for expansion and identifies specific priority projects, including Wau, Jebel Lado, and Rejaf East (South Sudan MWRI 2021).

Analysis of hydro-climatic data further confirms the potential benefits of improved agricultural water management. Map 2.5 shows areas of South Sudan that face, on average, some water deficit conditions during the May–September rainy season. This is the main crop-growing season in the Greater Upper Nile and Greater Bahr el Ghazal areas, and thus any water

MAP 2.5

Aridity index during the main growing season (May to September), average 2006–19

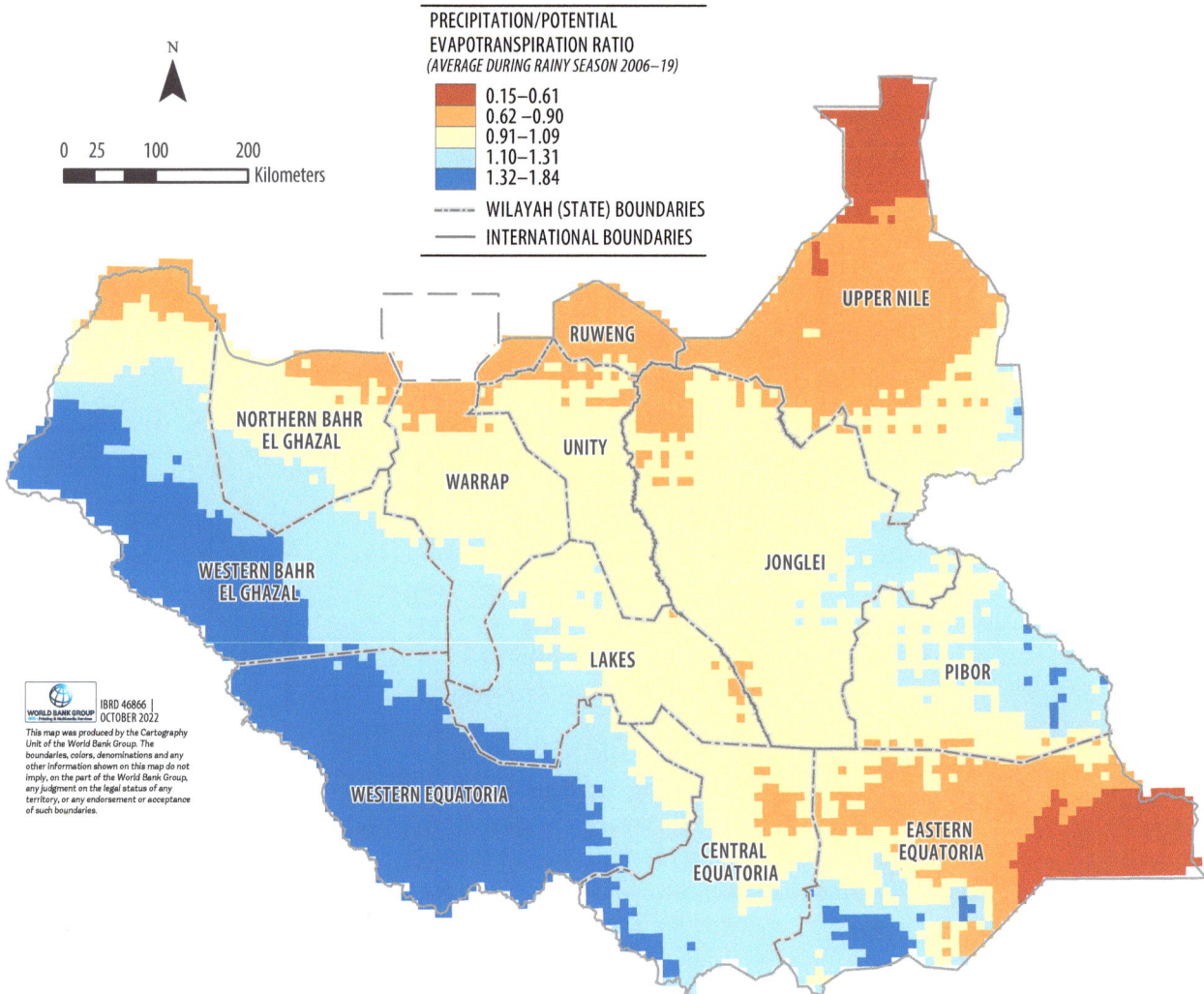

PRECIPITATION/POTENTIAL
EVAPOTRANSPIRATION RATIO
(AVERAGE DURING RAINY SEASON 2006–19)

- 0.15–0.61
- 0.62–0.90
- 0.91–1.09
- 1.10–1.31
- 1.32–1.84

WILAYAH (STATE) BOUNDARIES
INTERNATIONAL BOUNDARIES

Source: World Bank.

deficit is likely to affect harvests that take place from September onward. The risk of water deficits is quantified using the aridity index, which compares the long-term average of precipitation to the long-term average of climatic water demand (known as potential evapotranspiration). When this ratio is less than one, especially during the growing season, water deficits might occur and hinder plant growth, reducing harvests. Eastern Equatoria and Upper Nile emerge as the two key states facing severe aridity conditions during the main growing season (red areas in map 2.5). When population distribution is overlaid on this information on aridity, it emerges that about 7.5 million people live in areas facing some level of water deficit during the growing season, especially in the Greater Upper Nile and Greater Bahr el Ghazal areas and Eastern Equatoria (World Bank 2022a).

Improved water availability during the main crop-growing seasons can enhance yields and bolster food production. South Sudan's yields are well below average yields in neighboring countries. In 2018, for example, South Sudan's cereal yield (in kilograms per hectare) was about 18 percent of the average in

South Africa, and about a third (31–41 percent) of that of Kenya, Uganda, or Ethiopia (World Bank 2022b). This low agricultural performance is confirmed by data for South Sudan's major crops, whose average yields are well below yield potential for both rainfed and irrigated systems estimated for the country (table 2.3). Although potential for yield improvement is location-specific and depends on a range of biophysical and human-related factors, table 2.3 clearly shows significant opportunities for agricultural water management to enhance food production. In rainfed systems, yield improvements could materialize through measures to retain more water in soils (for example, use of cover crops, no-till systems, and soil water management practices such as terraces). Irrigation expansion is another solution; however, its adoption will depend on whether use of irrigation is sustainable (withdrawal rates in line with recharge rates and environmental requirements) or economically feasible (for example, depth of groundwater and associated pumping costs).

Innovations in irrigation service provision offer opportunities to enhance water's contribution to livelihoods and food security. First, processes such as farmer-led irrigation development could help accelerate the uptake of irrigation in the country and enhance the chances of social and economic sustainability (Izzi, Denison, and Veldwisch 2021). Small-scale farmer-led irrigation practices are a cost-effective and scalable agricultural water management solution that have been proven to enhance the food security and livelihoods of smallholders in Sub-Saharan Africa (Lefore, Closas, and Schmitter 2021). Another opportunity for expansion of irrigated agriculture in South Sudan is small-scale solar-powered irrigation systems. In the context of underdeveloped electricity infrastructure, off-grid solar photovoltaic irrigation presents an important alternative for pumping and for improving rural communities' livelihoods. The solar suitability framework developed by the International Water Management Institute (Schmitter et al. 2018) is used here to quantify the suitability for solar-based irrigation in South Sudan. South Sudan has some of Sub-Saharan Africa's highest solar adoption potential (Xie et al. 2014), with a suitable area for solar-based irrigation of 6–10 million and 1–3 million hectares, using groundwater and surface water, respectively, as shown in figure 2.9. Within South Sudan, areas with the highest potential for groundwater-based solar pumping are in the east and northeast of the country, and for surface water–based pumping in the northwest and east. Although irrigation has significant potential, including through solar pumping, more careful assessments are required to prioritize investments for rehabilitation and expansion. Particular attention is needed for issues of equity in access to technologies for poor farmers and women, and sustainability of

TABLE 2.3 **Comparison of average yields for major crops and yield potential under well-managed irrigated and rainfed systems in South Sudan**

MAJOR CROPS	YIELD ESTIMATES, 2018 (TONS/HA)	YIELD POTENTIAL UNDER IMPROVED AGRICULTURAL WATER MANAGEMENT PRACTICES	
		RAINFED SYSTEMS (TONS/HA)	IRRIGATED SYSTEMS (TONS/HA)
Groundnuts	0.5–0.7	2.0–3.0	3.5–4.5
Cassava	11.0–17.0	12.5–30.0	12.5–30.0
Sorghum	0.7–1.3	0.3–2.0	3.5–5.0
Maize	0.7–1.3	2.0–3.0	6.0–9.0

Source: World Bank, based on FAO 2019 and SORUDEV 2021.
Note: Data on average yields are for 2018 and come from FAO (2019). Data on yield potential are from SORUDEV (2021). Ha = hectare.

FIGURE 2.9

Area identified as suitable for small-scale solar irrigation with surface and groundwater resources

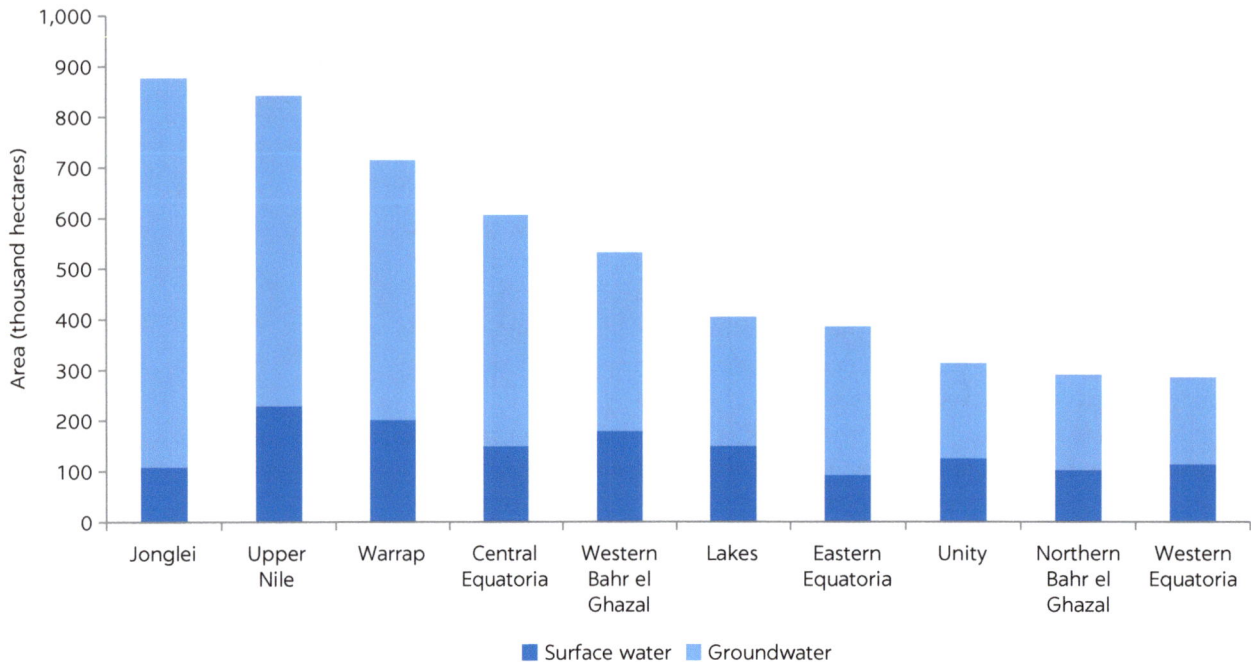

Source: International Water Management Institute 2022.
Note: No data available for Abyei AA, Greater Pibor AA, and Ruweng AA.

water use to avoid water resources depletion. In addition, problems facing South Sudan's agricultural sector are not going to be solved by irrigation expansion alone, requiring a comprehensive food systems approach to ensure that all important links are pursued (World Bank 2022d).

Even though improvements in agricultural water management can also benefit livestock systems, investments in this area need to be particularly cognizant of related social and conflict dynamics. FAO (2019) estimates that there are at least 11.7 million to 13 million head of cattle in South Sudan, plus about 24 million sheep and goats. Although the accuracy of these estimates is low and difficult to assess, the sheer scale of the numbers suggests that water-livestock interactions need to be considered in the country's water resources development. In most countries, water-livestock interactions are dominated by the large quantity of water used in the production of feed. Across the world, only about 2 percent of water consumption related to livestock production goes into animal drinking (Heinke et al. 2020). In South Sudan, however, there are many more ways in which livestock and water interact (box 2.2).

The converging effects of climate change, environmental degradation, and conflict on livelihoods and ecosystems

Even though natural capital–based livelihoods have evolved to adapt to hydrological variability, many adaptation strategies have broken down in the past few decades because of increasing external and internal pressures. Conflict and climate change emerge as two key pressures that are having profound effects on livelihoods. Livelihoods are also one of the main channels through which the impacts of climate change interact with social and political factors, such as elite

Livestock and water resources interactions

The One Health approach provides a framework with which to analyze livestock and water resources interactions in South Sudan. Animal and human health are interrelated, and in turn they depend on a healthy environment. As shown in figure B2.2.1, water is a core determinant and connector shaping interactions between human, livestock, and environmental health in South Sudan.

Water resources engender risks and opportunities at the interface between environmental and livestock health. Most livestock feed on rangelands whose water consumption is met through rainfall. Hence, improvements in pasture management and soil moisture retention can enhance the productivity of these rainfed systems, halting land degradation and contributing to sustaining forage availability. With regard to risks, flooding leads to livestock losses and disease. For example, at least 800,000 head of cattle, goats, and sheep and an unknown quantity of poultry died because of drowning, lack of livestock feed, and diseases following the 2021 flooding event (FAO 2021).

Livestock can also significantly degrade the country's water resources, thus requiring careful coordination between water and livestock management interventions and community management of water points. Livestock grazing and watering along the edges of water bodies such as rivers and dams leads to removal of riparian vegetation and greater channel siltation, increasing the chances of localized flooding and hindering navigation.

Water resources also play a key role at the interface of human and livestock interactions. Uncontrolled livestock grazing close to community drinking water points can lead to contamination of drinking water supplies and disease transmission. Conversely, more controlled and strategic placement and use of livestock water points can contribute to livestock health and community well-being. As discussed in chapter 3, absence of livestock water points induces herders to move into new areas in search of water, putting them in contact with other population groups and heightening the risk of conflict. Strategic placement of

FIGURE B2.2.1

One Health framework summary of livestock and water resources interactions in South Sudan

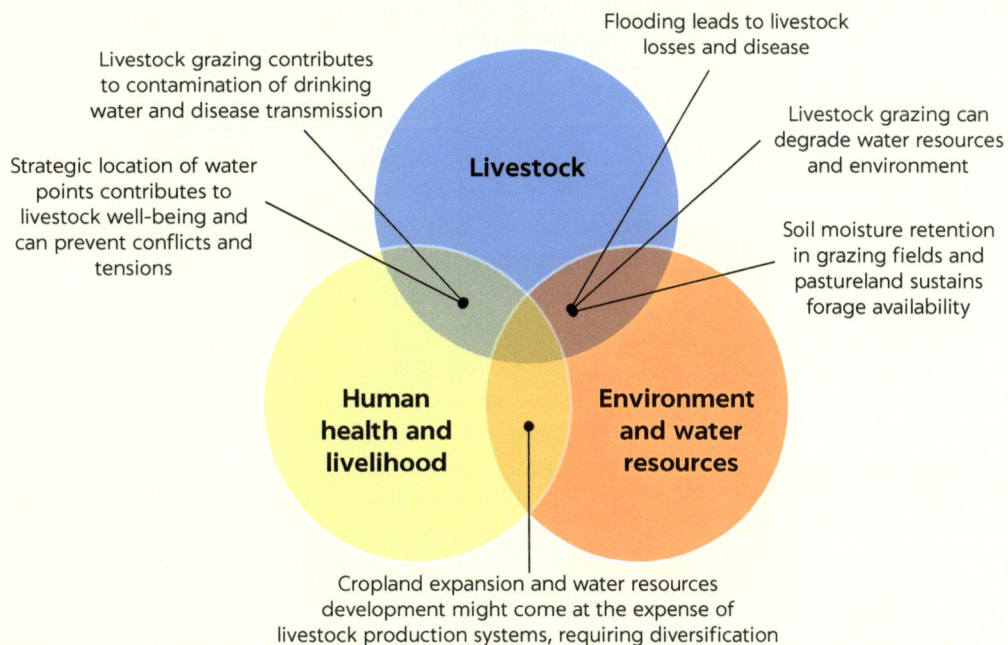

Source: World Bank.

continued

Box 2.2, *continued*

groundwater points, especially in the arid southeast, can prevent excessive mobility and can enable pastoralists to take advantage of rangeland areas currently unusable because of the lack of watering facilities (Peden et al. 2005). Strategic placement of water points along routes to markets can further improve livestock production because it reduces the risk of animal weight loss and mortality, thus overcoming market access constraints caused by animals' poor health.

Human and environmental interactions, especially in relation to water resources development, can further strain livestock systems. For example, any anticipated expansion of rainfed or irrigated cropland might come at the expense of pastoralists' access to land and water resources. To avoid future tensions and marginalization, investments need to carefully navigate customary land access practices to diversify community livelihoods to rely less on livestock and pasture.

exploitation of local grievances, to compound existing vulnerabilities and tensions.

Decades of conflict and insecurity have disrupted many livelihood systems and altered related production and trade patterns. Since at least the Second Sudanese Civil War, which started in 1983, livelihood systems have changed in response to conflict, displacement, resettlements, reduced kinship ties, and humanitarian aid. These factors and, to a lesser extent, demographic pressures and associated changes in population density, have seriously disrupted mobility patterns and access to water and land resources over the years. These disruptions have had ripple effects on food security, heightening the risk of food shortages, particularly for pastoralists. Conflict and insecurity are expected to remain the major pressure on livelihoods moving forward, as resettlements continue, risks of cattle raids or predation remain high, and security of land tenure, whether legally or customarily defined, remains low (Diing et al. 2021).

Climate change is also straining livelihoods through its impacts on water resources availability and extremes. Although livelihoods have adapted to South Sudan's high levels of hydrological variability, the frequency and intensity of floods and droughts under climate change well exceed this envelope of variability and cause unprecedented stress on livelihoods. Droughts lead to fodder and water shortages, which lead to higher mortality among animals and decreased crop production. Droughts might also lead pastoralists to sell more of their livestock, causing an oversupply of typically undernourished animals that fetch low prices in markets and thus make people more prone to finding alternative means of recouping their losses, including cattle raiding or joining violent groups (Maystadt, Calderone, and You 2014). This risk is particularly pronounced in the semiarid southwest of the country.

Degradation of the country's natural capital is also straining livelihoods. More than 99 percent of the population of South Sudan depends on forests as their source of energy (fuel wood and charcoal) and for construction and furniture (UNEP 2018). Deforestation, overgrazing, and plowing are the main causes of human-induced environmental degradation, especially soil erosion. In turn, these causes can have negative consequences on livelihoods, especially in the highlands and pastoralists' areas, where it triggers a series of cascading effects, such as fertility and nutrient loss, reduced carbon storage, and declining biodiversity. Soil erosion rates in South Sudan have been increasing since the start of the century, with global assessments pointing to a 5 percent increase in annual average soil erosion (Borrelli et al. 2017). By 2070 and without any adaptation measures, water erosion over land could increase by 2.5 percent across the country, with some areas in the highlands zone experiencing as much as a 7 percent increase in soil erosion and associated land degradation (Borrelli et al. 2020). The sustainability of water resources is also intertwined with the country's natural capital, with soil and catchment degradation causing river siltation, and increasing flood risk and oil spills causing public health incidents. The lack of environmental standards and guidelines to safeguard the exploration and exploitation in the extractive industry has led to pollution in the oil fields and in the surrounding areas (UNEP 2018).

As a result of the convergence of these pressures, livelihoods are being disrupted and new livelihood systems are emerging, some of which heighten vulnerability to water-related risks. Decades of conflict and forced displacement mean that humanitarian aid now plays a fundamental role for livelihoods, for both food provisioning and inputs, such as seeds. The forced displacement crisis has also influenced livelihoods, with refugees returning to South Sudan bringing new experiences of rural and urban living and livelihoods, which have contributed to the emergence of new markets, such as mining, charcoal, and brickmaking. Fuel wood and charcoal production supports income generation, but it also contributes to deforestation and land degradation, exacerbating vulnerability to droughts and pluvial flooding. Finally, remittances help populations face daily contingencies and disruptions to livelihood-generating activities. In 2021, the total inflow of remittances to South Sudan was equivalent to 30 percent of the national gross domestic product (World Bank 2021c).

WATER SECURITY FOR PROTECTION

Key points

- South Sudan ranks seventh in the world for share of the total country population exposed to river floods.
- Interactions between local and global climate patterns influence the occurrence of floods. Warming in the Western Equatorial Indian Ocean can bring excess precipitation to the African Great Lakes region and South Sudan, causing riverine flooding in the center and eastern parts of the country, where the largest rivers are located.
- One in two South Sudanese, or about 5.4 million people, live in areas exposed to moderate flood hazard (areas where water depths of a 1-in-100-year flood event reach or exceed 0.15 meters).
- One in four South Sudanese, or about 2.7 million people, live in areas exposed to high and potentially deadly flood hazard (areas where water depths of a 1-in-100-year flood event reach or exceed 0.5 meter).
- The southeastern and northeastern parts of the country have experienced more droughts compared with the rest of the country. In these areas, droughts can affect the mobility options of pastoralists and others who rely on natural resources for their livelihoods, bringing them into competition with neighboring communities and increasing the risk of cattle raids.
- Droughts are projected to become 60–100 percent more frequent by the end of the century compared with the 2020s.

Overview

This section focuses on the destructive force of water. Protection from water-related disasters, notably floods and droughts, is a key component of water security. Countries where lives, livelihoods, and economic performance are resilient to floods and droughts are relatively water secure. In contrast, countries are water insecure when floods and droughts impose social and economic costs, with ripple effects on economic performance and social stability. The impacts of floods and droughts in South Sudan are growing, not just because climate change is increasing their frequency and intensity, but also because protracted armed conflict and forced displacement are pushing more people and assets into harm's way.

South Sudan is a global hotspot for flood risk

South Sudan is one of the world's countries most exposed to river floods. It ranks seventh for share of total country population exposed to river floods, just behind countries such as Bangladesh and Myanmar, which are well-known flood risk hotspots (World Resources Institute 2019). Flood exposure is defined as the people, assets, or other elements located in harm's way (in hazard zones) and thereby subject to potential losses when the harm materializes (UNISDR 2009), while flood hazard is defined as a phenomenon that can cause loss of lives, livelihoods, disruption, and environmental damage. Exposure is mostly a function of the location of people and assets, while hazard is a function of hydrological and biophysical factors.

To analyze flood risk in South Sudan, this report uses the Fathom data set, which provides high-resolution information from a global hydrological model on the depth and extent of inundation from undefended floods during flood events of different frequencies (see appendix A for details). As shown in map 2.6, 1-in-20- and 1-in-100-year floods inundate large swaths of the country well beyond the areas close to the Sudd wetland. The map clearly shows that even under a 1-in-20-year flood event, that is, an event with an annual probability of occurrence of 0.05, all states apart from Western Bahr el Ghazal and Western Equatoria would face some flooding with depths of at least 0.15 meter. These flood depths are already sufficient to damage road infrastructure and considerably disrupt livelihoods. Under a more severe 1-in-100-year flood event, even more areas are expected to be inundated, including areas in central Unity and Ruweng Administrative Area (AA). Analysis of flood extents following the 2021 floods, shown in map 2.7, confirms the findings from the global hydrological model and the sobering assessment that even relatively frequent floods (for example, 1-in-20-year events) are expected to inundate all but 2 of the country's 13 states and administrative areas.

Mapping of flood depth further confirms that several states are confronted with very high and potentially deadly flood inundation depths, even for relatively frequent flood events. Under a 1-in-100-year flood event, large parts of the Greater Upper Nile and eastern Bahr el Ghazal regions would be submerged under a meter of floodwater. These areas are mostly, but not exclusively, located along the White Nile River and the Sudd wetland, as shown in map 2.8. Even under a 1-in-20-year event, that is, a relatively more frequent flood event, most areas around the Sudd and Machar wetlands and large parts of Unity, Warrap, and Jonglei states would be submerged under a meter of floodwater. Under

MAP 2.6

National flood extent map for 1-in-20- and 1-in-100-year flood events

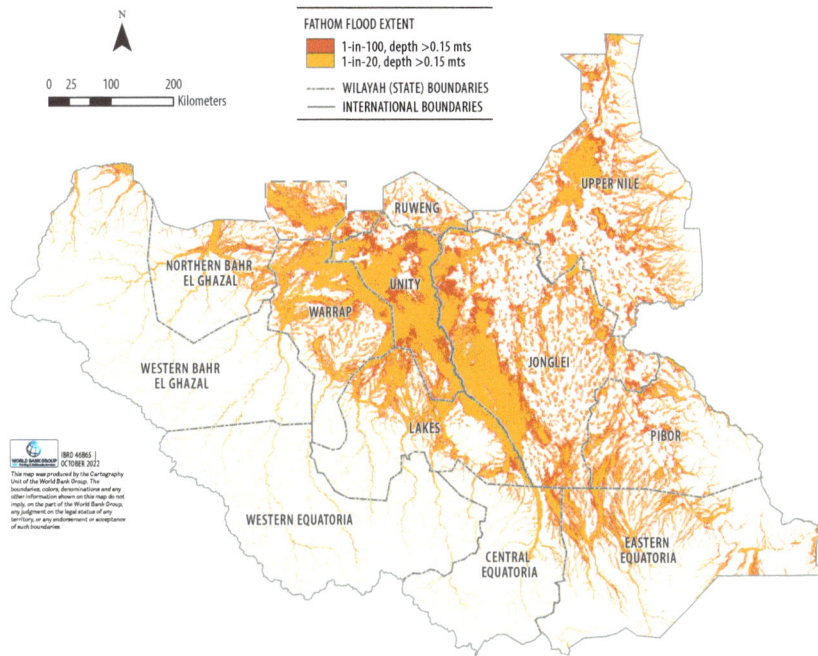

Source: World Bank using Fathom.

MAP 2.7

Flooded area as a proportion of total county area and flood extent of the May–October 2021 South Sudan floods

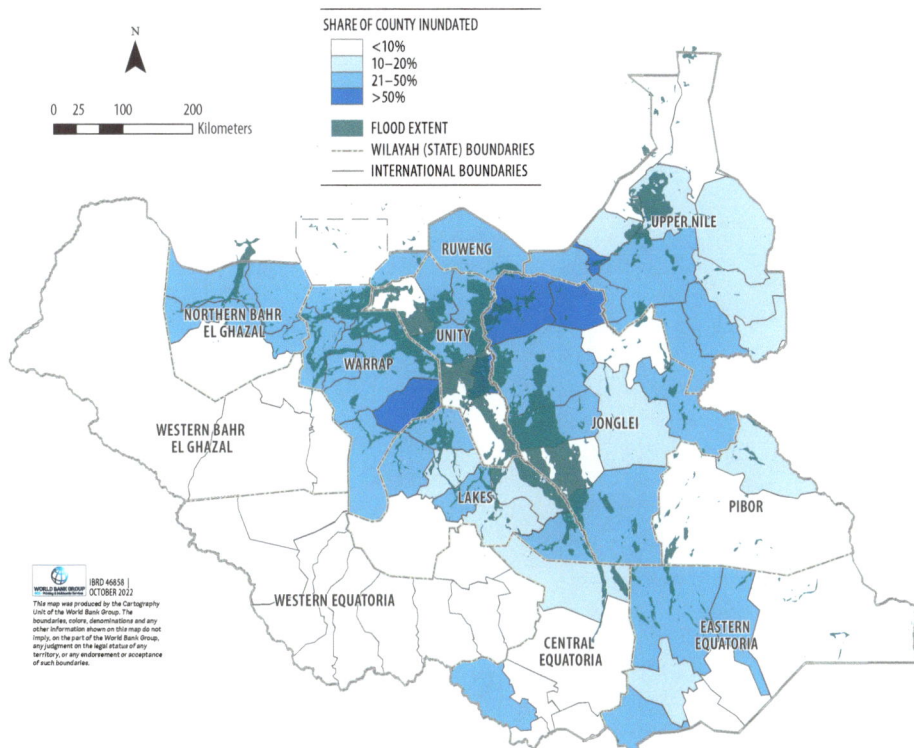

Source: World Bank.
Note: Darker blue counties are those that have experienced inundation over a greater proportion of their area. Note that overlain in green are the flood extents (that is, areas submerged) from September 19 through October 24.

MAP 2.8

Modeled flood depth for 1-in-20- and 1-in-100-year fluvial flood events

a. 1-in-20-year flood event

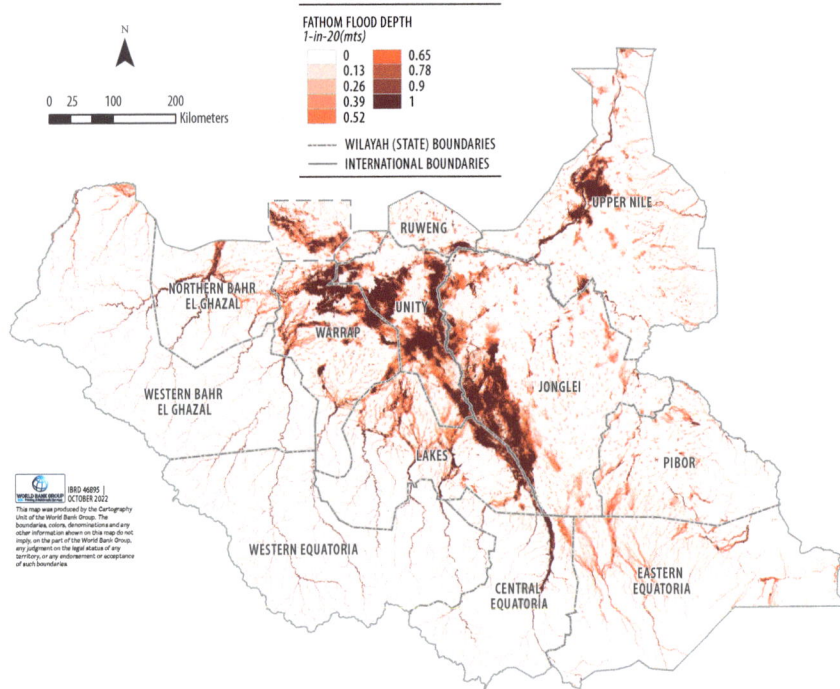

b. 1-in-100-year flood event

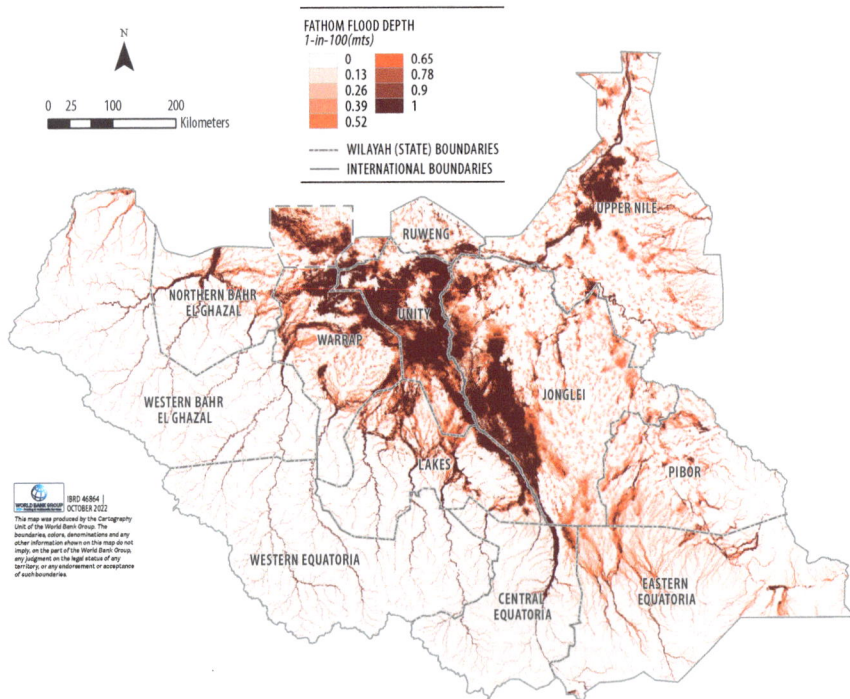

Source: World Bank using Fathom data.

these conditions, flood impacts on lives and livelihoods are catastrophic; even fit adults would have difficulty wading to safety, and all roads and evacuation routes would be completely submerged, requiring boats or helicopters to deliver relief and evacuate people.

This information on flood hazard (depth and extent) can be overlain with information on population and assets to map exposure to flooding. This combination helps provide a visual image of the locations where people are at risk and identifies counties with high numbers of people exposed to floods (that is, people living in harm's way). Map 2.9 shows population exposure to moderate or higher (that is, an inundation depth greater than or equal to 0.15 meter)[5] flood hazard relative to total county population. The central and eastern parts of the country have some of the highest exposure levels relative to their overall population. Table 2.4 shows the top 10 counties by relative exposure to flood hazard. Leer, Mayendit, and Twic East top the exposure ranking. These counties are near the Sudd wetland and are therefore highly exposed to the wetland's swelling following flooding. These findings are aligned with observations from the 2021 flood event, where, for example, water submerged nearly 90 percent of Mayendit's area (14 out of 16 payams) (World Bank 2021a).

In absolute terms, the top three counties with the most people exposed to moderate or higher flood hazard are Lafon, Kapoeta East, and Gogrial West (table 2.5). In a country such as South Sudan, where most counties face at least

MAP 2.9

Population exposure to moderate or higher flood risk relative to total county population

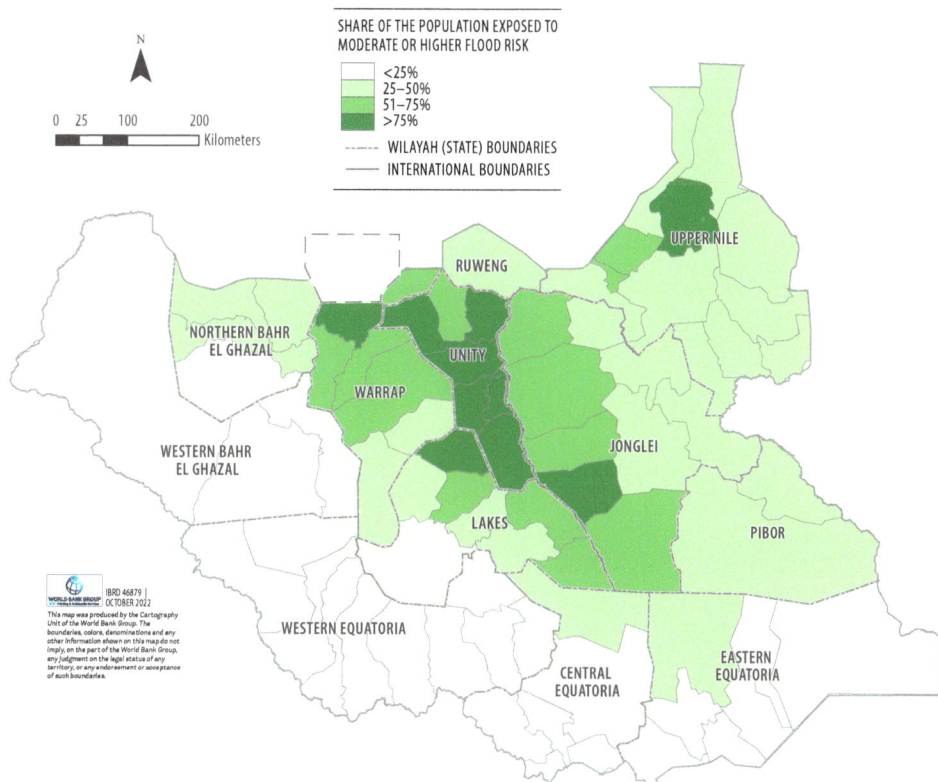

Source: World Bank using Fathom and WorldPop data.

TABLE 2.4 Top 10 counties by share of county population exposed to moderate or higher flood risk

COUNTY	STATE	POPULATION EXPOSED (% OF COUNTY POPULATION)	TOTAL POPULATION (THOUSANDS)
Leer	Unity	99	59
Mayendit	Unity	98	66
Twic East	Jonglei	90	118
Koch	Unity	89	105
Guit	Unity	86	66
Mayom	Unity	83	151
Panyijiar	Unity	80	109
Twic	Warrap	78	262
Melut	Upper Nile	78	125
Rumbek North	Lakes	77	70

Source: World Bank using Fathom and WorldPop data.

TABLE 2.5 Top 10 counties by total population exposed to moderate or higher flood risk

COUNTY	STATE	POPULATION EXPOSED (THOUSANDS)	POPULATION EXPOSED (% OF COUNTY POPULATION)
Lafon	Eastern Equatoria	294	40
Kapoeta East	Eastern Equatoria	195	18
Gogrial West	Warrap	191	67
Twic	Warrap	188	78
Bor South	Jonglei	174	51
Kapoeta North	Eastern Equatoria	169	24
Mayom	Unity	167	83
Magwi	Eastern Equatoria	145	13
Ayod	Jonglei	133	62
Aweil East	Northern Bahr el Ghazal	122	40

Source: World Bank using Fathom and WorldPop data.

some flood hazard, the absolute exposure map (map 2.10) more closely follows the country population map (map 2.9), with highly populous counties (for example, Gogrial West) also facing greater overall absolute risk because of their higher population.

The dramatic flood events of 2019, 2020, and 2021 are stark reminders of this extremely high exposure to flood hazards. South Sudan suffered three consecutive years of exceptionally severe flooding, and climate outlooks indicate that the 2022 rainy seasons will likely also bring above-average rainfall and flooding. The 2021 flood event damaged more than 100,000 buildings beyond repair, severely affecting about 1.24 million people (about 11 percent of South Sudan's population), with an additional 1.33 million people moderately affected.

MAP 2.10

Population exposure to moderate flood risk or higher (absolute)

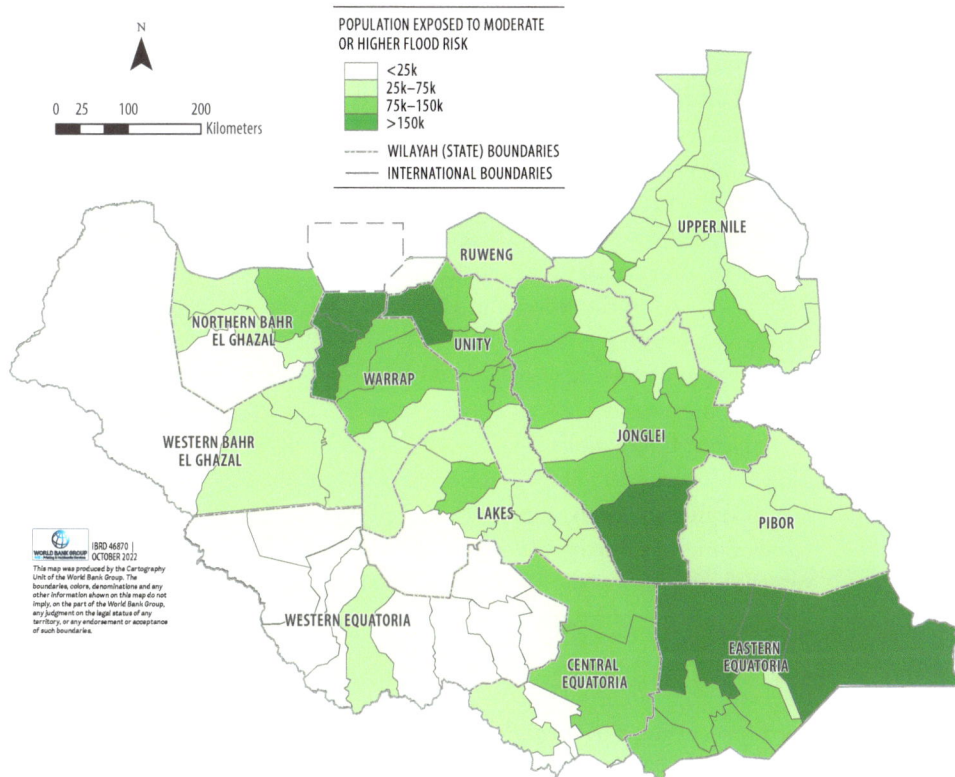

POPULATION EXPOSED TO MODERATE
OR HIGHER FLOOD RISK
- <25k
- 25k–75k
- 75k–150k
- >150k
- ----- WILAYAH (STATE) BOUNDARIES
- ——— INTERNATIONAL BOUNDARIES

0 25 100 200 Kilometers

RUWENG

UPPER NILE

NORTHERN BAHR EL GHAZAL

UNITY

WARRAP

WESTERN BAHR EL GHAZAL

JONGLEI

LAKES

PIBOR

WESTERN EQUATORIA

CENTRAL EQUATORIA

EASTERN EQUATORIA

IBRD 46870 | OCTOBER 2022

Source: World Bank using Fathom and WorldPop data.

The World Bank's damage assessment estimated the total direct economic damage from the 2021 flood event to be more than US$670 million (World Bank 2021a).

Catastrophic floods have devastating impacts on lives and livelihoods; however, more moderate floods can also have beneficial impacts. Rainfall occurring between April and October leads to seasonal floods, which are beneficial for soil fertility, grass and pasture growth, and fisheries (UNEP 2018). These events differ from the catastrophic floods just discussed because they occur with much higher frequency (annually) and lead to far less inundation than the less frequent events linked to variable continental and regional climate patterns. During this seasonal flooding, many parts of the country are left under water, including swaths of Jonglei, Unity, Upper Nile, Warrap, Northern Bahr el Ghazal, and parts of Western Equatoria and Eastern Equatoria (World Bank 2022c). Extensive seasonal flooding occurs particularly around the Sudd wetlands and along the rivers that flow into it from the south, east, and west, covering areas between 10 and 30,000 square kilometers and contributing to a significant difference in the size of the wetland between the dry and the rainy seasons. Despite different estimates for the size of the wetland (see chapter 1), all sources agree that seasonal hydrological variability is responsible for the considerable expansion and swelling of the wetland.

Determinants of flooding

South Sudan faces flood hazards from both fluvial and pluvial sources. Fluvial flooding occurs when water bodies (rivers, streams, lakes) overflow onto the surrounding banks and land. Pluvial flooding occurs when heavy rainfall saturates natural drainage (for example, soils unable to absorb the water) or artificial drainage (for example, urban drainage systems overwhelmed by the quantity of water), creating a flood independent of an overflowing water body. As shown in map 2.11, fluvial sources dominate in the central and eastern parts of the country, where the largest rivers are located. These floods are directly linked to rainfall patterns in the African Great Lakes region, where the Bahr el Jebel (White Nile) originates, and in the Ethiopian Highlands. Pluvial sources dominate in the southwest, where the steeper topography and the lack of large water bodies mean that most surface water floods occur following heavy rainfall events and not from the overflow of water bodies (map 2.12).

Complex interactions between climate patterns acting at local and global scales influence precipitation variability, and therefore the occurrence of floods and droughts, in South Sudan. At the continental scale, the El Niño–Southern Oscillation is a primary driver of variability. During an El Niño, the expected rainfall increase over most of the Lake Victoria catchment area is about 15–25 percent (Birkett, Murtugudde, and Allan 1999), which leads, in turn, to greater

MAP 2.11

Fluvial flood hazard (percentage of total depth of inundation for a 1-in-100-year undefended flooding event originating from fluvial sources)

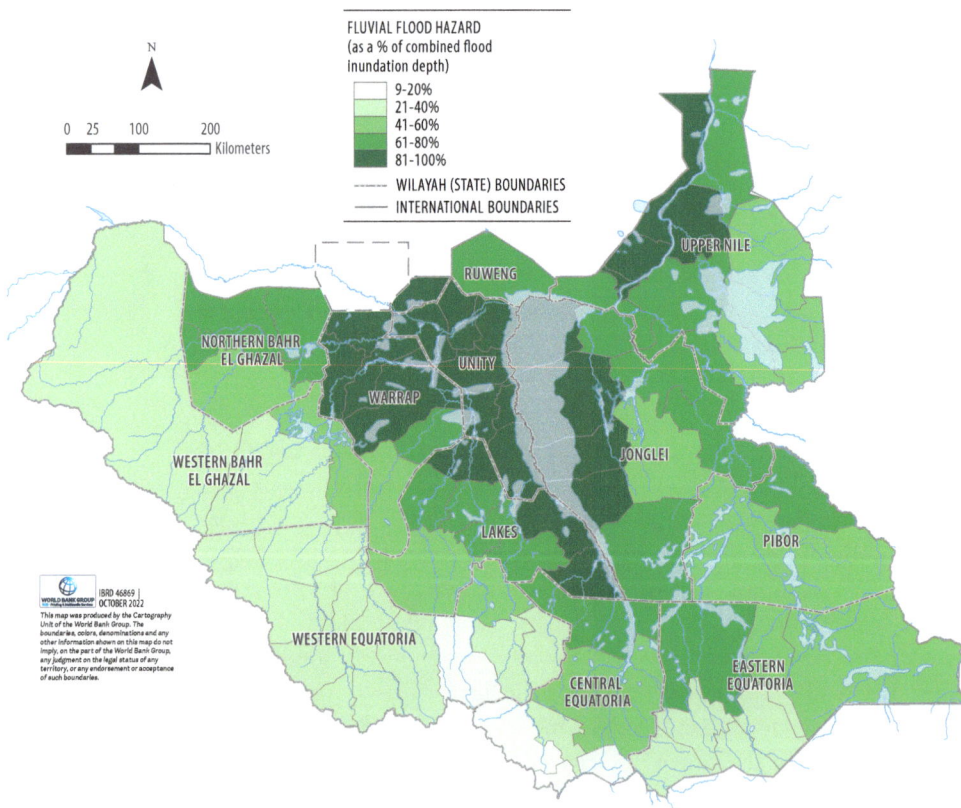

Source: World Bank using Fathom.

MAP 2.12
Pluvial flood hazard (percentage of total depth of inundation for a 1-in-100-year undefended flooding event originating from pluvial sources)

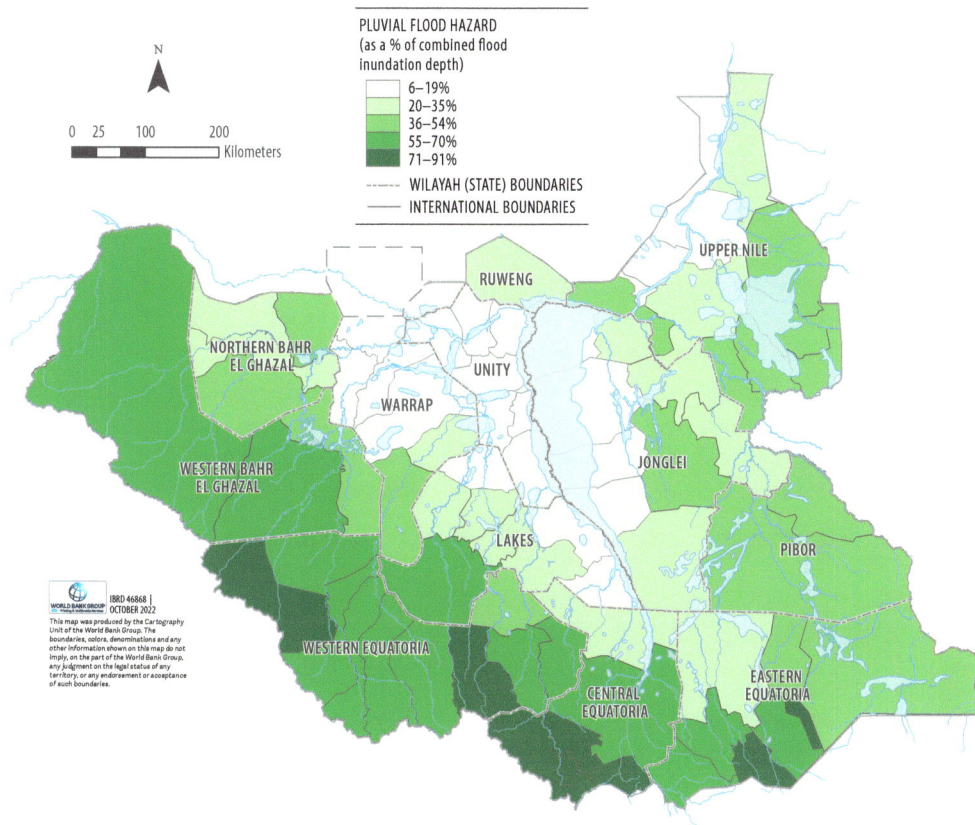

Source: World Bank using Fathom.

discharges downstream into South Sudan. Besides the El Niño–Southern Oscillation, changes in the sea-surface temperature in the Indian Ocean (known as the Indian Ocean Dipole) can further increase rainfall in South Sudan and upstream areas in Ethiopia and in the African Great Lakes region. More specifically, warming in the Western Equatorial Indian Ocean can bring excess precipitation to eastern Africa, as was observed during the 1997 floods, when the combination of El Niño with the Indian Ocean Dipole resulted in 20–160 percent excess precipitation in the African Great Lakes region (particularly Lake Victoria), which subsequently resulted in a major expansion of the Sudd wetland in South Sudan and related flooding (Birkett, Murtugudde, and Allan 1999). Similar patterns were also related to floods in 1961 and 2006 (Nicholson 2017) and, more recently, to floods in 2020, when warming of the western Indian Ocean[6] led to greater-than-average rainfall over the African Great Lakes area, contributing to increasing water levels and higher discharges out of Lake Victoria's main outlet in Jinja, Uganda.

The extent to which South Sudan floods then depends on the lagged effects of excessive rainfall in the Lakes region, particularly Lake Victoria, but also the Ethiopian Highlands, coupled with local rainfall events. Excessive rainfall in the Ethiopian Highlands is associated with flooding in Jonglei and Upper Nile, where streams belonging to the Baro-Akobo-Sobat basin drain. On the other hand, excessive rainfall in the African Great Lakes region is associated with flooding along the Bahr el Jebel, affecting Central and Eastern Equatoria, Jonglei, Lakes, Unity, and Warrap.

Lack of long-term and reliable gauged hydrological data severely hinders any comprehensive analysis of flooding patterns across South Sudan. Nonetheless, earth observation data can be applied to obtain a first-order understanding of the spatial dependence of flooding in the country. Satellite altimetry data can be used to measure water levels of lakes, reservoirs, and rivers, providing an indication of hydrological conditions in different parts of the country. For South Sudan, satellite-based water level data were retrieved from Schwatke et al. (2015). A simple correlation matrix of water levels confirms the strong relationship between flows entering South Sudan and hydrological conditions in the African Great Lakes (Lake Albert and Lake Kyoga). The locations shown in figure 2.10 are sorted from the most upstream (on the top) to the most downstream (at the bottom). There is a strong relationship between water levels in the African Great Lakes and the White Nile in Juba, which weakens downstream of the Sudd wetland in Malakal and Dawmayah. In this area, flows, and therefore flooding, are strongly influenced by rainfall in the catchment areas of the Sobat River in Ethiopia (that is, high correlation between Sobat and White Nile in Malakal and Dawmayah).

FIGURE 2.10

Correlation matrix of water levels for six locations in the Nile River basin using available satellite altimetry data

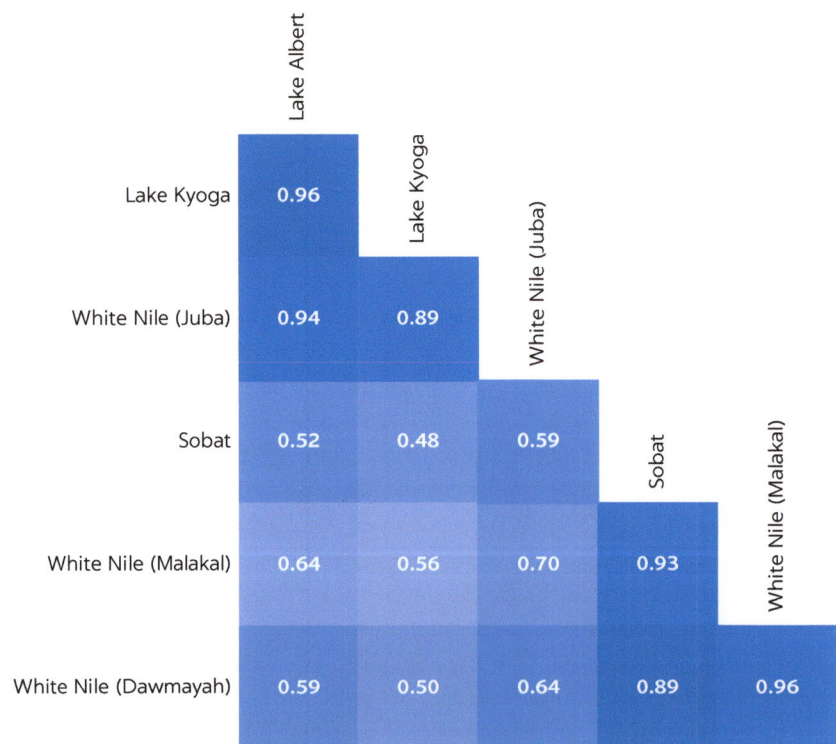

Source: World Bank using satellite altimetry data from Schwatke et al. (2015).
Note: The locations are sorted from the most upstream (Lake Kyoga) to the most downstream (White Nile at Malakal).

FIGURE 2.11

Horizon chart of historical monthly water height anomalies as a percentage of the water height average in select locations of South Sudan, 2008–22

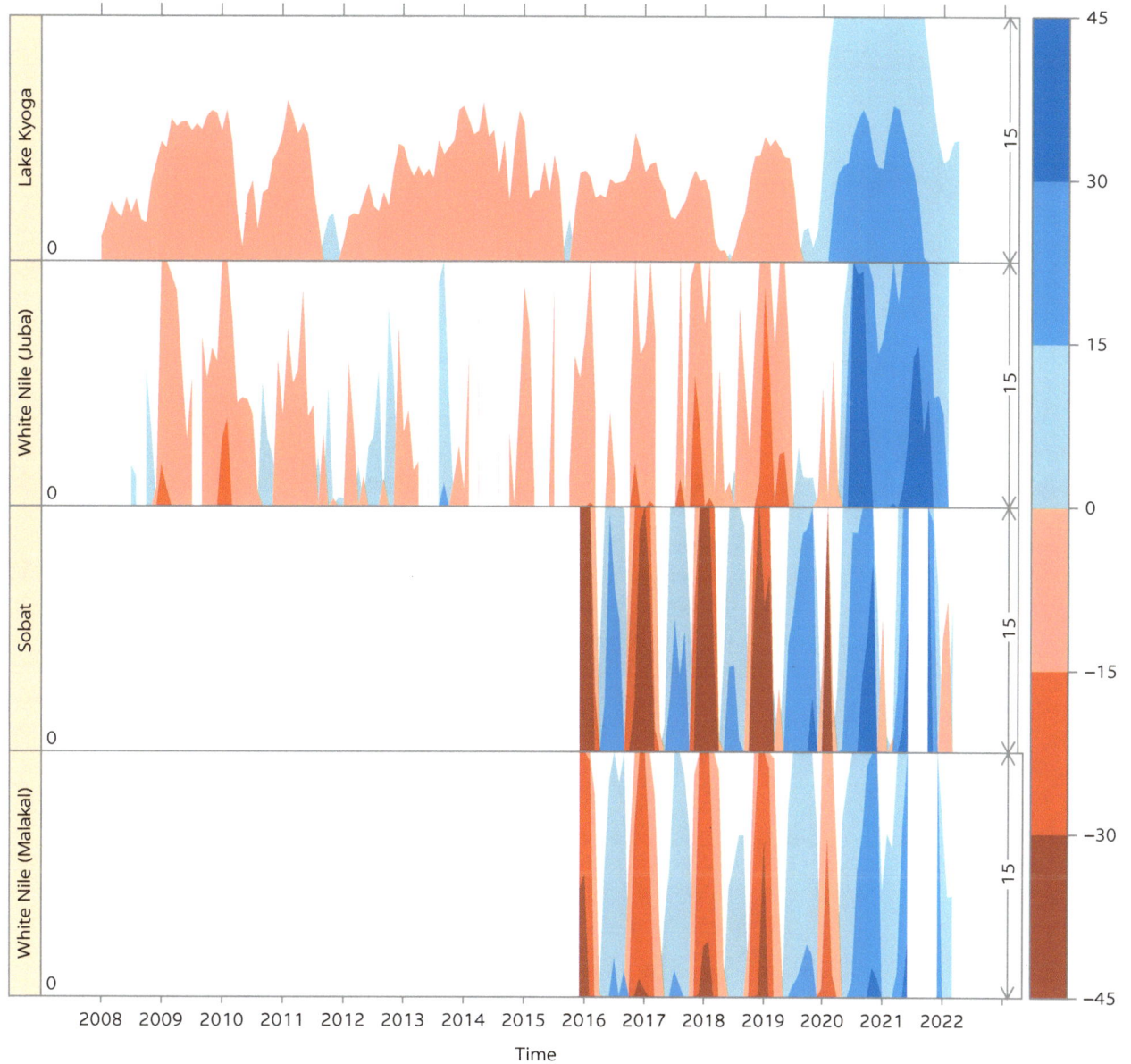

Source: World Bank with satellite altimetry data from Schwatke et al. (2015).
Note: Colored bars show percentage change from the average water height data for the period (2008–22). Data only available from July 2015 onward for Sobat and White Nile at Malakal. The paucity of data and short time series length mean that the figure only provides a broad comparison of the direction and magnitude of change of water heights across the four locations.

A comparison of water levels across select locations in South Sudan further highlights the scale of the 2019, 2020, and 2021 flood events. Figure 2.11 shows anomalies in water levels as a percentage of the average water level measured at four different locations in South Sudan. More intense shades of color represent greater percentage changes from the average, and a diverging color scheme is used to separate positive (blue) and negative (red) deviations for that location. The 2020 and 2021 high water levels are clearly visible, with water levels being 15–45 percent greater than the recorded average for the four locations, including in the upstream Lake Kyoga (located in Uganda). The figure also highlights the 2019 floods, with most flooding taking place in the Upper Nile region and caused by high flows from the Sobat River, and the seasonal element of the Sobat River hydrology and the influence of this seasonality on the White Nile flows at Malakal, which is located just downstream of the confluence of the White Nile and the Sobat Rivers.

Drought: A frequent, persistent risk

Hydrological variability also means that South Sudan is at risk from droughts. Figure 2.12 shows the Standardized Precipitation Index (SPI), a common metric used to track meteorological drought (that is, precipitation-related drought). The SPI values can be interpreted as the number of standard deviations by which the observed precipitation anomaly deviates from the long-term mean. Given the lack of long-term and reliable rain gauge station data in South Sudan, the report examines 40 years of rainfall estimates from CHIRPS: Rainfall Estimates from Rain Gauge and Satellite Observations (Funk et al. 2015). Figure 2.12 highlights the high temporal variability of drought in South Sudan, which is characterized by the alternation of drought-rich periods in the 1980s and in the 2000s (negative SPI) with relatively wetter periods in the 1990s and 2010s (positive SPI).

Droughts also display considerable spatial variability. Figure 2.13 shows the share of the country under different levels of drought between 1982 and 2021. The 1984–86 and 2008–09 droughts had very large spatial footprints, directly reducing rainfall levels across most of the country. Other episodes, such as the 2017 drought, were more concentrated in the northern and eastern states. For some states, droughts are a recurrent hazard. In the period considered in this

FIGURE 2.12

Standardized Precipitation Index (SPI-12) to characterize temporal drought patterns across South Sudan, 1982–2021

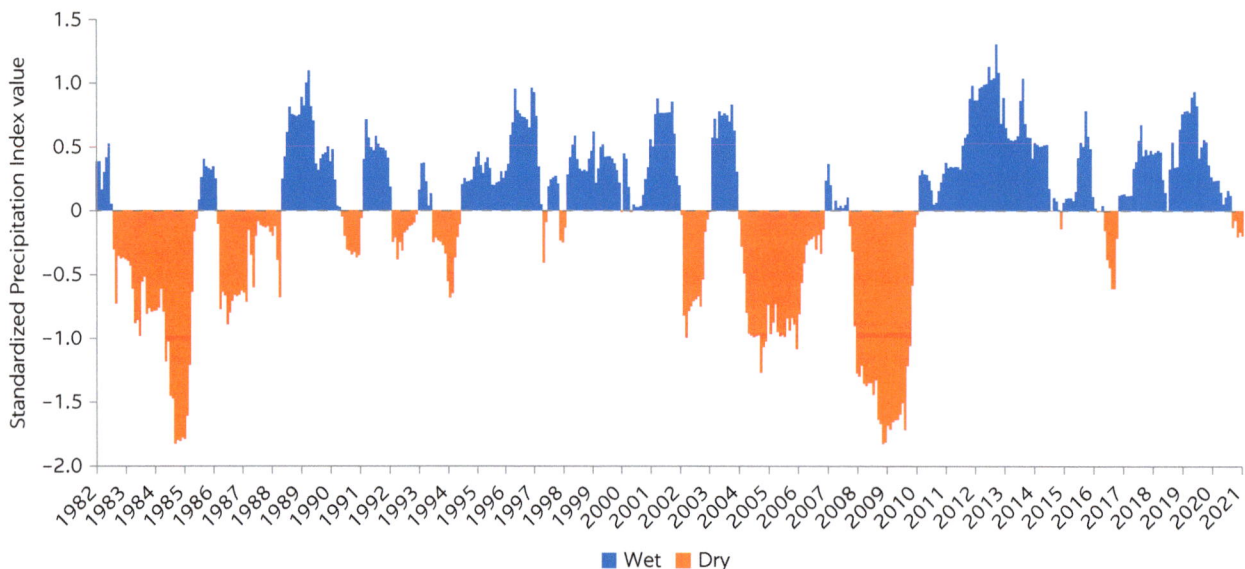

Source: World Bank, using CHIRPS data (https://data.chc.ucsb.edu/products/CHIRPS-2.0/).
Note: SPI shown for the 12-month accumulation time periods to capture the long-term trends of meteorological drought. Drought events defined as SPI-12 less than −1.

FIGURE 2.13

Share of South Sudan's area under drought conditions, 1982–2021

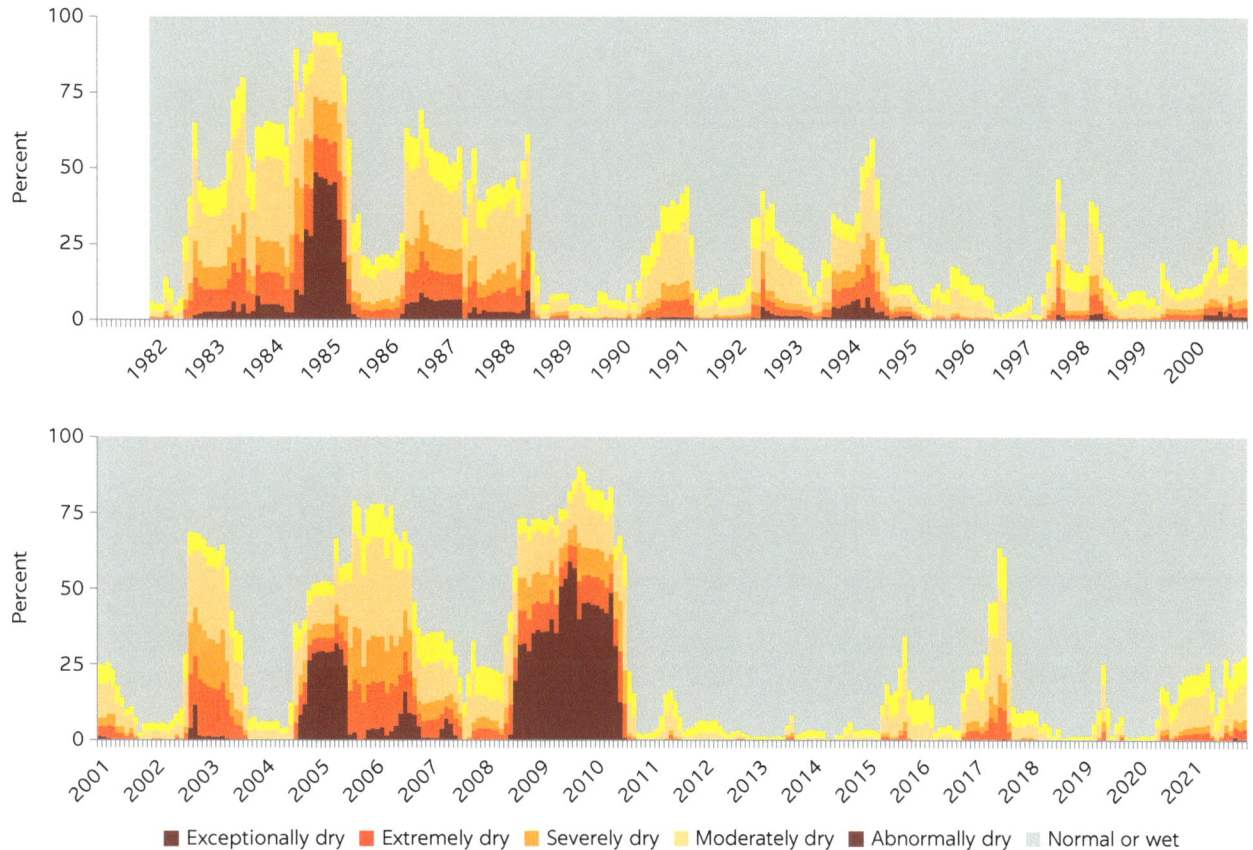

Source: World Bank, using CHIRPS data (https://data.chc.ucsb.edu/products/CHIRPS-2.0/).

analysis (1981–2021), Eastern Equatoria and Jonglei faced more than 10 drought events (figure 2.14), confirming the numerous reports of the frequent droughts affecting the southeast of the country (AVSI and Plan International 2017; Langton 1982). Droughts are less frequent but more persistent in the northern and western states. Over the past 40 years, Northern Bahr el Ghazal, Warrap, and Upper Nile states recorded fewer drought episodes; however, these events have tended to last longer and have been more intense (that is, the rainfall deficit has been greater). This difference can be partly explained by considering the different rainfall regimes in these areas, which are wetter than other states in the northeast and southeast. When a drought strikes in these areas, it typically leads to much greater departure from these areas' wetter conditions, as can be observed in figure 2.14, showing that drought characteristics vary among states.

The spatial pattern of drought characteristics is also confirmed by the analysis of the drought frequency relationship for different livelihood systems. The southeastern pastoralists, alongside livelihood systems in the northwest, have experienced more droughts compared with the rest of the other livelihood systems. In these areas, droughts can affect the mobility options of pastoralists and others who rely on natural resources for their livelihoods, bringing them into competition with neighboring communities and increasing the risk of cattle raids (NUPI and SIPRI 2021). Despite having experienced the highest number of

FIGURE 2.14

Drought duration and frequency relationship, by South Sudanese state, 1981–2021

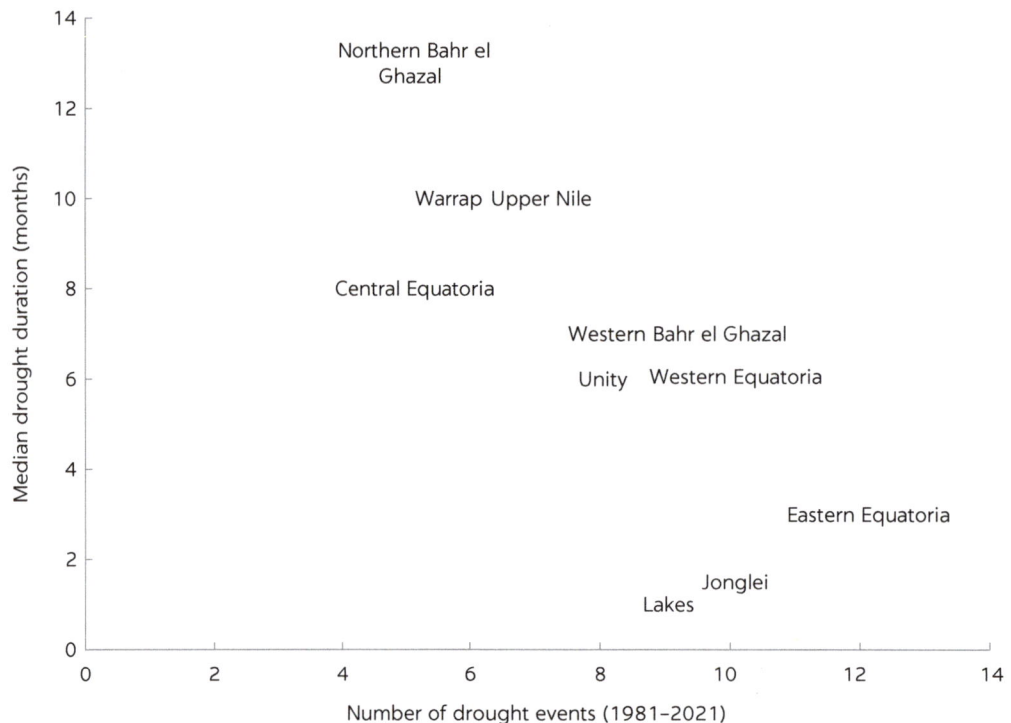

Source: World Bank using CHIRPS data (https://data.chc.ucsb.edu/products/CHIRPS-2.0/).
Note: Drought events are defined as SPI-12 less than −1.

drought episodes, these livelihood zones also have experienced shorter droughts compared with the rest of the country. When the duration of each drought episode is taken into account, it appears that the southern highland forest and sorghum and Nile basin agro-pastoralists face fewer, but longer, drought events.

While climatological studies suggest that the El Niño–Southern Oscillation influences drought occurrence in South Sudan and might partly explain the observed trend, there is still a lack of understanding about the broader climatic controls of drought occurrence (Awange et al. 2016; Elagib and Elhag 2011). As shown in figure 2.12, the prevalence of drought did not increase from 2009 to 2018. The 2017 drought was not more severe than preceding droughts in 2008–09. The 2017 famine was so catastrophic because drought conditions coincided with the harvesting period and an acute phase of the conflict, confirming that violent conflict and fragility exacerbate vulnerability to hydro-climatic hazards (Anderson et al. 2021).

The overall drought risk and impact are determined by the interplay of the drought characteristics described above with underlying vulnerabilities and exposure. In South Sudan, drought risks are particularly pronounced in the southeast and northeast of the country, particularly in Eastern Equatoria, Jonglei, Unity, and Upper Nile (map 2.13). In these areas, droughts led to poor crop growth or crop failure and reduced yields, as most recently observed in 2017, when failed rains led to an almost 10 percent reduction in aggregate food production (World Bank 2017). Although this drought event was relatively short, lasting for less than one year, it severely affected agriculture because it occurred during the harvest period. The drought mostly affected the northern part of the

MAP 2.13

Drought risk by county

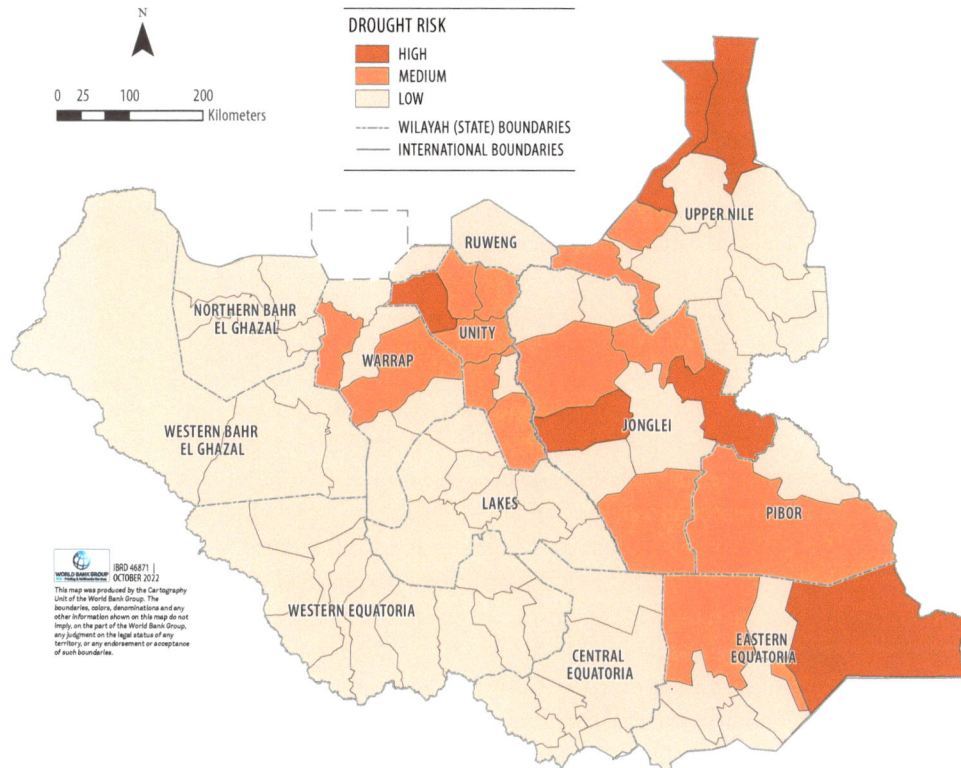

Source: ICA South Sudan, 2016 - Drought Risk, 1998–2014 (https://geonode.wfp.org/layers/geonode:ssd_ica_droughtrisk
_geonode_feb2016/metadata_detail).
Note: Counties classified into three categories (high, medium, low) based on the number of poor growing seasons and
percentage of area affected by droughts over the period 1998–2014.

country and, when combined with the impacts of conflict and violence, left
about 50 percent of the population facing severe food insecurity (WFP 2017).

Climate change is altering the frequency, magnitude, and duration of water-related disasters

Climate change is underway and already affecting both long- and short-term
patterns of hydrological variability that control the availability of water resources
and the occurrence of extreme events. South Sudan has already been warming at
one of the fastest rates around the world. Over the past 30 years, temperatures
have risen by 1.2°C, and are projected to increase a further 1°C to 1.5°C by mid-
century (South Sudan MEF 2021). These increasing temperatures will amplify
the impact of drought because warming typically leads to increased evaporation
and further reductions in the availability of water. For rainfall, climate model
projections over this part of Africa are less reliable, with climate model outputs
suggesting that rainfall could either increase or decrease in the long term
(Rowell et al. 2015).

Although the climate patterns responsible for floods and droughts in South
Sudan are not a consequence of climate change, their frequency, intensity, and
duration are expected to change as temperatures increase. Climate model analysis for South Sudan suggests that drought changes follow the "dry gets drier and

wet gets wetter" paradigm. Under all emissions scenarios, South Sudan is projected to experience more frequent, longer, and more intense drought events by the end of the century. Under a high emissions scenario, droughts are expected to become 60–100 percent more frequent compared with the 2020s by the end of the century, with droughts lasting for more than 30 months (Haile et al. 2020). With regard to flooding, the Indian Ocean Dipole and related extreme floods might occur with greater frequency, from one every 17.3 years, on average, to one event every 6.3 years, on average, under high emissions scenarios (Cai et al. 2014). This means that extremes such as the 2019 floods are likely to occur more frequently under global warming (Cai et al. 2021).

CONCLUSIONS

Although flood risks are capturing headlines, they are just one of the many threats from water insecurity. This chapter identifies several other threats from water insecurity, focusing on challenges for people, production, and protection. The chapter also shows that South Sudan can harness the ubiquity of water as a tool to advance national development and stability. For example, seasonal flooding sustains livelihoods for about 6 million people living along the Nile and Sobat Rivers and the wide eastern and western floodplains. Water security is achieved not by trying solely to control water and diverting its flow, but also by focusing on maintaining preparedness and delineating areas for water to reduce its destructive potential and making productive use of the water for household consumption, livelihoods, and development.

To address the destructive force of water described in this chapter, two broad sets of actions should be pursued. The first set of actions would address the water supply and sanitation crisis. The crisis can be addressed by strengthening service delivery models for rural households, bolstering the sustainable use and management of groundwater resources, and promoting climate-resilient solutions. The second set of actions should advance disaster risk preparedness and early warning, which can be achieved through a portfolio of infrastructure, institutions, and information, initially focusing on nonstructural measures to prevent populations from moving into harm's way and devising information systems and institutional arrangements to increase preparedness and early warning.

For managing water's productive force, the chapter highlights opportunities to harness floods for productive livelihoods, including enhancing flood-based livelihoods with investments supporting domestic fish production, wetland restoration, and flood-recession agriculture. The chapter also describes the potential for irrigation expansion to bolster food security, including through solar irrigation.

NOTES

1. In addition, the household survey uses Lot Quality Assurance Sampling (LQAS), which was developed by the WHO in 1991 as a practical management tool for conducting baseline surveys and monitoring health indicators. The main drawback to LQAS is the large error size of up to 10 percent due to the smaller sample size required for the methodology. In addition, the household survey provides estimates at the household level versus the population-level estimates that JMP provides, and it does not provide disaggregated estimates by urban and rural areas.

2. JMP estimates 41 percent of the population has at least basic drinking water service. Estimates are not available for year-round or seasonal access.

3. This calculation does not factor in waiting time at the water source, which can be substantial, especially during times of water scarcity.

4. Moreover, because the analysis uses the shortest distance between two points regardless of terrain or obstacles, the figures are likely a conservative estimate.

5. Any flood event causing a depth of inundation equal to or greater than 0.15 meter, following previous applications of the flood hazard data set (Rentschler and Salhab 2020).

6. National Oceanic and Atmospheric Administration data show a very positive Indian Ocean Dipole in 2019 and 2020 (http://psl.noaa.gov/gcos_wgsp/Timeseries/DMI/index.html).

REFERENCES

AfDB (African Development Bank). 2013. *South Sudan: An Infrastructure Action Plan—A Program for Sustained Strong Economic Growth*. Tunis, Tunisia: AfDB.

Anderson, W., C. Taylor, S. McDermid, E. Ilboudo-Nébié, R. Seager, W. Schlenker, F. Cottier, et al. 2021. "Violent Conflict Exacerbated Drought-Related Food Insecurity between 2009 and 2019 in Sub-Saharan Africa." *Nature Food* 2 (8): 603–15.

AVSI and Plan International. 2017. "Kapoeta Region Multi-Sector Survey." https://www .humanitarianresponse.info/sites/www.humanitarianresponse.info/files/assessments /avsi_kapoeta_region_multi-sector_report_.pdf.

Awange, J. L., M. Schumacher, E. Forootan, and B. Heck. 2016. "Exploring Hydro-Meteorological Drought Patterns over the Greater Horn of Africa (1979–2014) Using Remote Sensing and Reanalysis Products." *Advances in Water Resources* 94: 45–59.

Birkett, C., R. Murtugudde, and T. Allan. 1999. "Indian Ocean Climate Event Brings Floods to East Africa's Lakes and the Sudd Marsh." *Geophysical Research Letters* 26 (8): 1031–34.

Borrelli, P., D. A. Robinson, L. R. Fleischer, E. Lugato, C. Ballabio, C. Alewell, K. Meusburger, et al. 2017. "An Assessment of the Global Impact of 21st Century Land Use Change on Soil Erosion." *Nature Communications* 8 (1) : 1–13.

Borrelli, P., D. A. Robinson, P. Panagos, E. Lugato, J. E. Yang, C. Alewell, D. Wuepper, L. Montanarella, and C. Ballabio. 2020. "Land Use and Climate Change Impacts on Global Soil Erosion by Water (2015–2070)." *Proceedings of the National Academy of Sciences* 117 (36): 21994–22001.

Cai, W., A. Santoso, G. Wang, E. Weller, L. Wu, K. Ashok, Y. Masumoto, and T. Yamagata. 2014. "Increased Frequency of Extreme Indian Ocean Dipole Events Due to Greenhouse Warming." *Nature* 510 (7504): 254–58.

Cai, W., K. Yang, L. Wu, G. Huang, A. Santoso, B. Ng, G. Wang, and T. Yamagata. 2021. "Opposite Response of Strong and Moderate Positive Indian Ocean Dipole to Global Warming." *Nature Climate Change* 11 (1): 27–32.

Catley, A. 2018. "Livestock and Livelihoods in South Sudan." UK Department for International Development, London.

Diing, A., B. K. Majuch, C. Night, C. M. Anei, E. Abuk, E. N. Malou, J. G. Mut, et al. 2021. *South Sudan: Youth, Violence and Livelihoods*. Juba: Rift Valley Institute.

Elagib, N. A., and M. M. Elhag. 2011. "Major Climate Indicators of Ongoing Drought in Sudan." *Journal of Hydrology* 409 (3–4): 612–25.

FAO (Food and Agriculture Organization of the United Nations). 2015a. "Planning, Construction and Operation of Water Harvesting Structures in South Sudan." FAO, Rome. https://www .unep.org/resources/report/planning-construction-and-operation-water-harvesting -structures-south-sudan.

FAO (Food and Agriculture Organization of the United Nations). 2015b. "Water Harvesting for Peacebuilding in South Sudan. An Assessment of Livestock Water Harvesting Structures in Eastern Equatoria, Western Equatoria, and Lakes State." FAO, Rome. https://wedocs.unep .org/bitstream/handle/20.500.11822/19533/water_harvesting_peacebuilding_southSudan .pdf?sequence=1.

FAO (Food and Agriculture Organization of the United Nations). 2019. *Special Report. FAO/ WFP Crop and Food Security Assessment Mission to South Sudan.* Rome: FAO and World Food Programme.

FAO (Food and Agriculture Organization of the United Nations). 2021. "Flood Impact Report." FAO, Rome. https://www.fao.org/fileadmin/user_upload/faoweb/South-Sudan/FAOSS -Flood-Impact-Report-Dec-2021.pdf.

Fedele, G., C. I. Donatti, I. Bornacelly, and D. G. Hole. 2021. "Nature-Dependent People: Mapping Human Direct Use of Nature for Basic Needs across the Tropics." *Global Environmental Change* 71: 102368.

Funk, C., P. Peterson, M. Landsfeld, D. Pedreros, J. Verdin, S. Shukla, G. Husak, et al. 2015. "The Climate Hazards Infrared Precipitation with Stations—A New Environmental Record for Monitoring Extremes." *Scientific Data* 2 (1): 1–21.

Haile, G. G., Q. Tang, S. M. Hosseini-Moghari, X. Liu, T. G. Gebremicael, G. Leng, A. Kebede, X. Xu, and X. Yun. 2020. "Projected Impacts of Climate Change on Drought Patterns over East Africa." *Earth's Future* 8 (7): e2020EF001502.

Health of Mother Earth Foundation. 2019. "Assessing Clean Drinking Water Availability in Juba, South Sudan." Nile Initiative for Health and Environment. Health of Mother Earth Foundation, Juba.

Heinke, J., M. Lannerstad, D. Gerten, P. Havlík, M. Herrero, A. M. O. Notenbaert, H. Hoff, and C. Müller. 2020. "Water Use in Global Livestock Production—Opportunities and Constraints for Increasing Water Productivity." *Water Resources Research* 56 (12): e2019WR026995.

International Water Management Institute. 2022. "Solar Suitability Framework Application to South Sudan." Unpublished. International Water Management Institute, Colombo, Sri Lanka.

Izzi, G., J. Denison, and G. J. Veldwisch, eds. 2021. *The Farmer-Led Irrigation Development Guide: A What, Why and How-to for Intervention Design.* Washington, DC: World Bank.

Langton, P. 1982. "Drought in SE Sudan, January—July 1980." *Disasters* 6 (1): 16–20.

Lefore, N., A. Closas, and P. Schmitter. 2021. "Solar for All: A Framework to Deliver Inclusive and Environmentally Sustainable Solar Irrigation for Smallholder Agriculture." *Energy Policy* 154: 112313.

Magot, D. 2021. "The Drinking Trucks: In a City That Borders River Nile, Covid-19 Curbs Access to Clean Water for South Sudanese." *InfoNile,* December 1, 2021. https://www.infonile.org /en/2021/12/the-drinking-trucks-in-a-city-that-borders-river-nile-covid-19-curbs -access-to-clean-water-for-south-sudanese-photo-story/.

Martell, P. 2019. *First Raise a Flag: How South Sudan Won the Longest War but Lost the Peace.* New York: Oxford University Press.

Maystadt, J. F., M. Calderone, and L. You. 2014. "Local Warming and Violent Conflict in North and South Sudan." *Journal of Economic Geography* 15 (3): 649–71.

Mohamed, Y. A., B. J. J. M. Van den Hurk, H. H. G. Savenije, and W. G. M. Bastiaanssen. 2005. "Impact of the Sudd Wetland on the Nile Hydroclimatology." *Water Resources Research* 41 (8).

NBI (Nile Basin Initiative). 2012. "Assessment of the Irrigation Potential in Burundi, Eastern DRC, Kenya, Rwanda, South Sudan, Tanzania and Uganda Final Report," Appendix South Sudan. Nile Basin Initiative, Entebbe.

NBI (Nile Basin Initiative). 2020. *Sudd Wetland Economic Valuation of Biodiversity and Ecosystem Services for Green Infrastructure Planning and Development.* Entebbe: Nile Basin Initiative.

Nicholson, S. E. 2017. "Climate and Climatic Variability of Rainfall over Eastern Africa." *Reviews of Geophysics* 55 (3): 590–635.

NUPI and SIPRI (Norwegian Institute of International Affairs and Stockholm International Peace Research Institute). 2021. "Climate, Peace and Security Fact Sheet: South Sudan." NUPI and SIPRI. https://sipri.org/sites/default/files/Fact%20Sheet%20South%20 Sudan_HR.pdf.

OCHA (United Nations Office for the Coordination of Humanitarian Affairs). 2021. "South Sudan Flooding Situation Report No. 3: Inter-Cluster Coordination Group—As of 14 December 2021." Juba, UNOCHA.

Pape, U., and L. Parisotto. 2019. "Estimating Poverty in a Fragile Context: The High Frequency Survey in South Sudan." Policy Research Working Paper 8722, World Bank, Washington, DC.

Peden, D., A. Freeman, A. Astatke, A. Notenbaert, and D. Sheikh. 2005. "Investment Options for Integrating Water-Livestock-Crop Production in Sub-Saharan Africa." ILRI, Nairobi, Kenya, and IWMI, Addis Ababa, Ethiopia.

Rentschler, J., and M. Salhab. 2020. "People in Harm's Way: Flood Exposure and Poverty in 189 Countries." Policy Research Working Paper 9447, World Bank, Washington, DC.

RVI (Rift Valley Institute). 2022. "Fragility and Water Security in South Sudan." Study conducted for the World Bank by the Rift Valley Institute in collaboration with the Centre for Humanitarian Change. Background paper prepared for this report. Rift Valley Institute, Juba.

Rowell, D. P., B. B. Booth, S. E. Nicholson, and P. Good. 2015. "Reconciling Past and Future Rainfall Trends over East Africa." *Journal of Climate* 28 (24): 9768188.

Schmitter, P., K. S. Kibret, N. Lefore, and J. Barron. 2018. "Suitability Mapping Framework for Solar Photovoltaic Pumps for Smallholder Farmers in Sub-Saharan Africa." *Applied Geography* 94: 41–57.

Schwatke, C., D. Dettmering, W. Bosch, and F. Seitz. 2015. "DAHITI—An Innovative Approach for Estimating Water Level Time Series over Inland Waters Using Multi-Mission Satellite Altimetry." *Hydrology and Earth System Sciences* 19 (10): 4345–64.

South Sudan MEF (Ministry of Environment and Forestry). 2021. *South Sudan's Second Nationally Determined Contribution.* Juba: MEF.

South Sudan MWRI (Ministry of Water Resources and Irrigation). 2021. "Presentation on Irrigation Development Budget in the Republic of South Sudan." Ministry of Water Resources and Irrigation, Juba.

SORUDEV (South Sudan Rural Development). 2021. *Crop Production Farmer Extension Guide for Smallholders in South Sudan,* 2nd edition. https://knowledge4policy.ec.europa.eu /publication/crop-production-farmer-extension-guide-smallholders-south-sudan-2nd -edition_en.

SSCCSE (South Sudan Centre for Census, Statistics and Evaluation). 2011. "Southern Sudan Livelihood Profiles. A Guide for Humanitarian and Development Planning." SSCCSE, Juba.

UNEP (United Nations Environment Programme). 2018. *South Sudan: First State of Environment and Outlook Report 2018.* Nairobi: United Nations Environment Programme.

UNESCO (United Nations Educational, Scientific and Cultural Organization). 2017. "Sudd Wetland." UNESCO, Paris.

UNHCR (United Nations High Commissioner for Refugees). 2022. UNHCR WASH dashboard. https://wash.unhcr.org/wash-dashboard-for-refugee-settings/.

UNICEF (United Nations Children's Fund). 2008. "Southern Sudan Water Quality Guidelines, 2008." UNICEF, Juba.

UNISDR (United Nations Office for Disaster Risk Reduction). 2009. "UNISDR Terminology on Disaster Risk Reduction." UNISDR, Geneva.

WFP (World Food Program). 2017. "Integrated Food Security Phase Classification: The Republic of South Sudan." WFP, Rome. https://www.ipcinfo.org/fileadmin/user_upload/ipcinfo /docs/IPC_South_Sudan_AcuteFI_May2017_June-July2017.pdf.

WHO/UNICEF (World Health Organization/United Nations Children's Fund). 2017. *Progress on Drinking Water, Sanitation and Hygiene: 2017 Update and SDG Baselines.* Geneva: WHO and UNICEF.

WHO/UNICEF (World Health Organization/United Nations Children's Fund). 2021a. "Joint Monitoring Programme for Water Supply, Sanitation and Hygiene (JMP) for Households." WHO and UNICEF, Geneva. https://washdata.org/data/household#!/ssd.

WHO/UNICEF (World Health Organization/United Nations Children's Fund). 2021b. "Joint Monitoring Programme for Water Supply, Sanitation and Hygiene (JMP) in Schools." WHO and UNICEF, Geneva. https://washdata.org/data/school#!/ssd.

WHO/UNICEF (World Health Organization/United Nations Children's Fund). 2021c. "The Measurement and Monitoring of Water Supply, Sanitation and Hygiene (WASH) Affordability: A Missing Element of Monitoring of Sustainable Development Goal (SDG) Targets 6.1 and 6.2." WHO and UNICEF, New York. https://www.who.int/publications/i /item/9789240023284.

World Bank. 2013. "Republic of South Sudan: The Rapid Water Sector Needs Assessment and a Way Forward." World Bank, Washington, DC.

World Bank. 2017. "South Sudan Emergency Food and Nutrition Security Project (P163559)." Project Appraisal Document, World Bank, Washington, DC.

World Bank. 2021a. GRADE Note on May–October 2021 South Sudan Floods. World Bank, Washington, DC.

World Bank. 2021b. "South Sudan Economic Update, June 2021: Pathways to Sustainable Food Security." World Bank, Washington, DC.

World Bank. 2021c. "Annual Remittances Data." May 2021. https://www.worldbank.org/en /topic/migrationremittancesdiasporaissues/brief/migration-remittances-data.

World Bank. 2022a. "Agricultural and Food Insecurity Dynamics (2006–2020). South Sudan Conflict Economy." World Bank, Washington, DC.

World Bank. 2022b. *Directions for Reform: A Country Economic Memorandum for Recovery and Resilience in South Sudan*. Washington, DC: World Bank Group.

World Bank. 2022c. "South Sudan Climate Change Profile." Climate Change Knowledge Portal. World Bank, Washington, DC.

World Bank. 2022d. *Transforming Agriculture from Humanitarian Aid to a Development Oriented Growth Path in South Sudan*. World Bank: Washington, DC.

World Resources Institute. 2019. "Aqueduct 3.0: Updated Decision-Relevant Global Water Risk Indicators." World Resources Institute, Washington, DC.

Xie, H., L. You, B. Wielgosz, and C. Ringler. 2014. "Estimating the Potential for Expanding Smallholder Irrigation in Sub-Saharan Africa." *Agricultural Water Management* 131: 183–93.

3 Water Risks and Impacts: Links with Human and Social Development Outcomes

HEALTH AND NUTRITION

Key points

- Lower respiratory infections and diarrheal disease are the second- and third-largest causes of death, respectively, in South Sudan, with poor water supply, sanitation, and hygiene (WASH) the second-leading risk factor for all death and disability combined.
- Climate and environmental factors influence the emergence and dispersal of many infectious disease pathogens, and the risks are exacerbated by high levels of poverty, conflict, forced displacement, lack of access to WASH services, and poor-quality health services.
- WASH-related neglected tropical diseases are widespread across the country, and the persistence of the underlying factors that intensified successive cholera outbreaks in South Sudan between 2014 and 2017 puts the country at high risk for a resurgence of cholera.
- Conflict dynamics, population movement, displacement, and the presence of humanitarian aid confound the relationship between access to WASH and health and nutrition outcomes in South Sudan.

Overview

In its various roles for people, production, and protection, water is an upstream driver of better population health and nutrition and, when poorly managed, can lead to negative impacts. Consuming unclean water, whether contaminated with fecal pathogens or other pollutants, causes diarrhea and other ailments. In 2016, diarrheal diseases were the second-leading cause of death in low-income countries, killing nearly 60 out of every 100,000 people (WHO 2018). South Sudan has the third-highest rates of diarrheal deaths within the African continent (Oluwasanya et al. 2022). During periods of drought, farmers without reliable sources of water to grow food cannot feed their families or make income from selling crops. More frequent and heavier flood events attributable to a changing climate create breeding grounds for disease-carrying vectors, causing illness, anemia, and energy deprivation. Recognizing both the dramatic and subtle relationships between water, health, and nutrition underscores the need to formulate policy and investments that help mitigate risks and boost the benefits of water investments.

Low coverage of WASH services in South Sudan increases vulnerability to infectious disease

Diseases such as diarrhea and acute respiratory infections that affect young children are common in South Sudan. Lower respiratory infections and diarrheal disease are the second- and third-largest causes of death, respectively, with poor WASH the second-leading risk factor for all death and disability combined (IHME 2021). In the 2020 National Household Health Survey, 30.4 percent of households with children under 5 had experienced diarrhea in the two weeks before the survey. However, diarrhea prevalence is lower among households with access to an improved water source year-round (28.2 percent vs. 31.0 percent) and for households not using a surface water source in the rainy season (31.3 percent vs. 28.7 percent). Counterintuitively, households using improved sanitation and those that do not defecate in the open report higher prevalence of diarrhea (figure 3.1).

Poor access to WASH services is also linked to pneumonia. Suspected pneumonia, defined as the presence of cough and fast breathing, is reported in 14.7 percent of households in the survey. Higher rates are reported for households lacking access to improved and basic sources of water supply and improved sanitation, and for households practicing open defecation and using surface water sources during the rainy season (figure 3.2).

Climate change and the emergence and spread of water-related infectious disease

Climate change is predicted to lead to greater endemicity of some infectious diseases, while also putting new populations at risk (Tidman, Abela-Ridder, and de Castañeda 2021). Variations in temperature and rainfall and increasing humidity, along with increased frequency and intensity of flood and drought, influence the emergence of infectious pathogens and disease vectors. Outbreaks of infectious disease occur more often and are more deadly during water-related climate

FIGURE 3.1

Access to WASH and prevalence of diarrhea

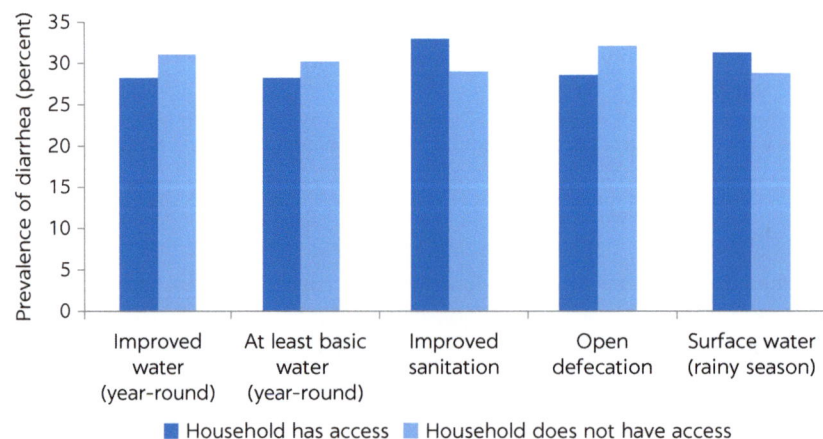

Source: World Bank using National Household Health Survey (2020).
Note: Prevalence defined as share of households with children under 5 experiencing diarrhea in the two weeks prior to the survey. WASH = water supply, sanitation, and hygiene.

FIGURE 3.2

Access to WASH and prevalence of suspected pneumonia

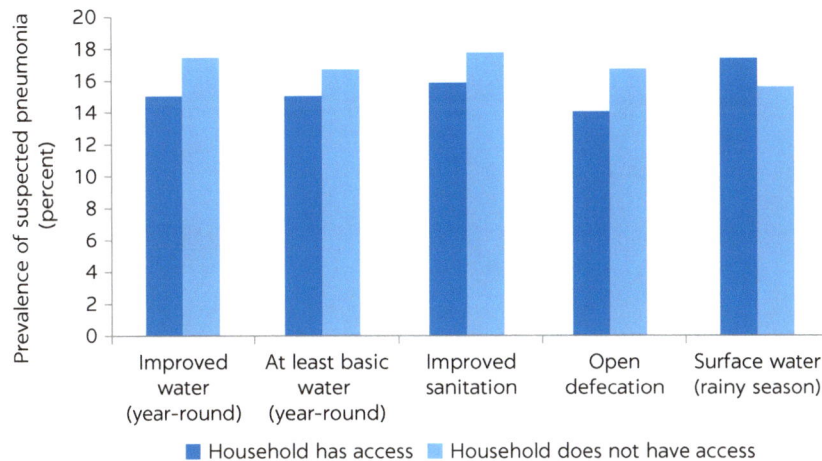

Source: World Bank using National Household Health Survey (2020).
Note: Suspected pneumonia is defined as cough and fast breathing. WASH = water supply, sanitation, and hygiene.

shocks such as flood and drought, while the capacity for a coordinated response is challenged by the emergency nature of these events. For example, cholera outbreaks were found to be more than 100 times more likely during periods of flooding in Sub-Saharan Africa when compared with nonflood periods between 1990 and 2010, and cholera outbreaks occurred during 30 percent of drought periods during these same years (Rieckmann et al. 2018). Climate and environmental factors influence the emergence and dispersal of a range of infectious disease pathogens, but socioeconomic conditions, such as poverty, conflict, lack of access to WASH services, poor-quality health services, and underlying vulnerabilities such as malnutrition exacerbate these naturally occurring factors and play a key role in the spread of infection.

Conflict and climate shocks and the associated effects on food and water security are also key factors that drive large-scale population displacement. Population movement is a significant driver of the emergence and spread of infectious disease, including among animals that harbor zoonotic diseases. For example, Rift Valley fever, a viral hemorrhagic fever in domesticated animals (for example, cattle, goats) that can also cause illness in humans, is endemic in South Sudan. Rift Valley fever is associated with repeated cycles of flood and drought, with outbreaks causing detrimental impacts on pastoral livelihoods through livestock mortality, production losses, and trade restrictions. Forced displacement triggered by conflict or natural disaster exposes populations to new disease risks, while inadequate public health infrastructure to accommodate displaced populations, including WASH services, exacerbates the spread of infectious disease and increases vulnerability to death and disease (Aagaard-Hansen, Nombela, and Alvar 2010; Errecaborde, Stauffer, and Cetron 2015). Figure 3.3 shows the links between the exposure and susceptibility factors driving risk of death and disease in the context of climate change.

More than 7 million people are estimated to be at risk of cholera in South Sudan (Ali et al. 2015) and successive cholera epidemics occurred between 2014 and 2017. These epidemics spread rapidly throughout the country within the context of civil war, large-scale population movement and forced displacement, flooding, and drought, causing more than 28,000 cases and more than 600 recorded deaths

FIGURE 3.3

Climate change effects, mediating factors, and waterborne disease risks

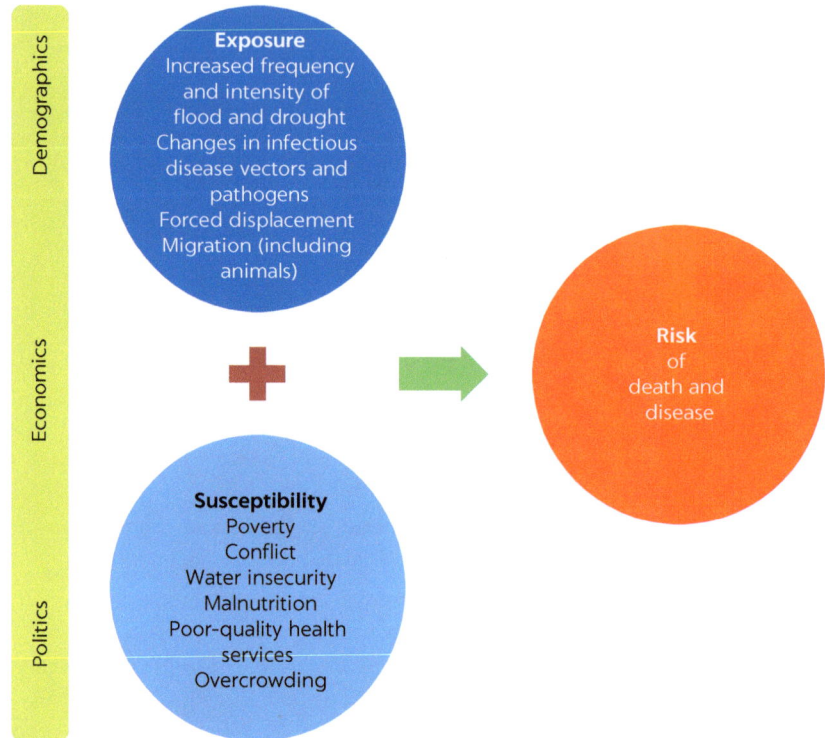

Demographics

Economics

Politics

Exposure
Increased frequency
and intensity of
flood and drought
Changes in infectious
disease vectors and
pathogens
Forced displacement
Migration (including
animals)

Susceptibility
Poverty
Conflict
Water insecurity
Malnutrition
Poor-quality health
services
Overcrowding

Risk
of
death and
disease

Source: World Bank.

(Jones et al. 2020). The persistence of the underlying factors that intensified previous outbreaks puts South Sudan at high risk for a resurgence of cholera.

South Sudan has one of the highest burdens of WASH-related neglected tropical diseases (NTDs) globally. NTDs are a group of parasitic and bacterial diseases that are more widespread among the world's poor and have received less attention and resources than other diseases of poverty, such as malaria.[1] In addition to death and disability, NTDs are associated with reductions in human capital, educational attainment, and economic productivity, particularly among the poorest. NTDs are associated with 40 percent of the burden of disease concentrated in Sub-Saharan Africa, with the top five NTDs[2] accounting for 510.1 DALYs (disability adjusted life years) per 100,000 inhabitants for all ages and both sexes in Sub-Saharan Africa in 2017 (table 3.1) (IHME 2018).

The presence of NTDs affects all counties across South Sudan. Although comprehensive burden of disease estimates are not available, survey data suggest that approximately 47 percent of the population is at risk of trachoma, with rates as high as 87 percent in some settings. In addition, there is widespread endemicity of onchocerciasis and schistosomiasis, suspected endemicity of lymphatic filariasis in all 10 states, and prevalence of soil-transmitted helminths ranging from 10 percent to 35 percent based on surveys covering Central Equatoria and Eastern Equatoria states (South Sudan Ministry of Health 2016). Across the country, recent data from the World Health Organization's Expanded Special Project for Elimination of Neglected Tropical Diseases indicate that at least one of these NTDs is endemic to all counties, with the southern counties, particularly those bordering the White Nile River, having prevalence of at least five NTDs (map 3.1).

Poor WASH access plays an important role in the spread of NTDs while also increasing vulnerability to disease once infected (Grimes et al. 2014; Stocks et al.

2014; Strunz et al. 2014). For example, trachoma, which is the leading infectious cause of blindness globally, is transmitted through exposure to infected feces, with access to water for personal hygiene and access to sanitation helping to prevent exposure and transmission (Esrey et al. 1991). Data from the Expanded Special Project for Elimination of Neglected Tropical Diseases combined with coverage of basic water supply and improved sanitation for counties in South Sudan indicate that high NTD prevalence coexists with poor WASH coverage in Ayod, Duk, Fangak, Juba, Koch, Pibor, and Tong North counties, among other counties concentrated in the center of the country (map 3.2).

TABLE 3.1 Top WASH-related NTDs in Sub-Saharan Africa, by DALYs, 2017

NEGLECTED TROPICAL DISEASE	DALYS PER 100,000 INHABITANTS	AS SHARE OF TOTAL DALYS (%)
Schistosomiasis	148.4	29
Onchocerciasis	160.4	31
Trachoma	13.9	3
Lymphatic filariasis	111.8	22
Soil-transmitted helminthiasis	75.6	15
Total	**510.1**	**100**

Source: IHME 2018.
Note: DALYs = disability adjusted life years; WASH = water supply, sanitation, and hygiene.

MAP 3.1

Number of endemic NTDs, by county, 2020

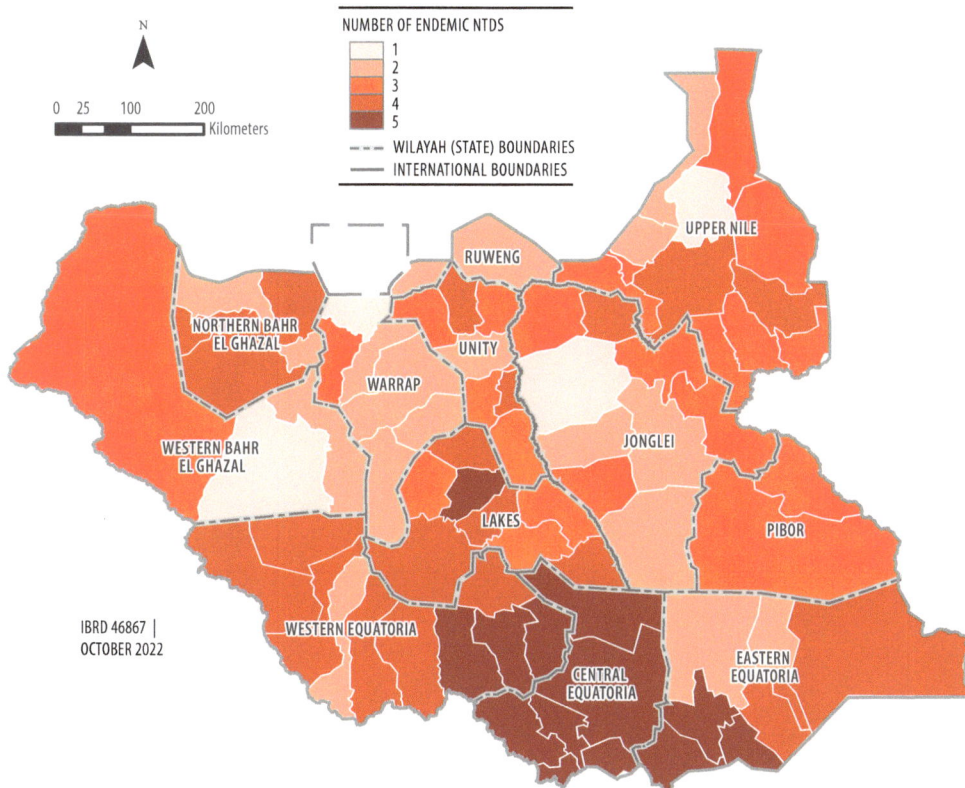

Source: World Bank using World Health Organization, the Expanded Special Project for Elimination of Neglected Tropical Diseases (2020) (https://espen.afro.who.int/).
Note: NTDs = neglected tropical diseases (trachoma, soil-transmitted helminths, schistosomiasis, onchocerciasis, lymphatic filariasis).

MAP 3.2

Coverage of basic water supply and improved sanitation and prevalence of NTDs, by county, 2020

a. Coverage of basic water supply

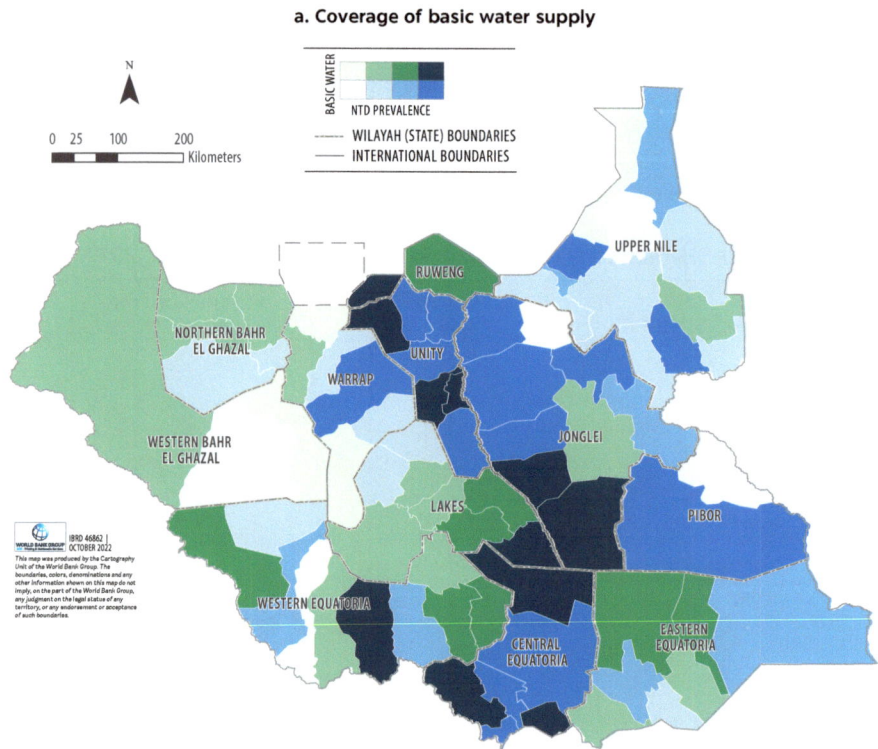

b. Improved sanitation

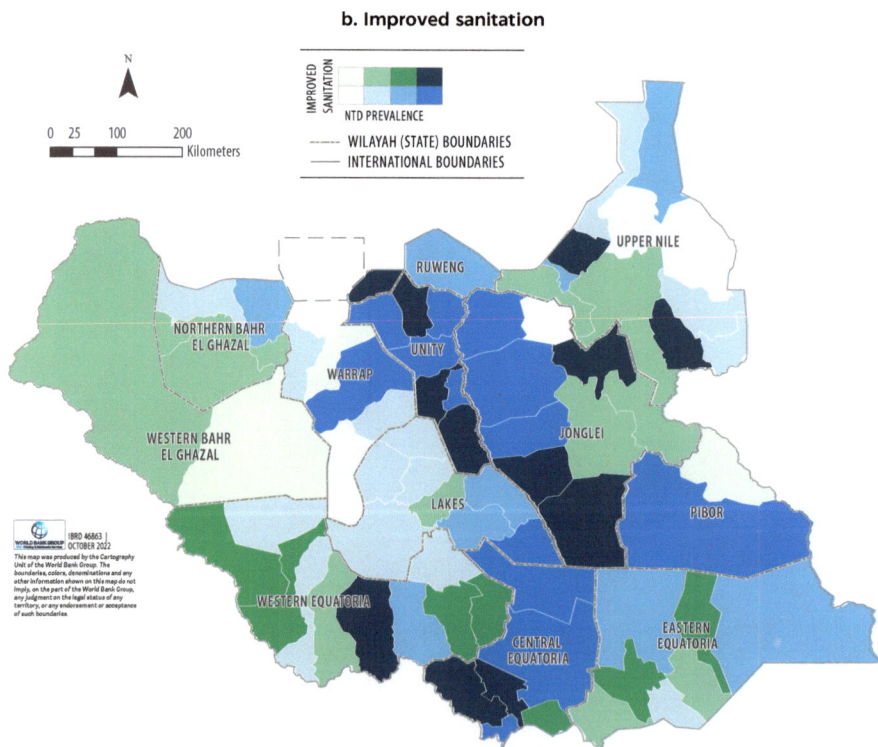

Source: World Bank using World Health Organization, the Expanded Special Project for Elimination of Neglected Tropical Diseases (2020) (https://espen.afro.who.int/) and National Household Health Survey (2020).
Note: NTDs = neglected tropical diseases.

Water insecurity is a binding constraint to food and nutrition security

Water is a fundamental driver of the availability, access, stability, and utilization of food, but its role is often overlooked (figure 3.4). Poor access and quality of water supply affect utilization of food by interrupting the body's capacity to physically retain and absorb nutrients when suffering from diarrhea and other enteric infections. Water also affects availability and access to food as a direct input into agricultural productivity and food distribution, and the stability of food security is affected by water management practices and infrastructure such as irrigation and storage. Human activities, including agriculture, deforestation, and overexploitation of natural resources, disrupt ecosystems and threaten the ability to draw on them for food and nutritional needs, including water for drinking and livelihoods.

Nearly a third of children under 5 in South Sudan are stunted, with prevalence of undernutrition highest in the borderland areas. The most recent nationally representative data on child undernutrition is from the 2010 Multiple Indicator Cluster Survey. Nationally, 31.3 percent of children under 5 in South Sudan are stunted and 22.7 percent are wasted. This is about the average prevalence of stunting for the Africa region (30.7 percent), but higher than the average for wasting in the region (6.0 percent) (Global Nutrition Report 2021). An estimated 27.6 percent of children under 5 are underweight. Map 3.3 presents

FIGURE 3.4

Water, food security, and nutrition

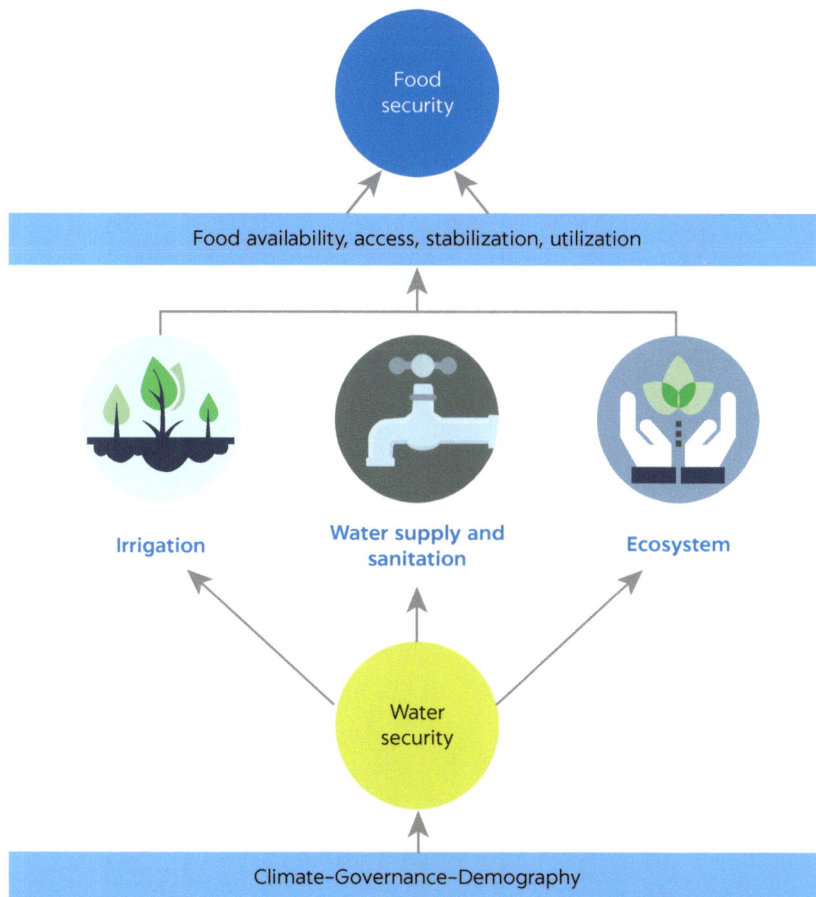

Source: Chase et al. 2019.

MAP 3.3

Prevalence of underweight, stunting, and wasting in South Sudan, 2020

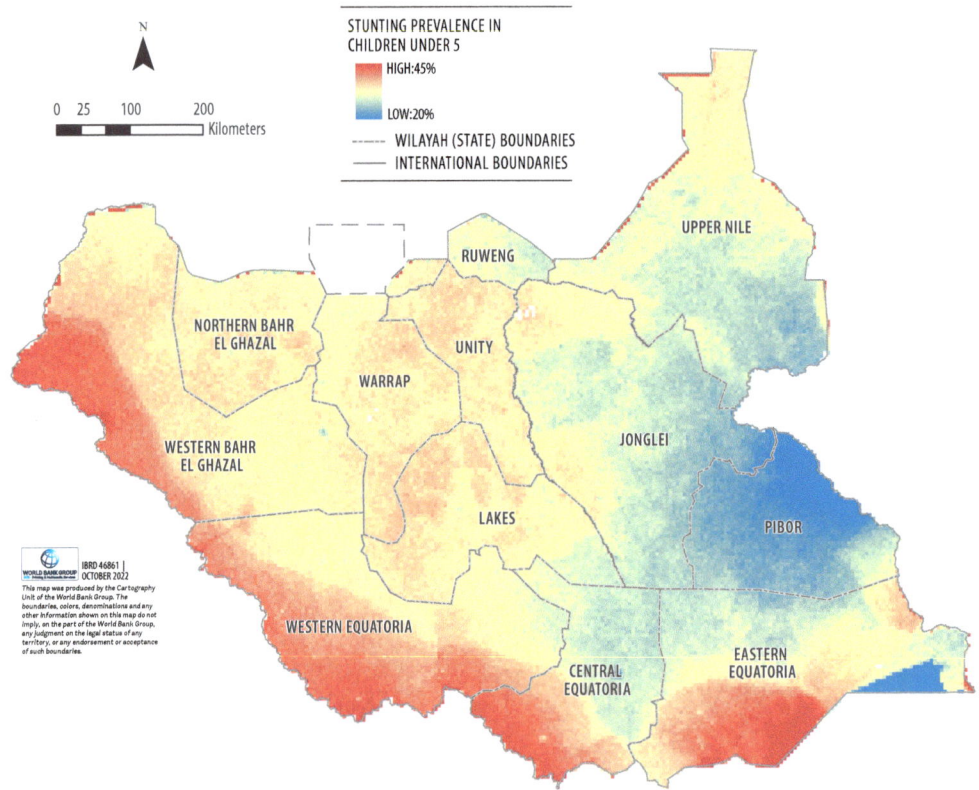

STUNTING PREVALENCE IN
CHILDREN UNDER 5

HIGH: 45%

LOW: 20%

------ WILAYAH (STATE) BOUNDARIES
——— INTERNATIONAL BOUNDARIES

IBRD 46861 |
OCTOBER 2022

This map was produced by the Cartography
Unit of the World Bank Group. The
boundaries, colors, denominations and any
other information shown on this map do not
imply, on the part of the World Bank Group,
any judgment on the legal status of any
territory, or any endorsement or acceptance
of such boundaries.

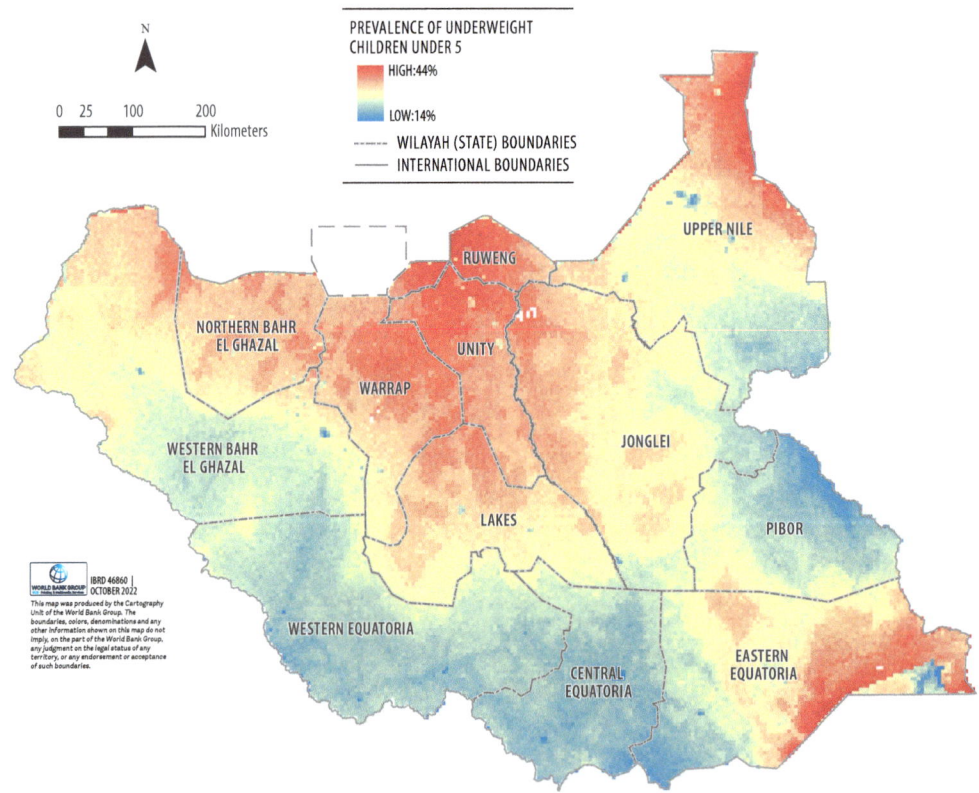

PREVALENCE OF UNDERWEIGHT
CHILDREN UNDER 5

HIGH: 44%

LOW: 14%

------ WILAYAH (STATE) BOUNDARIES
——— INTERNATIONAL BOUNDARIES

IBRD 46860 |
OCTOBER 2022

This map was produced by the Cartography
Unit of the World Bank Group. The
boundaries, colors, denominations and any
other information shown on this map do not
imply, on the part of the World Bank Group,
any judgment on the legal status of any
territory, or any endorsement or acceptance
of such boundaries.

continued

MAP 3.3, *continued*

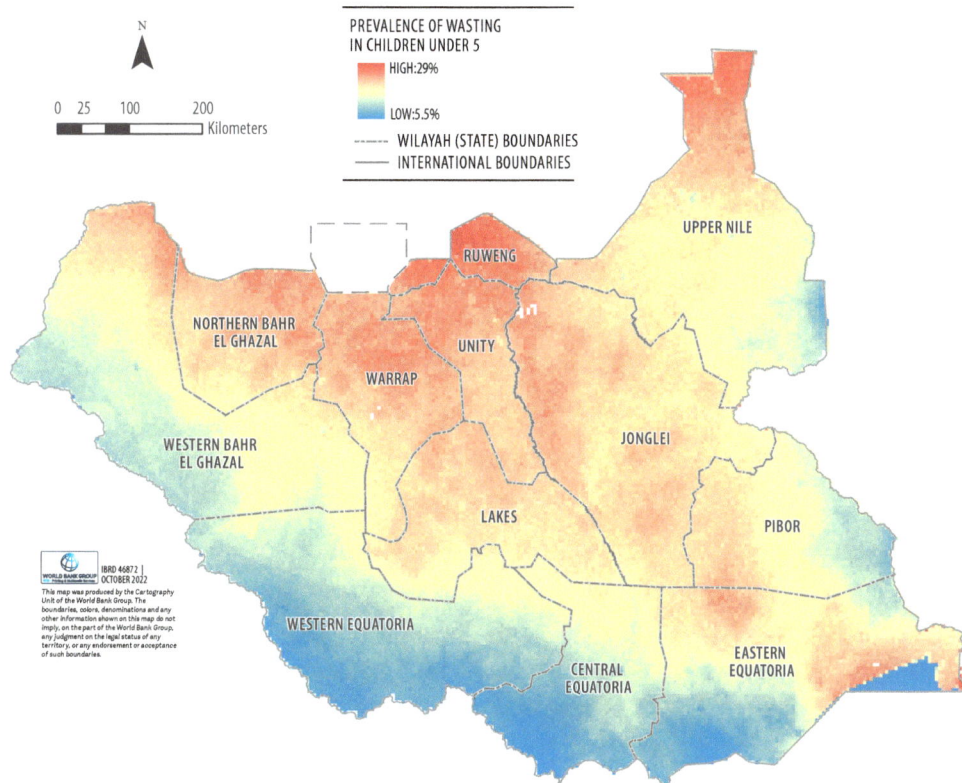

PREVALENCE OF WASTING
IN CHILDREN UNDER 5

HIGH: 29%

LOW: 5.5%

------- WILAYAH (STATE) BOUNDARIES
———— INTERNATIONAL BOUNDARIES

0 25 100 200
Kilometers

N

UPPER NILE

RUWENG

NORTHERN BAHR
EL GHAZAL

UNITY

WARRAP

WESTERN BAHR
EL GHAZAL

JONGLEI

LAKES

PIBOR

WESTERN EQUATORIA

CENTRAL
EQUATORIA

EASTERN
EQUATORIA

IBRD 46872 |
OCTOBER 2022
This map was produced by the Cartography
Unit of the World Bank Group. The
boundaries, colors, denominations and any
other information shown on this map do not
imply, on the part of the World Bank Group,
any judgment on the legal status of any
territory, or any endorsement or acceptance
of such boundaries.

Source: Institute for Health Metrics and Evaluation; Global Child Growth Failure Geospatial Estimates 2000–2019.

geospatial estimates of undernutrition, which suggest that underweight and wasting are most prevalent in the north-central and northeast regions of the country, whereas stunting prevalence is highest in the western and southern states. Undernutrition across all indicators is highest in border-land areas.

The complexity of conflict dynamics, population movement, and displacement make it difficult to disentangle the relationship between WASH, health, and nutrition outcomes in South Sudan. For example, states such as Western Equatoria, with higher-than-average reported access to improved sanitation at 22 percent compared with 10 percent nationally, have among the highest levels of stunting (33.4 percent vs. 31.3 percent nationally) and diarrhea (48 percent vs. 30 percent nationally) prevalence in the country.

The presence of humanitarian aid may further skew the relationship between WASH access, health, and nutrition outcomes. Recipients of humanitarian aid are often among the most vulnerable, yet in South Sudan they have access to services that exceed those for the rest of the population. A survey of internally displaced persons (IDPs) in urban areas of 7 of South Sudan's 10 former states in 2017 found that although just 46 percent had access to basic water supply before displacement, this number had jumped to 73 percent at the new residence.[3] A similar survey conducted in four of the largest IDP camps with defined boundaries in Bentiu, Bor, Juba, and Wau showed 98 percent of households had access to at least basic water supply. In comparison, access to at least basic water supply nationally is estimated to be 40 percent (see chapter 2).

GENDER

Key points

- South Sudanese women and girls generally lack ownership over water resources in the country's highly patriarchal society. However, certain women can be more deprived than others, based on a host of factors, including age, ability, ethnicity, and area of residence.
- Despite carrying much of the responsibility for ensuring households' water supplies, women are excluded from key decisions about siting, design, and maintenance of water points and allocation of water resources. This often leads women and girls to walk longer distances in search of water, or use water from unsafe sources, leading to increased risks of sexual and gender-based violence and disease.
- Water collection has intangible benefits for social capital, with women perceiving queuing and collecting water as an opportunity for exchanging news and socializing.
- Women play a predominant role in farming, providing 80 percent of farm labor in the country, and are therefore more vulnerable to floods and droughts than men, who have control over and access to "movable" livestock assets.

Overview

South Sudan is one of the most unequal societies in the world along gender lines, ranking third worst on the global Women Peace and Security Index (GIWPS 2021). South Sudanese society is highly patriarchal, dominated by elders in communities (Giovetti 2022). However, decades of conflict have meant that, in the absence of men, women often assume decision-making roles within communities. There is a national-level electoral quota for women that requires that women represent at least 25 percent of legislative and executive bodies. Women account for 32 percent of the current Transitional National Legislative Assembly (IPU Parline 2021). Despite these developments, women continue to be underrepresented in state and community leadership bodies, face restrictions from participating in community institutions, have high illiteracy rates and poor reproductive health outcomes, and are more exposed to early and forced marriage, as well as gender-based violence, than women in other parts of the world (BRACED 2017; Edward 2014; Mai 2015).

Against this backdrop, this section examines the relationship between water and gender in South Sudan. Building on existing frameworks that study water and gender (Das 2017), this section describes three ways in which the relationship between water and gender plays out in South Sudan. First, there are large gender inequalities in water security, notably in accessing water services and in confronting water-related risks. Second, women's ownership and control over water resources, and participation in the water sector, mirrors existing patterns of gender inequality. Third, gender inequality in water reflects belief systems and social norms that exacerbate and often determine water insecurity for women and girls.

Gender shapes how people access WASH services and confront water-related risks

Lack of access to water services for households and other uses affects males and females differently. Women and girls are the primary harvesters of water, firewood, and other natural resources in South Sudan (Oxfam 2019b). This is especially true of water, which is primarily collected by women in 85.6 percent of households, followed by young women (under age 15) in 8.8 percent of households (USAID 2017). Despite no countrywide estimate of the average time spent fetching water, evidence from some states suggests that women and girls walk up to eight hours or more to fetch water, particularly in the dry season when nearby surface water sources have been exhausted (World Vision 2022). These data align well with global evidence that shows women spend 2.6 times more time on unpaid domestic and care work relative to men (UN WOMEN 2018).

Even though water collection poses a significant time burden on women and girls, compromising their human development, and increases risks of sexual and gender-based violence (SGBV), queuing at communal water points also has some positive aspects. Women going together are safer and less likely to be attacked. Girls appreciate the opportunity to meet other girls and exchange news and gossip and make friends. Women feel time at the water point is time away from household chores and enjoy socializing. They conduct most of their meetings under the "borehole tree," suggesting that water collection has intangible benefits for social capital and mental health. In the three areas surveyed as part of a background paper prepared for this report (Juba, Kapoeta, Rumbek), women perceived water points as the equivalent of the "big tree" gathering,"[4] with the difference that when meeting at a water point, women are able to express themselves freely (RVI 2022).

Water from available water sources is often not safe to drink and can pose health risks to communities, especially women and girls involved in water collection (Oxfam 2017). Most *haffirs* (Arab word for ponds), for example, lack functional silt traps, leading women to collect water that poses several disease risks (diarrhea, Guinea worm, bilharzia, typhoid, and zoonotic diseases from livestock and wildlife) (Wathorne 2015). Inadequate or absent sanitation facilities across South Sudan, particularly in IDP camps that shelter those fleeing conflict or environmental shocks, also increase health risks among women and children (UNICEF 2020). Sanitation facilities usually lack safety features, such as locks and adequate lighting, that can reduce exposure to gender-based violence (GBV) while in use (Ellsberg et al. 2020; Ellsberg et al. 2021).

The differential impacts of poor access to water services for women and girls become even more pronounced during menstruation. It is well known that lack of appropriate sanitation and hygiene facilities affects women's participation in education and employment. An estimated 33 percent of schools in South Sudan have no drinking water service and 21 percent lack sanitation (WHO/UNICEF 2021). Lack of access to WASH, including sanitary pads, is a common reason for girls to drop out of school or avoid school enrollment altogether (Oxfam 2017).

Surveys of men's and women's perceptions about household water insecurity confirm these statistics on unequal access to water services. Women interviewed in rural areas in Juba, Kapoeta, and Rumbek perceive themselves as being water insecure with a much greater frequency than male respondents. This is to be expected as the questions relate to the "experience" of water insecurity in the household. Because men are not responsible for household water supply, they typically experience less water insecurity. Among the three locations surveyed, Juba (both women and men) reported much higher levels of water insecurity than Kapoeta and Rumbek, which could be due to a higher reliance on surface water, intermittent water tanker supplies, and saline boreholes.

Lack of access to water services is intertwined with women's perceptions and experiences of personal safety. Water collection, especially when it requires women and girls to walk long distances, increases the risk of nonpartner SGBV, which is experienced by women in South Sudan at about four times the global average. Furthermore, violence, conflict, and forced displacement mean that women must collect water from rivers away from the village, where there is more risk of SGBV. Evidence also shows that household water and food insecurity are linked to increased exposure to sexual and physical violence perpetrated by domestic partners (Ellsberg et al. 2020; Ellsberg et al. 2021). Focus group discussions in Juba, Kapoeta, and Rumbek highlight that these events are common but usually not reported (RVI 2022). Water points are used as a target for young men to obtain wives. Following a rape, a young man may demand that the family give the girl to him. Women reported using a number of coping strategies to reduce the risks experienced while collecting water from faraway and unsafe sources. These include going out in large groups, avoiding nighttime water collection, and sharing information on the best times and access points for water collection.

The perception and type of SGBV risks in relation to water collection changes depending on the season. In the dry season, men are busy finding grazing land and water away from hand pumps and water points, meaning that there is less likelihood of them approaching communal water points where women collect water. In turn, this makes women feel safer during water collection activities, at least in relation to the risk of nonpartner violence. Women interviewed in Kapoeta also mentioned that in the dry season the vegetation is low, making it more difficult for attackers to hide. Although the dry season reduces perceptions of risk, overall perceptions of insecurity connected to water access are still high, with about 40 percent of women respondents suggesting that they fear for their safety when fetching water. Risk perceptions for nonpartner violence are much higher in the wet season. Conversely, the risk of partner violence is likely to be higher in the dry season, when household water and food insecurity peaks (Ellsberg et al. 2020; Ellsberg et al. 2021).

The consequences of poor access to water services are particularly severe for forcibly displaced women and girls. Incidents of SGBV, including sexual violence and intimate partner violence (IPV), abductions, and killings, are pervasive in and around areas of settlement, with common reports of abductions and sexual violence. Almost all (97 percent) of these incidents are perpetrated against women or girls. Most incidents occur during routine water and firewood harvesting activities. Basic GBV risk-mitigation measures taken around water and sanitation facilities are extremely rare (Bill and Melinda Gates Foundation 2018; OCHA 2021a). As a result, almost a third of IDPs and returned refugees live in communities where women and children avoid certain areas because of safety concerns. Indeed, perceptions of safety are largely concentrated in the immediate town or area of settlement and rapidly diminish when venturing further to collect water or firewood, thus limiting women's access to services and income-earning opportunities, reducing their overall resilience and adaptive capacity (Oxfam 2019b).

Beyond confronting differential challenges related to access to water services, women are particularly vulnerable to flood risk. Successive years of flooding have destroyed homes and crops, leading to particularly debilitating impacts on women and members of female-headed households. Women play a predominant role in farming, providing 80 percent of farm labor in the country (AfDB 2013), and are therefore more vulnerable to floods than men, who are comparatively more likely to own and control movable livestock assets (BRACED 2017). Aside from the elevated risk of exposure, women and girls also face additional challenges on account of floods. In 2019 and 2020, for example, floods destroyed a fifth of women- and girl-friendly spaces nationwide, as well as more than 56 percent of health facilities and some 400 schools (OCHA 2021a). Flooding also disrupts firewood collection activities—the major source of energy in 96 percent of households—leading women to traverse ever longer distances and, hence, encounter greater safety risks in search of these critical resources (BRACED 2017). Access to housing, land, and property rights (including inheritance) also shapes vulnerability to floods, especially among women and female-headed households whose limited access to land and property rights is extremely constrained under both customary and statutory law. Forcibly displaced women and girls tend to be disproportionately more affected by floods. More than half of all IDPs and returned refugees live in partially damaged housing or makeshift shelters, increasing women's exposure to GBV as well as their vulnerability to flood events (Oxfam 2019b).

When families are confronted by disasters, they often force their girls into marriage to provide some material relief (World Vision 2021a). Child marriage is most prevalent among IDPs living with a host community, in comparison with IDPs living in a camp setting or among residents (that is, nondisplaced persons) (Krystalli et al. 2019). Child marriage may be an important coping strategy used by IDP households living among the host community to increase their social capital and thereby their access to critical resources in times of distress caused by conflict and external shocks, such as flood or droughts (Mazurana, Marshak, and Spears 2019).

Women's participation in the water sector mirrors existing gender inequalities

The combination of gender inequalities and water insecurity shapes women's and girls' empowerment and agency in several ways. Amid conditions of extreme water insecurity and a highly patriarchal society, South Sudanese women experience stark disparities in ownership of water resources compared with men. Customary laws, which often negate women's land and property rights, are widely in force and enshrined in the Constitution of South Sudan (JICA 2017). Findings from focus group discussions show that ownership of water resources is often tied to land tenure, giving men de jure precedence in ownership over women (RVI 2022). This finding is also consistent with evidence from other regions (CEPAL 2021; IUCN 2019).

Women's lack of land tenure also constrains their ability to influence water management and obtain a fair share of water resources. Senior men tend to take precedence at meetings and gatherings, such as big tree meetings, which are highly structured by hierarchy and convention as to who can participate or speak (Leonardi 2015). Under such circumstances, the role of women and youth in community decision-making (including that relevant to management and distribution of water) is inhibited (Smith, Olosky, and Fernández 2021). Findings from focus group discussions support this: although women are part of water management committees, their active participation is low. Interviews also reveal that, although women represent 30 percent of water committee members, they tend not to speak or make decisions during meetings, while men tend to dominate leadership roles and often resist the participation of more assertive women (RVI 2022), resulting in severe implications for women's time use and productivity. For example, global evidence shows that women farmers could improve their yields by up to 30 percent if they received the same access as men to land and water (WWAP 2019).

Gender inequalities are also reflected in employment patterns within the water sector, where women's representation in higher-level, technical, and higher-paid positions is low compared with that of men, but higher across unpaid and voluntary positions (IOM 2020a). Barriers to women's participation include lack of professional and family support for career progression, job recruitment processes that limit women applicants or that do not equitably recognize their experience, inadequate or nonformalized maternity leave policies and practices, and assumptions that many water-related roles are physically too hard for women (for example, drilling, pump mechanic). Beyond preventing women from working in the water sector, these barriers also have consequences for women who do manage to enter the sector and face lower salaries, lack of training opportunities, and lack of safety in the workplace. Although overall women's employment in the sector is low, there are some notable exceptions, including the presence of a woman as the managing director of the South Sudan Water Corporation as of 2022.

Inequalities in ownership and control over water resources are also influenced by the intersection of gender with other factors, such as age, ability, ethnicity, area of residence, and so on. (Das 2017). Women and girls with disabilities, for example, are particularly disadvantaged in access to water and hygiene facilities, which are typically not built according to universal accessibility standards (UN WOMEN 2020). Conversely, older women (especially those who have surpassed reproductive age) have more agency and decision-making authority in the context of water resource decisions, according to both water experts and water users in South Sudan (RVI 2022).

Social norms and belief systems determine the water and gender relationship

Social norms on the types of roles, occupations, and decisions in which women can engage often underpin their low participation and lack of involvement in water management. Owing to norms around the gendered division of household labor and caregiving, women serve as the primary collectors of water in South

Sudanese households, followed by girls. Performing this role often comes at a severe cost given that women and girls are expected to sacrifice their water and food consumption in favor of male members of the household during times of scarcity and must also contend with retributory violence by husbands and fathers (IPV) if they are unable to perform this role (Huser 2018; Oxfam 2017). Hence, social norms that require women to take responsibility for household water supply could be a significant driver of IPV, malnutrition, and other health and well-being challenges for women and girls (Ellsberg and Contreras 2017).

Social norms and customs around land ownership also serve to exclude women from key decisions around siting water points and allocation of water resources (whether made by customary or formal institutions). In South Sudan's patriarchal society, these decisions are the responsibility of men, because they "own" the land and livestock, and because they are tasked with watering and feeding the livestock. These rules are meant to assert status and power and rein-force established hierarchies, such as men's control of the two most valued pro-ductive assets: land and livestock. These norms also result in water points that are often in areas not appropriate for women (too far or too unsafe). In turn, this location increases risks for women who must travel longer distances and to unsafe areas to collect water. This is particularly the case for siting of haffirs. Although haffirs are mainly intended for livestock, they are often the only source of domestic water, meaning that their location can significantly influence the time women spend collecting water and the related exposure to SGBV (RVI 2022).

Social norms also shape distinct patterns of youth involvement in water man-agement along gender lines. Young women are quite engaged in water issues and often responsible for collecting water for the household. In addition, young women carry out crucial operation and maintenance functions, including find-ing resources within communities to pay mechanics when hand pumps break down. Young men are involved in watering livestock but not in making decisions about water development and allocation. More specifically, young men have responsibility for ensuring access to river water for livestock, including digging wells in the dry riverbeds during the dry season. These wells are also used by women for domestic water. Youths are excluded from customary institutions but, where necessary, young men are sometimes used as "secretaries" to elders in the customary institutions (RVI 2022).

In addition, norms around marriage intersect with water and sanitation con-ditions to compound women's exposure to different risks. The Social Norms Assessment (Bukuluki et al. 2022) shows that early marriage is culturally con-doned in most parts of South Sudan, and the decision of when and whom to marry is typically made by fathers. Obtaining bridewealth to offset household welfare needs is often a key motivation for such decisions, which may explain why certain families in South Sudan use early marriage as a coping strategy amid food and water scarcity (Plan International 2022; World Vision 2021a). There are also reports of early marriage being adopted, primarily among IDP families, to protect young girls from the risk of violence during routine food and water collection activities, which could potentially reduce the dowry received by the family (Oxfam 2019a).

Similarly, social norms and beliefs around menstruation and menstrual hygiene increase girls' vulnerability from limited access to WASH. According to the South Sudan Social Norms Assessment (Bukuluki et al. 2022), most women and girls are either unaware of modern hygiene products or believe that use of such products would disrupt their regular menstrual cycle, leading many girls to restrict school attendance during their periods. Finally, customary practices around hygiene, including open defecation, which is widely practiced, can increase health risks for women and children. In certain areas, open defecation is practiced despite the availability of improved sanitation facilities, suggesting that part of the issue may be cultural rather than purely a matter of infrastructure availability (UNICEF 2020).

In addition, GBV is often accepted as a normal part of life by both men and women. The prevalence of inequitable gender norms and harmful cultural practices, such as bridewealth, reinforces women's subordinate status in the marital home, and therefore drives exposure to spousal violence and abuse. Perpetrators of nonpartner violence are similarly emboldened by entrenched patriarchal norms, which typically place the burden of assault on the victims and survivors (Ellsberg et al. 2020; Ellsberg et al. 2021). On the other hand, survivors are constrained in reporting or seeking help against violence because of the stigma associated with rape and sexual assault as well as the lack of professionalism and confidentiality in available reporting mechanisms (Ellsberg and Contreras 2017; UNICEF 2019).

Despite these sobering trends, there is evidence that some social norms regarding women's participation are changing. For example, older women, who are perceived to know more, are given the opportunity to influence decisions with respect to community water management in Kapoeta (RVI 2022). Even in pastoralist communities in Lakes state, there are examples where women are active in committees. They are seen to be more responsible because they are more reliably present. It was reported that the chair and treasurer of committees are now frequently women. Despite these advances, these gains can be erased in the face of disasters, escalating conflict, and displacement. As households are displaced by floods and conflict, women typically lose their roles in the new areas where they settle, where social norms and arrangements for water management might be different. See box 3.1.

BOX 3.1

Overview of lessons and good practices from gender and natural resource interventions

Integration of gender is widely recognized as a key ingredient of successful water and natural resource interventions given the multidimensional roles of women in relation to the environment and as resilience actors, particularly during crises (Tantoh et al. 2021). This discussion reviews key lessons and good practices for water and natural resource interventions that integrate gender considerations within their design and implementation. The reviewed interventions include measures on women's voice and agency and their capacity to manage and use natural resources or start related businesses. Certain interventions also engage with women alongside a host of other stakeholders from the public or private sectors or at the community level.

Women's voice and agency

Global evidence highlights the merits of enhancing women's voice and agency in natural resource interventions, particularly in the context of resource user associations and related service providers (IUCN 2019, 2020; Joint Regional Initiative for Women's Inclusion in REDD+ 2013). However, this elevation of women's voices is often difficult to achieve in highly

continued

Box 3.1, *continued*

patriarchal societies such as South Sudan because of constraints on women's mobility, skills, and ownership and control of resources.

Some interventions address these constraints by reserving a share of seats in water and natural resource user associations for women. However, as the experience of the World Bank–financed Revitalizing the Sudan Gum Arabic Production and Marketing Project shows, simply reserving a share of seats in such groups or associations is often not sufficient because women can be overshadowed in such settings by male members (Abdel Magid 2020). Hence, certain interventions, such as the Nepal community forestry program, adopt accompanying measures to ensure women's quotas are meaningfully implemented, including grassroots advocacy for reformed government guidelines as well as rotation of leadership positions on a periodic basis and joint listing of male and female household members in the community forestry user group membership rolls. Such measures help address the exclusionary effects of gender and other forms of discrimination, which typically allow land-rich males to dominate community forestry user group membership. They can also be instrumental in allowing women to take up roles previously performed by male family members in a context of high male out-migration (Joint Regional Initiative for Women's Inclusion in REDD+ 2013). Other interventions, such as World Vision's Humbo (Forestry) Project,[a] make explicit attempts to include female-headed households and women in forest regeneration efforts by engaging them in forest management groups and cooperatives. Such inclusion not only provides women with an alternate source of household income, it also encourages the sustainable management of the forest resources they rely on (Dejene and Ogega 2021; FMNR, n.d.).

However, in many cases, the chief barrier to women's voice and agency in natural resource management is a lack of land tenure rights, which are typically denied to women in countries with deeply embedded customary laws, such as South Sudan. Hence, certain interventions adopt innovative strategies to extend secure land-use rights to women without necessarily dismantling the customary laws in place within target areas. A project in the Philippines did so by supporting local governments in extending land to women through long-term leases. This is a useful and innovative strategy for ensuring women's participation in contexts where there is a tight link between formal land tenure and participatory usage rights alongside weak or nonexistent land ownership rights for women. As seen in the Philippines' project , the strategy can also open avenues for women's participation in technical training and livelihood support projects as well as their leadership in resource management planning (Joint Regional Initiative for Women's Inclusion in REDD+ 2013).

However, extending land-use rights to women may not always be possible at the outset of an intervention, thus necessitating more gradual strategies. An example is the Namati Project in Kenya, which set up gender-balanced community dialogue forums where problems related to land management, gender inclusion, and customary practices were discussed. As a result, the involved communities issued multiple bylaws strengthening women's land governance rights, including bylaws requiring families with registered land to obtain joint land ownership certificates held by both husband and wife; requiring 50 percent of the major and minor leadership positions within community forest user groups be held by women; enabling women to be elected as traditional leaders; and requiring that women be represented in all community-level committees (Keene 2019). Adopting a slightly different approach, the USAID Kenya Integrated Water, Sanitation and Hygiene Project designed and delivered training to water service providers on gender equality mainstreaming and development of gender action plans and policies. As a result, several of the trained water service providers went on to draft and implement new recruitment policies stipulating a minimum share of female staff (USAID 2020).

Building the capacity of women

Despite being the primary users of water and natural resources in their communities, women may lack the

continued

Box 3.1, *continued*

skills and entitlements to meaningfully participate in related interventions. Conversely, women can contribute substantially to community resilience and sustainable natural resource management if their skills are adequately enhanced (IUCN 2019). Hence, many such interventions aim to build women's capacity in relation to natural resource management by enhancing their skills and their access to credit, finance, and social networks (Independent Evaluation Office 2020; Joint Regional Initiative for Women's Inclusion in REDD+ 2013).

For example, in India, women's participation in tendu leaf picking operations was increased through extension services offered by the Indian Forest Service. Even though the project offered mixed-gender extension training, it offset the risk of women's exclusion by holding sessions at appropriate venues and times and supporting culturally sensitive seating arrangements, having well-trained female facilitators from Forest Service staff or women-focused nongovernmental organizations, as well as meeting protocols to ensure women's voices were heard. Women's participation was also enhanced, in both qualitative and quantitative ways, through the use of context-specific media and training materials, external accountability measures involving women's professional groups or government audit units, and organization of women-only pre-meetings in advance of the mixed-gender extension sessions. Adopting a more holistic approach, the Nepal Irrigation and Water Resource Management Project focused on building women's skills, savings, and social capital, which resulted in a 60 percent increase in women's participation in project-related water user associations over the first year of operations (Joint Regional Initiative for Women's Inclusion in REDD+ 2013).

Some interventions take a more long-term approach to capacity-building by giving women a stake in the long-term sustainability of project activities. The Chivi WASH Project in Zimbabwe, for example, trained women to repair water pumps and build latrines and motivate local communities to achieve open defecation–free status. This project led to tremendous gains in drinking water availability and storage, hygienic practices, and community health outcomes. It also drove a change in social norms, as evidenced by near universal support expressed by local communities for women's leadership in WASH interventions at project end (CARE International 2021). Similarly, the Women's Well Repair Initiative built the capacity of women to engage in well maintenance work and launch related businesses (Water Is Basic 2020).

Women's entrepreneurship

Supporting women's livelihood diversification and entrepreneurial activities is a successful strategy for maximizing the positive gender impacts of natural resource interventions. This support can be achieved through technology transfer and establishment of women-only or women-led producer associations (Joint Regional Initiative for Women's Inclusion in REDD+ 2013).

For example, the Women, Water and Work Project in India established rainwater harvesting systems near homes owned by women to reduce the time they spent on water collection, especially during the dry seasons, thereby opening up avenues for their engagement in livelihoods diversification activities. Likewise, the Solar Sister Project in East Africa supports rural women in off-grid communities with time-saving technologies (portable solar lights, mobile phone chargers, and radio chargers) through a direct sales network of female entrepreneurs. The project uses a micro-consignment approach to support entry into the direct sales network (Joint Regional Initiative for Women's Inclusion in REDD+ 2013). This example is particularly useful because the renewable energy sector offers an unprecedented opportunity to support women's employment and livelihoods diversification: globally, women's participation in the sector is 10 percentage points higher than in the traditionally male-dominated fossil fuel industry (IRENA 2019). In the context of South Sudan, there might be synergies to support rural women through solar irrigation (see chapter 2).

continued

Box 3.1, *continued*

Alternatively, natural resource interventions can also support networks of women producers. For example, the NUNUNA Federation in Burkina Faso, a women-only union of shea butter producers now comprising 4,000 members, was assisted by Tree Aid and other partners in gaining secure rights to forest areas and obtaining credit, training, and business development support, which eventually helped them increase production capacity and reduce production costs substantially, and to obtain fair-trade and organic certification (Joint Regional Initiative for Women's Inclusion in REDD+ 2013).

Engagement of external stakeholders

Effective participation of external stakeholders can be critical to interventions seeking to engage women in natural resource management. For example, the SOS Sahel Project made explicit efforts to incorporate women's and youth's perspectives, including from oft-neglected nomadic communities. This effort revealed a number of conflict triggers and mitigation strategies that proved instrumental in regulating use of pasture and water resources between communities and different types of users (nomadic and settled). For example, in 2015, women and youth in Abusafifa managed to stop two armed conflicts before they escalated into widespread tribal conflict. In addition, after experiencing challenges in women's inclusion during the first stage of the project, the second stage of the project engaged traditional leaders and obtained their assent before organizing local women and youth into committees, which were trained to support demarcation of a livestock corridor, watershed management, and conflict mitigation and resolution in Sudan (Abdel Magid 2020).

a. HumboForestry Project (https://fmnrhub.com.au/projects/humbo/#.Y5i5DXbMJPY).

FORCED DISPLACEMENT

Key points

- South Sudan is the main source of refugees in Sub-Saharan Africa and hosts one of the world's largest internally displaced populations. More than 90 percent of the refugee population live in camps in two states (Upper Nile and Unity), and more than 70 percent of the IDPs live with host communities.
- The provision of clean drinking water in areas of return or local integration is one of the Six Priority Areas under the 2021 South Sudan Durable Solutions Strategy. Without water and water services, durable solutions cannot materialize.
- In South Sudan, water scarcity not only triggers tensions and conflict, but creates opportunities for cooperation between the forcibly displaced and their hosts.
- Forcibly displaced women and girls experience distinctive WASH-linked needs and risks over the different phases of the displacement cycle. If unattended, such needs and risks can increase their vulnerability to GBV and IPV and contribute to deepening gender inequalities.
- Groundwater is the main source of water in refugee camps and in multiple IDP settlements across South Sudan. Promoting sustainable use and management of South Sudan's aquifers is of paramount importance to respond to the forced displacement crisis.

Overview

South Sudan is the main source of refugees in Sub-Saharan Africa and hosts one of the world's largest internally displaced populations. The country presents a multilayered mix of IDPs, asylum seekers, refugees, returnees, stateless persons, and persons at risk of statelessness. Despite the 2018 Revitalized Agreement on the Resolution of Conflict in the Republic of South Sudan (R-ARCSS) that resulted in reduced hostilities among the main conflicting parties, violence in multiple areas across the country persists. Forced displacement was traditionally associated with armed conflict, but in recent years water-related disasters, notably floods, have triggered large-scale internal and cross-border displacement (UNHCR 2021b). Since the outbreak of conflict in December 2013, more than 4 million South Sudanese have been displaced, and the country persists as Africa's largest and the world's third-largest refugee crisis (UNHCR 2022a).

As of March 2022, there were more than 2 million IDPs and more than 335,000 registered refugees in South Sudan (UNHCR 2022a) (table 3.2). The IDP population increased significantly from 1.7 million in 2020 to more than 2 million in 2022. More than 70 percent of IDPs live in informal and formal IDP settlements. Central Equatoria, Unity, and Warrap host the largest numbers of IDPs (OCHA 2022a). Until 2020, a significant number of IDPs lived in the UN Protection of Civilian (PoC) sites established by the United Nations Mission in South Sudan in 2013. In 2020, after an assessment suggesting that security risks had decreased, four out of the five PoCs were gradually transformed into conventional displacement camps under the sovereignty of the government of South Sudan (Mold 2020).

The refugee population in South Sudan is concentrated in the north, where it poses multiple development challenges to the states where they reside. As of March 2022, Unity (including Ruweng Administrative Area) and Upper Nile were hosting the largest numbers of refugees (figure 3.5). Together, these states host more than 90 percent of the refugee population, 92 percent of who are from Sudan. Central Equatoria and Western Equatoria in the south also host refugees. South Sudan has an open-door and nonencampment policy toward refugees, and they are allowed to live with host communities. Most refugees, unlike IDPs, live in the nine refugee settlements established in the country (World Bank 2022). Prima facie asylum procedure applies for Congolese, Ethiopian Anuak, and Sudanese asylum seekers.

South Sudan is the main country of origin of refugees in Sub-Saharan Africa, with at least 2.2 million South Sudanese having crossed international borders. South Sudanese fleeing the conflict enjoy prima facie refugee status in all

TABLE 3.2 Forcibly displaced people in South Sudan and South Sudanese refugees in neighboring countries

PROFILE	NUMBER	STATES OR COUNTRIES WITH LARGEST NUMBERS OF DISPLACED POPULATIONS
Internally displaced persons	2,017,236	Central Equatoria, Unity, Warrap
Refugees (from neighboring countries in South Sudan)	335,317	Central Equatoria, Unity, Upper Nile, Western Equatoria
Refugees (from South Sudan in neighboring countries)	2,240,082	Central African Republic, Democratic Republic of Congo, Ethiopia, Kenya, Sudan, Uganda

Source: UNHCR 2022a.

FIGURE 3.5

Refugees and asylum seekers, by South Sudanese hosting state and administrative area, March 2022

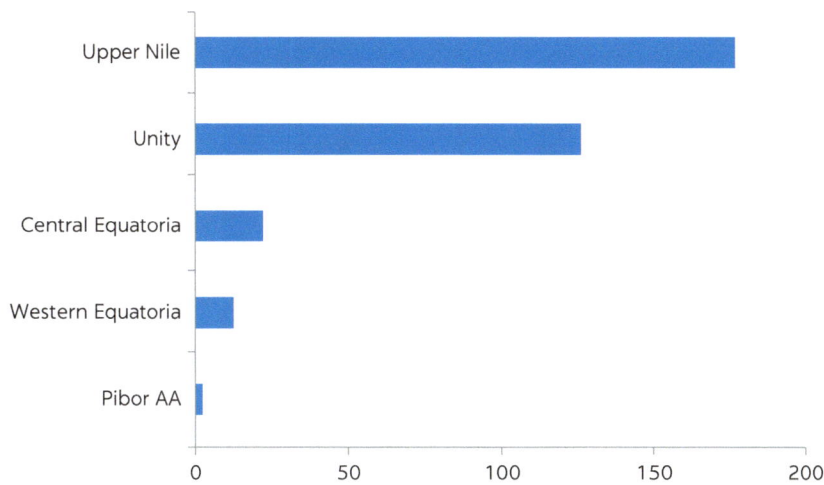

Source: UNHCR 2022b.
Note: AA = Administrative Area. Unity includes refugees in Ruweng AA.

countries of the East, Horn, and Great Lakes regions of Africa. The main countries of asylum for South Sudanese refugees are the Central African Republic, the Democratic Republic of Congo, Ethiopia, Kenya, Sudan, and Uganda (UNHCR 2020). The UNHCR estimates that 95 government, development, and humanitarian partners are involved in the response to South Sudanese in need of international protection. About 83 percent of the overall South Sudanese refugee population comprises women and children, and some 65 percent of refugees are younger than 18. More than 66,000 children have been registered as unaccompanied or separated from their parents or usual caregivers. The South Sudanese refugee situation has been defined as a women, girls, and youth crisis (UNHCR 2020).

Only a small percentage of the 2.2 million South Sudanese refugees have returned or are planning to return to the country permanently in the short and medium term (UNHCR 2020). The UNHCR estimates that as of May 2021 more than 300,000 refugees from neighboring countries have returned home spontaneously and are settling into their villages or surrounding areas to start rebuilding their lives. Some of these returnees return permanently, and others temporarily, creating a phenomenon of pendular migration in some parts of the country (Schots and Smith 2019). The deterioration of the protection environment for South Sudanese refugees in two of the main countries of asylum, Ethiopia and Sudan, has triggered spontaneous returns to South Sudan.

Between November 2017 and June 2019, more than 213,000 self-organized returns occurred, mostly from Sudan following the 2019 political unrest there (UNHCR 2020). The UNHCR estimates that 42 percent of the South Sudanese who participated in a 2019 survey[5] do not plan to return to South Sudan in the foreseeable future (UNHCR 2019). The number of IDPs who return to their hometowns must be added to the number of returnees who have crossed an international border. It is estimated that 1.3 million IDPs returned to their hometowns between 2017 and 2020 (UNHCR 2021a). Decisions about return are increasingly dependent on water-related risks, as described in the next section.

Flooding, drought, and water-related forced displacement

Although conflict and insecurity are the most important push factors for displacement, water-related risks increasingly contribute to forced displacement. Of the half a million people who were displaced in 2021, 40 percent left their homes because of armed clashes and subnational violence (UNHCR 2022c). Beyond conflict and insecurity, water and access to water services can underlay people's decision to move from one place to another and also people's decisions on where to settle (Nagabhatla et al. 2020). Water can thus "push" and "pull" people, thereby influencing displacement patterns. Push factors are defined as those conditions that force people to move from the place where they reside, for example, armed conflict, natural disasters, lack of food, or poor access to natural resources required for subsistence. Pull factors are defined as those conditions that attract people to certain locations and are the opposite of push factors (Lee 1966).

Floods are a major cause of internal displacement in South Sudan. Between July and October 2020, 856,000 people were affected by floods and 389,000 were forcibly displaced (OCHA 2020). In 2021, flooding had affected 466,000 people in areas along the Nile and Lol Rivers and Sudd marshlands since May, reflecting a 23 percent increase in the number of people reported to be affected since the end of August 2021, with Jonglei, Northern Bahr el Ghazal, Unity, and Upper Nile the worst affected states (OCHA 2021b). As of April 2022, hundreds of thousands of people remain displaced by floods, particularly in the Greater Upper Nile region. The country is also vulnerable to droughts, and droughts are increasingly influencing displacement patterns (UNHCR 2022c).

Water challenges in contexts of forced displacement

Displaced persons are often hosted in areas with limited water sources and water supply infrastructure, and where water scarcity and climate change are already affecting the host population (WWAP 2019). The World Health Organization's recommended amount of at least 20 liters of water per capita per day to meet basic hygiene needs and ensure basic food hygiene is rarely met in contexts of protracted displacement. In South Sudan, the overcrowding and poor sanitation conditions of the settlements where refugees and IDPs find shelter, coupled with inadequate water supply, often affect the education, nutrition, health, and human development outcomes of the forcibly displaced (WASH Cluster South Sudan 2022). Waterborne diseases are prevalent in some formal and informal settlements as well as in some refugee camps (Flachberg 2014). The use of wood for cooking and for the construction of temporary and transitional shelters contributes to the environmental degradation of the surrounding areas—including the sources of fresh water—where the forcibly displaced are settled, often creating tensions with the hosts (IDMC 2017). Table 3.3 summarizes the main types of water-related challenges faced by forcibly displaced populations.

In South Sudan, as in most Horn of Africa countries, groundwater is often the main source of water available in locations where refugees find shelter (Scherrer, Schweitzer, and Bünzli 2021). In the Kakuma refugee camp in Kenya, for example, more than 187,000 refugees are entirely dependent on

TABLE 3.3 **Water-linked challenges and impacts**

	WATER-LINKED CHALLENGE	IMPACTS AND LOCATION	SOURCE
Water security for people	Reliance on water provision by humanitarian actors. States have services delivery responsibilities but lack sufficient capacity and resources.	Lack of public sector ownership of the agenda, poor health, malnutrition. Protection of Civilians camp in Malakal (Upper Nile)	WASH Cluster South Sudan 2021
	Extensive tanker water provision in urban and semi-urban areas.	Lack of incentives for medium- and long-term water investments, profit model, affordability issues, poor quality water and disease. Juba (Central Equatoria)	Magot 2021
	Inadequate access to sanitation and poor waste management.	Waterborne diseases, poor health outcomes, snake bites. Mahad camp (Juba)	World Vision 2021b
Water security for production	Environmental degradation of places hosting large numbers of forcibly displaced.	Overexploitation of aquifers, deforestation by cutting of wood for firewood, poor waste management. Yambio (Western Equatoria)	IOM 2021b
	Lack of formal or informal institutions guiding allocation of water sources between forcibly displaced and their hosts.	Resource competition, tensions between new and old neighbors, contested land use, violence. Malakal (Upper Nile)	Conflict Sensitivity Resource Center 2021
	Security risks experienced by the most vulnerable groups (women, girls, youth) during water collection activities.	SGBV, unwanted pregnancy, forced recruitment. Bentiu (Unity)	OCHA 2022b
	Lack of water harvesting structures to sustain livelihoods and water points.	Durable solutions not consolidated, failed returns and relocations, food insecurity. Akobo (Jonglei)	Oxfam 2019a
Water security for protection	Inadequate shelter.	Waterborne diseases, large-scale disease outbreaks, rapid urbanization. Kajokeji (Eastern Equatoria)	OCHA 2022b
	Location of informal settlements in floodplains.	Second and third displacements, loss of lives. Bor (Jonglei)	Team visits in March 2022, Bor county; IOM 2021a

Source: World Bank.
Note: SGBV = sexual and gender-based violence.

groundwater pumped from 12 wells (UNHCR 2016). In South Sudan, the Sudd and Baggara aquifers are two of the main sources of water in the two northern states hosting more than 90 percent of the refugee population. In the Bentiu camp (Unity) alone—South Sudan's largest refugee camp—more than 120,000 refugees rely on groundwater (Seequent 2022). In the Ajuong Thok and Pamir camps (Unity), 60 percent of water demand is met with solar-powered pumps (United Nations 2017). Making groundwater available through boreholes and other water harvesting techniques has been instrumental in promoting development in areas hosting large numbers of IDPs, refugees, and returnees (United Nations 2017); in reducing conflicts for water access; and in transforming the lives of the forcibly displaced and their hosts (Seequent 2022). For example, of the roughly 5,000 households in Gumbo, located to the east of Juba, about 80 percent of the population are IDPs and refugees, and they rely heavily on groundwater (Lasagna et al. 2020).

Groundwater management will be critical for addressing the development and humanitarian needs of the forcibly displaced and their hosts (Scherrer, Schweitzer, and Bünzli 2021). Sustainability plays a key role in groundwater use and management, and the operation and maintenance of groundwater-linked infrastructure can be a source of cooperation between new and old neighbors. Evidence demonstrates that water scarcity not only triggers tensions and conflict, but also cooperation between the forcibly displaced and host communities, and that cooperation around water is more likely to occur in contexts of water scarcity and violence (Döring 2020). In South Sudan, water management committees frequently bring together forcibly displaced people and their hosts, and joint efforts to operate and maintain water pumps, kiosks, and plants, for example, have contributed to peaceful coexistence between the forcibly displaced and the host communities.

Water and gendered challenges and opportunities in contexts of forced displacement

Forcibly displaced women and girls frequently find more challenges during water collection–linked activities than do nondisplaced women and girls. Deteriorated health conditions caused by displacement, disputes with host communities, negative coping mechanisms, weaker social networks, and unattended psychological wounds produced by the violence experienced as they fled their homes are some of the additional challenges that forcibly displaced women have to cope with (English 2017). In the overcrowded settlements and camps, women struggle to give a sense of normality and dignity to their children while coping with huge limitations to washing clothes, long queues at water points, and fear about their physical security every time they travel far to visit a latrine, defecate in the open, or collect water (English 2017).

Displaced women and girls continue to bear high levels of GBV, and water-linked challenges increase their levels of vulnerability. A third of people displaced live in communities where women and girls avoid certain areas because of fear for their safety, and basic GBV risk-mitigation measures around sanitation facilities remain extremely rare outside large IDP camps (IOM 2020b). IDP women also reported feeling unsafe because of congestion in the camps, given that it leads to a lack of privacy, which contributes to increased risk, and actual occurrence, of sexual violence (United Nations Secretary-General High Level Panel on Internal Displacement 2020). The Women Peace and Security Index results for five African countries, including South Sudan, indicate that displaced women experience an average disadvantage of about 24 percent compared with host community women. Displaced women face greater economic marginalization, financial exclusion, and much higher risks than host community women of IPV at home, rising as high as 42 percent in South Sudan (GIWPS 2021). About 73 percent of women in Rumbek, most of who are IDPs, had experienced IPV in their lifetimes (GIWPS 2021). Co-wives and their children live with their husband in the same tent. Women living in the PoCs even reported having to be in the same bed and turn their faces to the wall while their husbands engage in sexual intercourse with one of their co-wives (George Washington University, CARE International, International Rescue Committee 2017). The disproportionate amount of time that forcibly displaced women spend in WASH-linked activities shortens the time available for leisure, education, child care, or income-generating activities. Given the prevalence of GBV in South Sudan, multiple humanitarian and development actors (IOM, USAID, and UNICEF) have linked GBV prevention efforts with WASH actions and with employment-generation opportunities for women in camps and settlements.

Women and children make up 83 percent of the overall South Sudanese refugee population in neighboring countries (UNHCR 2020). Often decisions about relocation or return, when made by women, are made in a context of incomplete information and amid a complex interplay of push and pull factors related to physical safety and material security, including availability of water supply and sanitation (Oxfam 2019b). Data suggest that women are on the move more frequently than men, both for temporary relocation and attempts at more permanent resettlement (Oxfam 2019b). Availability of clean water supply and access to WASH services are among the major factors that influence return and relocation decisions, particularly in rural areas where livelihoods are intimately linked to natural resource access. Access to WASH services, including menstrual hygiene awareness and sanitary kits, is also noted by female IDPs and refugees as a factor that affects the decision to return or relocate (Oxfam 2019b).

Water is an enabler of durable solutions

Water availability is an enabler of the durable solutions available to the forcibly displaced. Durable solutions to forced displacement are defined as the alternatives that refugees and IDPs have to break the displacement cycle and settle permanently in a place (Research and Evidence Facility 2019). There are three solutions available to IDPs (local integration, voluntary relocation, and voluntary return[6]), and three to refugees (voluntary return to the country of origin, integration into the country of asylum, and voluntary resettlement in a second country of asylum). Durable solutions are achieved when individuals no longer have specific assistance or protection needs linked to displacement, and represent the closure of the displacement cycle. The achievement of durable solutions is a state responsibility, and humanitarian and development actors play a complementary role (World Bank 2017). Although the fragile security situation in multiple states across the country hinders the possibility of achieving durable solutions, the government of South Sudan, in cooperation with humanitarian, development, and peace actors, is working in this direction.

The provision of clean drinking water in areas of return or local integration is one of the Six Priority Areas under the 2021 Durable Solutions Strategy, highlighting that water availability is a governing factor in the government response to forced displacement. Water is a fundamental variable in the durable solutions equation in South Sudan. Without access to water supply and sanitation services, local integration processes, voluntary returns, and relocations cannot materialize (World Bank Group 2019). The enjoyment of an adequate[7] standard of living is achieved when the forcibly displaced have sustained access to essential food and potable water; basic shelter and housing; essential medical services, including post–sexual assault care and other reproductive health care; sanitation; and at least primary school education (Inter-Agency Standing Committee 2010). The challenge is complex given that the security conditions in multiple parts of the country remain fragile, and that in the absence of security conditions durable solutions cannot materialize.

A WASH Transition Strategy for Former PoC Sites[8] was developed to ensure that the responsibility for maintaining and operating WASH facilities is progressively transferred to local populations and to the responsible local authorities. The WASH Transition Strategy for Former PoC Sites, through the WASH ex-PoC Task Force, is contributing to building the capacity of the responsible local authorities who should become responsible and accountable for ensuring regular services to eventually promote suitable solutions for IDPs by creating the service conditions conducive to durable solutions (returns and local integration) (WASH Cluster South Sudan 2021). In several locations, multisectoral plans are being developed at the site level, including transition plans for security, services, and community engagement.

South Sudan's durable solutions agenda is fully aligned with a development approach to situations of protracted displacement. The World Bank characterizes a development approach to forced displacement as one that is complementary to humanitarian efforts; focuses on medium-term socioeconomic aspects; is government-led and places particular attention on institutions and policies; aims to build partnerships with and between governments, the private sector, and civil society; and includes a strong focus on host communities (World Bank 2021).

Policy responses to forced displacement in South Sudan

The provision of clean drinking water is one of the Six Priority Actions under the 2021 Durable Solutions Strategy and Plan of Action for Refugees, Internally Displaced Persons, and Host Communities in South Sudan. Other policy documents reviewed do not contain provisions on water supplies for the forcibly displaced specifically. The strategy is the guiding framework for supporting refugees, returnees, IDPs, and host communities in finding sustainable durable solutions to displacement; it follows a whole-of-government and a whole-of-society approach and is anchored on and guided by the R-ARCSS. It was developed in the context of the Intergovernmental Authority on Development–led Solutions Initiative for South Sudan and Sudan, and builds upon the 2017 National Framework for Return, Reintegration and Relocation of Displaced Persons.

Similarly, the Revised National Development Strategy (R-NDS) for South Sudan 2021–2024 (Government of South Sudan and United Nations Development Programme 2021) sets multiple objectives in the area of forced displacement. The goals set by the R-NDS for IDPs, returnees, refugees, and their hosts fall mostly under two clusters: governance and services (social development). First, in the context of the governance cluster, the government of South Sudan aims at "[e]nsuring the resettlement and reintegration of returnees and refugees, and the provision of reconstruction and recovery services." The R-NDS emphasizes the need to ensure effective and sustainable implementation of the R-ARCSS to achieve the multiple development goals established under the governance cluster. Second, under the services (social development) cluster, the R-NDS acknowledges that the provision of services (including water) is critical in building and strengthening the government-citizen relations and makes special reference to the importance of social inclusion of IDPs, returnees, refugees, and their hosts.[9] The R-NDS gives special attention to the investments required in the areas of return for the potential arrival of returnees that can occur in the 2021–24 period. South Sudan has signed on to the relevant regional and international refugee conventions and protocols and has also taken concrete steps to make it possible for refugees to enjoy their rights, including enacting a Refugee Act in 2012 and establishing a Commission for Refugee Affairs to manage issues related to refugees (World Bank 2022).

The R-ARCSS states the required provisions and commitments necessary to address the development and protection gaps of IDPs, returnees, and refugees in the country. Chapter 3 of the R-ARCSS calls on the government to create an enabling environment for the safe and dignified return of the South Sudanese who fled hostility in their original home areas or places of habitual residence and ended up in other parts of the country or other countries. By enabling a protective environment, the parties agreed to (a) protecting and providing secure access to the civilian population in need of humanitarian assistance; (b) providing physical, legal, and psychosocial protection to refugees and IDPs to return in safety and dignity, including the re-unification of families separated during the conflict; (c) granting rights to citizenship, civil registration, and issuance of appropriate identification documents to refugees and IDPs; and (d) allowing refugees and IDPs to return to their places of origin or live in areas of their choosing.

CONFLICT

Key points

- Despite the intuitive narrative that water disasters heighten the risk of conflict because they disrupt livelihoods and mobility patterns, forcing populations to resort to violence to access land and water, evidence suggests that community vulnerability to water-conflict issues differs widely and is mediated by political and social factors.
- Water is often a weapon and casualty of conflict: warring parties systematically destroyed or stole pumps used by communities, depriving them of access to water.
- South Sudan is trapped in a vicious cycle of water insecurity and conflict, exacerbated by climate change.

Overview

Over the past two decades, research and policy debate on the impact of water-related hazards on conflict risk has expanded significantly, with several studies focusing on South Sudan, both before and after independence (NUPI and SIPRI 2021; Verhoeven 2011). The potential for water to contribute to conflict and unrest has long been recognized, with recent reports of violence erupting over access to water resources and often closely intertwined with conflicts over access to land for crop production and livestock grazing (Brottem and McDonnell 2020). The development of extractive industries is posing new water-related risks, including water pollution, which are expected to further strain the country's fragile environments and social fabric. The effects of water on conflict vary greatly across space and time, and social context, economic development, and governance systems shape this interaction and variation.

Scholars and policy analysts highlight the importance of relying on complementary approaches to understand the links between water and conflict (Borgomeo et al. 2021; Mach et al. 2019). A first approach is based on quantitative assessments and empirical analysis that draw inferences based on data on water availability and variability, such as rainfall, and conflict occurrences. A second approach uses qualitative methods, including coding of events related to water, historical documents, and interviews. This section builds on both approaches to summarize the existing evidence on the intersection between water and conflict in South Sudan. The section examines two core aspects of the water-conflict nexus, first, the role of water as a contributing factor to conflict, and second, the impact of conflict on water resources and services, whereby water itself becomes a casualty—and even a weapon—of conflict.

Water as a contributing factor to conflict and violence

Quantitative and qualitative assessments highlight the significant links between water availability and the occurrence of violence. Empirical analysis of drought and conflict data suggests that there are statistically significant links between the occurrence of drought and violence, with more severe drought associated with higher levels of violence. Building on the methods developed in Khan and Rodella (2021) and Harari and Ferrara (2018), figure 3.6 shows that over the period 1997–2011, drier periods in South Sudan were associated with increased violence and conflict. Sudan is also shown for comparison. The negative slope for Sudan indicates that higher levels of conflict also occur during dry periods in that country; however, its position below South Sudan's line means that it experiences lower levels of violent conflict, on average.

There are numerous potential channels with which to explain the relationship observed in figure 3.6. First, dry periods negatively affect livelihoods. Given the high proportion of South Sudan's population directly dependent on water resources for their basic needs, it is not surprising that any long-term or short-term change in water availability has an impact on livelihoods. More specifically, droughts affect two core components of South Sudanese livelihoods: cattle and mobility. Drought disrupts livestock grazing activities by limiting land and water resources available for rearing, which, in turn, can induce tensions as herders try

FIGURE 3.6

Relationship between conflict and drought for South Sudan and Sudan, 1997–2011

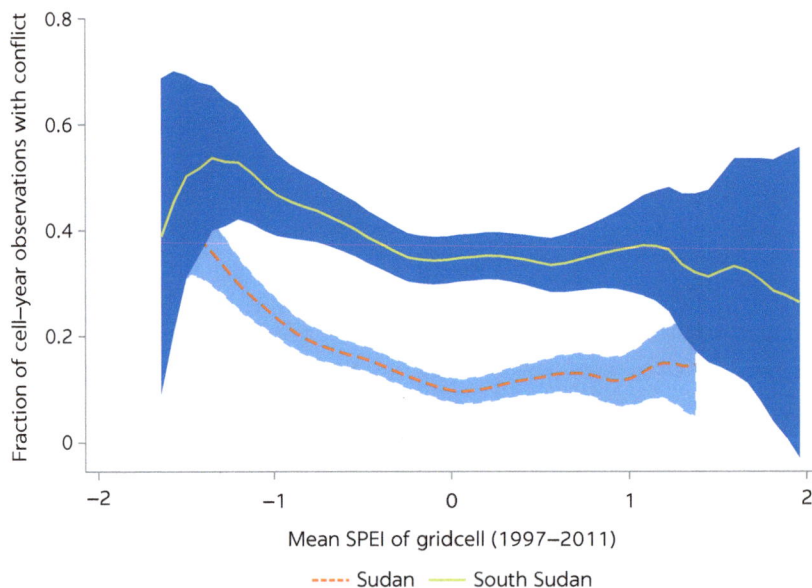

Source: World Bank using data from Harari and Ferrara (2018).
Note: The relationship between conflict and drought is measured with the Standardized Precipitation Evapotranspiration Index (SPEI) for South Sudan and Sudan using data from Harari and Ferrara (2018). No controls in regression. Sudan is included for comparison only. The shaded area is the 95 percent confidence interval of the estimated (polynomial) curve. See appendix A for details on the regression methodology.

to access limited supplies of these resources. These conditions can also lead to an oversupply of livestock in local markets, as herders sell cattle in times of hardship, causing an overall decline of livestock prices and a related increase in the price of other food items, thus further affecting household incomes (Maystadt, Calderone, and You 2014; Maystadt and Ecker 2014). To manage these price shocks, households might resort to cattle raiding, increasing the probability of violent conflict. Additionally, drought affects mobility patterns. Pastoralist routes adapt to the changing availability of water, moving groups closer together in areas with remaining water and pasture. By moving away from customary mobility routes, pastoralists are more likely to end up closer to groups from other areas or ethnicities, with which they lack shared customary institutions and mechanisms to settle disputes (Van Baalen and Mobjörk 2018). In turn, the absence of shared institutions might increase the chances of conflict.

Qualitative research provides further nuance to the findings from this empirical assessment, suggesting that the links between water and conflict also materialize during floods. When water is overly abundant, pastoralists may depart from negotiated access and customary institutions for accessing water resources and land, which, in turn, could move them closer to other groups, inciting competition over shared resources or making them more vulnerable to cattle raiding (Van Baalen and Mobjörk 2018). Areas close to the Sudd wetland that experience high variation in land cover, from standing waters during times of floods to grasslands when the waters recede, also experience frequent conflicts (Sosnowski et al. 2016), particularly at the boundary between Unity and Warrap states. This situation again highlights the multifaceted links between water and conflict, with water scarcity being just one potential channel through which water combines with social and political factors to increase conflict risk.

Despite these links between water and conflict, it is important to emphasize that droughts or floods rarely, if ever, explain the occurrence of conflict and violence. The impacts of water on conflict and violence dynamics are intertwined with other pressures on livelihoods, mobility, and incomes. In other words, important political and social factors mediate and often exacerbate these water-conflict links. Table 3.4 summarizes existing academic studies on the subject and identifies the moderating factors explored in each study. In the context of South Sudan, three factors emerge as more prominent. First is small arms proliferation among civilians. A 2016 survey suggests that civilians hold between 232,000 and 601,000 firearms (with automatic weapons being the most common type), with the higher estimate likely to be more accurate (SSBCSSAC and UNDP 2017). Widespread access to and misuse of firearms fueled an increased militarization and violence of cattle raiding and exacerbated perceptions of insecurity (Wild, Jok, and Patel 2018). Second, government interventions further restrict mobility, for example, through restrictions along the international border with Sudan (Davies et al. 2018). The establishment of the border between Sudan and South Sudan cut through existing livestock migration routes, separating pastoralists living north of the border from favored dry season pastures south of the border, creating a potential source of tension during each migration season (Cormack and Young 2012; Craze 2013). Third is elite exploitation of extreme climatic conditions. Although conflicts over water resources take place at the community level, they are often escalated by state policies. Political elites exploit local grievances and tensions over water resources to inflict damage on political opponents, influence national political struggles, or promote top-down water resources development to

TABLE 3.4 Studies examining the link between water-related risks and conflict in South Sudan

FINDINGS	MEDIATING FACTOR	SUGGESTED RESPONSE	CASE STUDY LOCATION	SOURCE
Resource scarcity has had a limited effect on violent conflict, whereas water abundance is related to violence	Political economy factors at local, national, and global level	Focus on the impacts of resource abundance and political economic forces in water and conflict assessments	National, Sudd wetlands	Selby and Hoffmann 2014
Conflict locations and regions with high interannual changes in wetland extents are spatially related	Worsening of livelihood conditions alters mobility patterns	Monitor land use change as a potential indicator of worsening livelihoods and conflict risk	Sudd wetlands and floodplains	Sosnowski et al. 2016
Top-down development approach to water resources development contributes to tension and instability	Elite attempts to maintain exclusive power and to marginalize and exclude areas and populations at the state's periphery	Develop legal and institutional frameworks to deal with land tenure, water rights, and conflict resolution at all levels (interstate, state, regional, and local)	National, Greater Upper Nile	Cascão 2013
Warmer temperatures increase the frequency of violent conflict by about a third	Worsening of livelihood conditions leading to, among other things, competition between herders and farmers and explosion of grievances in relation to food prices	Support livestock destocking and restocking processes at times of drought through improved access to markets; development of weather insurance schemes; and provision of income diversification opportunities (irrigation, education)	National (includes Northern Sudan)	Maystadt, Calderone, and You 2014

Source: World Bank.

exclude populations from development opportunities. This exploitation occurred both before and after independence (Assal 2006; El Zain 2006; Selby and Hoffmann 2014).

Water as a casualty and weapon of conflict

Heavy fighting with explosive weaponry and intentional sabotage means that the country's water and sanitation infrastructure, alongside the electricity infrastructure on which it largely depends, has suffered long-lasting damage. This destruction has immediate impacts on conflict-affected populations, who identify drinking water as the most serious problem they face, before food or health care (Ayazi et al. 2015). Following independence, access to drinking water supply services in rural areas declined. According to data from the UNICEF Joint Monitoring Programme, access to at least basic drinking water sources (an improved source within 30 minutes roundtrip) declined from 38.8 percent in 2011 to 33.6 percent in 2020, with the population shifting to limited access (where collection takes more than 30 minutes roundtrip) (figure 3.7; see chapter 2). Many reasons are behind this decline, including forced displacement, infrastructure damage, and pump failure. The pump failure issue is exacerbated by brain drain, whereby water utility staff and pump operators either did not work or left the country because of security reasons.

Violence and conflict have been intentionally targeted toward water resources or human-built water systems to inflict damage on opponents in several instances. United Nations Human Rights Council investigations report that access to water was used as a weapon to inflict damage on opponents

FIGURE 3.7

Share of rural population spending more than 30 minutes collecting drinking water, 2015 and 2020

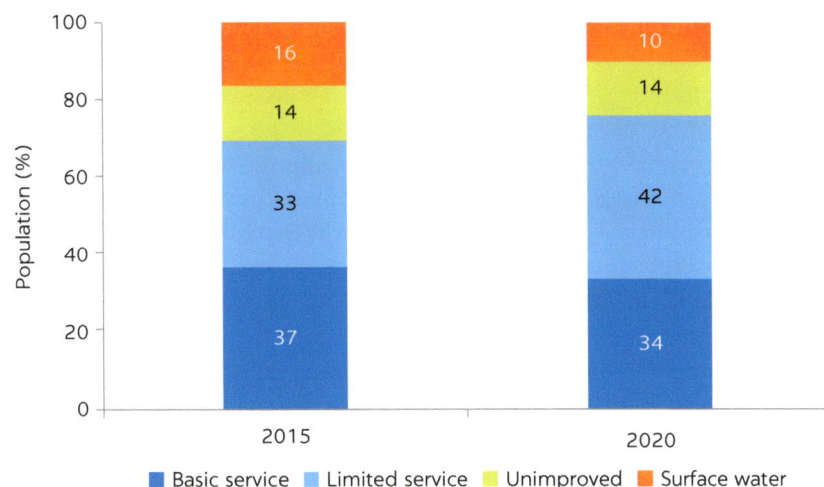

Source: UNICEF Joint Monitoring Programme data for South Sudan (2015, 2020).

(UN Human Rights Council 2020a). In Lakes state, deliberate tactics weaponized water to weaken communities, with warring parties systematically destroying or stealing pumps used by locals, depriving them of access to water (UN Human Rights Council 2020b) for both consumption and sanitation. For example, water infrastructure was a casualty of war in the northern town of Malakal. The town's piped water supply system was largely destroyed during the war, with the remaining pipes being either blocked or looted (The New Humanitarian 2018).

Breaking the vicious cycle of water insecurity and fragility

Water security is more difficult to achieve in fragile contexts—and the failure to achieve water security has greater consequences in fragile contexts (Sadoff, Borgomeo, and De Waal 2017). South Sudan is currently confronted with this vicious cycle, which risks undermining development and peace-building efforts, and will be further exacerbated by climate change. Protracted armed conflict is the starting point of this vicious cycle: it increases poverty, halts economic activities, disrupts livelihoods, and damages social networks and formal and informal institutions. These political and socioeconomic impacts, in turn, increase vulnerability to climate change. In the context of South Sudan, this vulnerability is further compounded by the large share of the population relying directly on water resources and other natural assets, whose availability and variability is influenced by climate, for their basic needs and livelihoods. This climate sensitivity combines with social and political factors to undermine the coping capacity of populations to respond to climate change, so that once floods or droughts strike, damage is even greater. Humanitarian emergencies around the world demonstrate this vicious cycle, with most food crises taking place in locations with high vulnerability to climate change and experiencing protracted armed conflict (Buhaug and von Uexkull 2021).

In South Sudan, this vicious cycle materializes, for example, when people forcibly displaced by conflict and violence end up settling in flood-prone areas.

Because they reside in these marginal, hazard-prone areas, they are the first to be affected by flood events, which can lead to further displacement. This repeated displacement cycle increases the risk of negative impacts, including loss of life from floods and droughts, and prevents populations from building their coping capacity to adapt to future shocks.

Breaking this cycle is the entry point for water sector and climate change adaptation interventions, with at least two implications for water sector investments. First, they should be carried out following the do-no-harm principle, to avoid exacerbating fragilities and tensions and therefore paradoxically increasing vulnerability to climate change and water insecurity. Second, water management and related customary institutions should be leveraged to promote cooperation and peace-building. For example, following the independence of South Sudan and the creation of the northern border, communities living along the border conducted a series of meetings and reached an agreement on sharing of access to water resources despite the tensions between the two countries (Abdalla 2013). Without restored social relations conducive to cooperation, water sector interventions are unlikely to succeed. Although existing localized systems of dispute resolution and resource management can be effective in helping to manage conflict, they are not a panacea. In an analysis of local responses to conflict in Lakes state, Ryle and Amoum (2018) suggest that the greater level of peace in eastern Lakes state can be partly explained because of the different responses by community leaders. Although both eastern and western parts of Lakes state experienced similar sources of conflict relating to cattle theft, the constructive response of community leaders in the eastern part of the state allowed for a greater level of peace than in neighboring areas (Brottem and McDonnell 2020).

CONCLUSIONS

To examine the far-reaching implications of water insecurity in South Sudan, this chapter illustrates links with key aspects of human development, inclusion, and fragility. Unless these links are considered, water-related interventions are likely to fail and potentially exacerbate existing challenges. To advance inclusive and conflict-sensitive interventions, government and donors should promote alternative and more inclusive modalities for decision-making and water management at the community level in accordance with relevant country legislation (such as the Local Government Act 2009). Alternatives for community-level institutions include Payam Development Committees and Boma Development Committees, as envisaged in the Local Government Act 2009, which typically include representation of women, youth, the displaced, elders, and people with disabilities. These community-level institutions provide mechanisms for inclusion and for reducing and managing social tensions that might arise because of interventions.

NOTES

1. Addressing NTDs is a priority under the Sustainable Development Goals, with goal 3.3 to end the epidemics of AIDS, tuberculosis, malaria, and neglected tropical diseases and combat hepatitis, waterborne diseases, and other communicable diseases by 2030.
2. Schistosomiasis, onchocerciasis, trachoma, lymphatic filariasis, and soil-transmitted helminths (STH).

3. A survey of 375 IDPs in the 2017 round of high-frequency surveys in Central Equatoria, Eastern Equatoria, Lakes, Northern Bahr el Ghazal, Warrap, Western Bahr el Ghazal, and Western Equatoria states.
4. Large trees are gathering places for community meetings and celebrations.
5. The survey further indicates that 31 percent of respondents do plan to return but have no clear timeline, 7 percent plan to return in the next 18 months, and 20 percent remain undecided on their return plans.
6. Local integration refers to the sustainable local integration into areas IDPs take refuge; relocation refers to the sustainable integration in another part of the country; and voluntary return refers to the sustainable reintegration at the place of origin. There is no global legally binding framework, but there are principles and instruments that guide actions directed at promoting durable solutions to internal displacement.
7. In this context, adequacy means that these minimum goods and services are available, accessible, acceptable, and adaptable.
8. The WASH action plan is divided into three sections: (a) critical or urgent needs to resume and maintain essential services with a short-term timeframe, (b) medium-term needs that include the strengthening of community engagement and ownership and progressive shift toward more robust and durable WASH facilities, and (c) long-term needs that include activities and resources needed to ensure all WASH services are sustainable, standards are in place for sustainability, and communities are fully engaged in maintenance of services. Short-term and a portion of the medium-term needs should be funded through the humanitarian framework, whereas a portion of the medium-term needs and the long-term needs should be funded through the development framework.
9. Cluster Five Gender and Youth acknowledges the disproportionate impacts of conflict and climate change on girls, women, and youth and discusses how vulnerabilities are exacerbated in contexts of forced displacement.

REFERENCES

Aagaard-Hansen, J., N. Nombela, and J. Alvar. 2010. "Population Movement: A Key Factor in the Epidemiology of Neglected Tropical Diseases." *Tropical Medicine and International Health* 15 (11): 1281–88.

Abdalla, A. J. 2013. "People to People Diplomacy in a Pastoral System: A Case from Sudan and South Sudan." *Pastoralism: Research, Policy and Practice* 3 (1): 1–7.

Abdel M., T. D. 2020. *Lessons Learned and Good Practices in Natural Resource Management.* Nairobi: United Nations Environment Programme. https://postconflict.unep.ch/Sudan /NRM_2020_EN.pdf.

AfDB (African Development Bank). 2013. *South Sudan: An Infrastructure Action Plan— A Program for Sustained Strong Economic Growth.* Tunis: African Development Bank.

Ali, M., A. R. Nelson, A. L. Lopez, and D. A. Sack. 2015. "Updated Global Burden of Cholera in Endemic Countries." *PLoS Neglected Tropical Diseases* 9 (6): e0003832.

Assal, Munzoul. 2006. "Sudan: Identity and Conflict over Natural Resources." *Development* 49: 101–5.

Ayazi, T., L. Swartz, A. H. Eide, L. Lien, and E. Hauff. 2015. "Perceived Current Needs, Psychological Distress and Functional Impairment in a War-Affected Setting: A Cross-Sectional Study in South Sudan." *BMJ Open* 5 (8): e007534.

Bill and Melinda Gates Foundation. 2018. "Gender and the Sanitation Value Chain: A Review of the Evidence." Bill and Melinda Gates Foundation, Seattle, WA. https://www .gatesgenderequalitytoolbox.org/wp-content/uploads/Gender-and-Sanitation-Evidence -Review-May-2018.pdf.

Borgomeo, E., A. Jägerskog, E. Zaveri, J. Russ, and R. Damania. 2021. *Ebb and Flow: Volume 2. Water in the Shadow of Conflict in the Middle East and North Africa.* Washington, DC: World Bank.

BRACED (Building Resilience and Adaptation to Climate Extremes and Disasters). 2017. "Building Climate Resilience in Fragile Contexts: Key Findings of BRACED Research in South Sudan—Improving Resilience to Climate Change in South Sudan." BRACED, London.

Brottem, L., and A. McDonnell. 2020. "Pastoralism and Conflict in the Sudano-Sahel: A Review of the Literature." Search for Common Ground, Washington, DC. https://www.sfcg.org/wp-content/uploads/2020/08/Pastoralism_and_Conflict_in_the_Sudano-Sahel_Jul_2020.pdf.

Buhaug, H., and N. von Uexkull. 2021. "Vicious Circles: Violence, Vulnerability, and Climate Change." *Annual Review of Environment and Resources* 46: 545–68.

Bukuluki, P., M. Okwii, K. Hoffman, and M. Pavin. 2022. "South Sudan Social Norms Assessment." USAID/Momentum Integrated Health Resilience, Washington, DC. https://usaidmomentum.org/wp-content/uploads/2022/03/MOMENTUM-IHR-South-Sudan-Social-Norms-Assmt-01-21-22.pdf.

CARE International. 2021. "Evaluation Brief: Post Project Sustainability Evaluation of Chivi WASH Project in Zimbabwe." CARE Food and Water Systems, USA and Zimbabwe. https://www.careevaluations.org/wp-content/uploads/CWP-brief-for-dissemination-updated-may-2022.pdf.

Cascão, A. E. 2013. "Resource-Based Conflict in South Sudan and Gambella (Ethiopia): When Water, Land and Oil Mix with Politics." In *State and Societal Challenges in the Horn of Africa: Conflict and Processes of State Formation, Reconfiguration and Disintegration*, edited by Alexandra Magnólia Dias, 144–65. Lisbon: Center of African Studies (CEA)/ISCTE-IUL, University Institute of Lisbon.

CEPAL. 2021. "Implications of Gender Roles in Natural Resource Governance in Latin America and the Caribbean." *Natural Resources in Latin America* 2. https://www.cepal.org/en/insights/implications-gender-roles-natural-resource-governance-latin-america-and-caribbean.

Chase, C., A. Bahuguna, Y. Chen, S. Haque, and M. Schulte. 2019. "Water and Nutrition: A Framework for Action." World Bank, Washington, DC.

Conflict Sensitivity Resource Center. 2021. "Conflict Sensitivity Analysis: United Nations Mission in South Sudan (UNMISS) Protection of Civilian (PoC) Sites Transition: Bentiu, Unity State, and Malakal, Upper Nile State." Conflict Sensitivity Resource Center, South Sudan.

Cormack, Z., and H. Young. 2012. "Pastoralism in the New Borderlands: Cross-Border Migrations, Conflict and Peace-Building." Feinstein International Center, Tufts University, Boston. https://fic.tufts.edu/assets/Pastoralism-in-the-New-Borderlands.pdf.

Craze, J. 2013. "Dividing Lines: Grazing and Conflict along the Sudan–South Sudan Border." Small Arms Survey, Geneva.

Das, M. B. 2017. "The Rising Tide: A New Look at Water and Gender." World Bank, Washington, DC.

Davies, J., C. Ogali, L. Slobodian, G. Roba, and R. Ouedraogo. 2018. *Crossing Boundaries: Legal and Policy Arrangements for Cross-Border Pastoralism*. Rome: Food and Agriculture Organization.

Dejene, A., and J. Ogega. 2021. "A Gender-Responsive Approach to Natural Resources." *Blog, Global Food for Thought*. The Chicago Council on Global Affairs, July 16, 2021. https://www.thechicagocouncil.org/commentary-and-analysis/blogs/gender-responsive-approach-natural-resources.

Döring, S. 2020. "From Bullets to Boreholes: A Disaggregated Analysis of Domestic Water Cooperation in Drought-Prone Regions." *Global Environmental Change* 65: 102147.

Edward, J. K. 2014. "A Strategy for Achieving Gender Equality in South Sudan." Sudd Institute, Juba.

Ellsberg, M., and M. Contreras. 2017. "No Safe Place: A Lifetime of Violence for Conflict-Affected Women and Girls in South Sudan, Summary Report." The Global Women's Institute, Washington, DC. https://globalwomensinstitute.gwu.edu/sites/g/files/zaxdzs1356/f/downloads/No%20Safe%20Place_Summary_Report.pdf.

Ellsberg, M., M. Murphy, A. Blackwell, M. Macrae, D. Reddy, C. Hollowell, T. Hess, and M. Contreras-Urbina. 2021. "'If You Are Born a Girl in This Crisis, You Are Born a Problem': Patterns and Drivers of Violence against Women and Girls in Conflict-Affected South Sudan." *Violence against Women* 27 (15–16): 3030–55. https://www.ncbi.nlm.nih.gov/pmc/articles/PMC8521375/.

Ellsberg, M., J. Ovince, M. Murphy, A. Blackwell, D. Reddy, J. Stennes, T. Hess, and M. Contreras. 2020. "No Safe Place: Prevalence and Correlates of Violence against Women and Girls in Conflict-Affected South Sudan." *PLoS ONE* 15 (10). https://www.ncbi.nlm.nih.gov/pmc /articles/PMC7549805/.

El Zain, M. 2006. "Ruling Elite, Frontier-Caste Ideology and Resource Conflicts in the Sudan." *Journal of Peacebuilding and Development* 3 (1): 36–47.

English, J. 2017. "Keeping Women Safe in South Sudan's Displacement Camps." *ReliefWeb Blog*, May 6, 2017.

Errecaborde, K. M., W. Stauffer, and M. Cetron. 2015. "Neglected Tropical Disease Control and Elimination: Is Human Displacement an Achilles Heel?" *PLoS Neglected Tropical Diseases* 9 (3): e0003535.

Esrey, S. A., J. B. Potash, L. Roberts, and C. Shiff. 1991. "Effects of Improved Water Supply and Sanitation on Ascariasis, Diarrhoea, Dracunculiasis, Hookworm Infection, Schistosomiasis, and Trachoma." *Bulletin of the World Health Organization* 69 (5): 609–21.

FMNR (Farmer Manager Natural Regeneration). n.d. Humbo Forestry Project. https://fmnrhub .com.au/projects/humbo/#.Yn4Mk-hBxEb.

Flachberg, F. 2014. "Hygiene Promotion in Emergencies: A Fortuitous Comparison—The Case of Bentiu IDP Camps, Unity State, South Sudan." In *Sustainable Water and Sanitation Services for All in a Fast Changing World: Proceedings of the 37th WEDC International Conference, Hanoi, Vietnam*, 15–19.

George Washington University, CARE International, and International Rescue Committee. 2017. "No Safe Place: A Lifetime of Violence for Conflict-Affected Women and Girls in South Sudan." What Works, UKAid.

Giovetti, O. 2022. "Gender Equality in South Sudan: What We Know in 2022." Concern Worldwide. https://www.concern.net/story/gender-equality-in-south-sudan.

GIWPS (Georgetown Institute for Women, Peace and Security). 2021. "The Women Peace and Security Index: A New Lens on Forced Displacement." GIWPS, Washington, DC.

Global Nutrition Report. 2021. "2021 Global Nutrition Report: The State of Global Nutrition." Development Initiatives, Bristol, UK.

Government of South Sudan and United Nations Development Programme. 2021. *Revised National Development Strategy 2021–2024: Consolidate Peace and Stabilize the Economy*. Juba: Government of South Sudan and United Nations Development Programme.

Grimes, J. E., D. Croll, W. E. Harrison, J. Utzinger, M. C. Freeman, and M. R. Templeton. 2014. "The Relationship between Water, Sanitation and Schistosomiasis: A Systematic Review and Meta-Analysis." *PLoS Neglected Tropical Diseases* 8 (12): e3296.

Harari, M., and E. L. Ferrara. 2018. "Conflict, Climate, and Cells: A Disaggregated Analysis." *Review of Economics and Statistics* 100 (4): 594–608.

Huser, C. 2018. "Conflict and Gender Study—South Sudan. Addressing Root Causes Programme." ACORD International. https://www.acordinternational.org/silo/files/conflict-and-gender -study--south-sudan.pdf.

IDMC (Internal Displacement Monitoring Centre). 2017. "South Sudan Mid-Year Update 2017 (January–June)." Internal Displacement Monitoring Centre, Geneva.

IHME (Institute for Health Metrics and Evaluation). 2018. *Findings from the Global Burden of Disease Study 2017*. Seattle, WA: IHME.

IHME (Institute for Health Metrics and Evaluation). 2021. "South Sudan." IHME. http://www .healthdata.org/south-sudan.

Independent Evaluation Office. 2020. "Lessons from Evaluations: UNDP Environment and Natural Resource Management Support to Countries in Crisis." UNDP, Geneva. http:// fgvclear.org/site/wp-content/uploads/environment-sector.pdf.

Inter-Agency Standing Committee. 2010. "IASC Framework on Durable Solutions for Internally Displaced Persons." Inter-Agency Standing Committee, April 5, 2010. https://interagencystandingcommittee.org/other/iasc-framework-durable-solutions -internally-displaced-persons.

IOM (International Organization for Migration). 2020a. "Closing the Gender Gap in the Humanitarian Water, Sanitation and Hygiene Sector in South Sudan." IOM, Juba.

IOM (International Organization for Migration). 2020b. "South Sudan—Protection Summary: Site and Village/Neighborhood Assessment—Mobility Tracking R8 (February–March 2020)." IOM Displacement Tracking Matrix. https://migration.iom.int/reports/south -sudan-%E2%80%94-protection-summary-site-and-villageneighborhood-assessment -%E2%80%94-mobility-tracking.

IOM (International Organization for Migration). 2021a. "Construction of Dike Brings Hope to Flood-Affected Communities in Bor." IOM, May 28, 2021.

IOM (International Organization for Migration). 2021b. "Deforestation in South Sudan." IOM South Sudan, Juba. https://environmentalmigration.iom.int/sites/g/files/tmzbdl1411/files /documents/deforestation-report-in-s.-sudan-2021.pdf.

IPU Parline. 2021. "South Sudan. Data on Women." IPU Parline. https://data.ipu.org/node/160 /data-on-women?chamber_id=13580.

IRENA (International Renewable Energy Agency). 2019. *Renewable Energy: A Gender Perspective*. Abu Dhabi: IRENA. https://www.irena.org/publications/2019/Jan/Renewable -Energy-A-Gender-Perspective.

IUCN (International Union for Conservation of Nature). 2019. "Gender and Natural Resource Governance: Addressing Inequalities and Empowering Women for Sustainable Ecosystem Management." IUCN, Gland, Switzerland. https://portals.iucn.org/union/sites/union/files /doc/iucn-srjs-briefs-gender-nrg-en_0.pdf.

IUCN (International Union for Conservation of Nature). 2020. "Strategies for Integrating Gender in Sustainable Ecosystem Management." *IUCN Blog*, March 8, 2020. https://www.iucn.org /news/gender/202003/strategies-integrating-gender-sustainable-ecosystem-management.

JICA (Japan International Cooperation Agency). 2017. "Country Gender Profile: Republic of South Sudan." JICA, Tokyo. https://land.igad.int/index.php/documents-1/countries/south -sudan/gender-5/981-country-gender-profile-republic-of-south-sudan-2017/file.

Joint Regional Initiative for Women's Inclusion in REDD+. 2013. "Scoping Study of Good Practices for Strengthening Women's Inclusion in Forest and Other Natural Resource Management Sectors." UN-REDD Programme, Geneva. https://www.uncclearn.org/wp -content/uploads/library/scoping_study_gender_redd_wocan-unredd-leaf_dec_2013-v2.pdf.

Jones, F. K., J. F. Wamala, J. Rumunu, P. N. Mawien, M. T. Kol, S. Wohl, L. Deng, et al. 2020. "Successive Epidemic Waves of Cholera in South Sudan between 2014 and 2017: A Descriptive Epidemiological Study." *The Lancet Planetary Health* 4 (12): e577–e587.

Keene, S. 2019. "Strengthening Indigenous and Rural Women's Rights to Govern Community Lands: Ten Factors Contributing to Successful Initiatives." Rights and Resources Initiative, Washington, DC. https://rightsandresources.org/wp-content/uploads/2019/05 /Governance-Brief_RRI_Apr-2019.pdf.

Khan, A. M., and A.-S. Rodella. 2021. "A Hard Rain's a-Gonna Fall? New Insights on Water Security and Fragility in the Sahel." Policy Research Working Paper 9805, World Bank, Washington, DC.

Krystalli, R., E. Stites, A. Humphrey, and V. Krishnan. 2019. "The Currency of Connections: The Impact of Weddings and Rituals on Social Connections in Bentiu, South Sudan." Feinstein International Center, Tufts University, Boston.

Lasagna, M., S. M. R. Bonetto, L. Debernardi, D. A. De Luca, C. Semita, and C. Caselle. 2020. "Groundwater Resources Assessment for Sustainable Development in South Sudan." *Sustainability* 12 (14): 1–21.

Lee, E. 1966. "A Theory of Migration." *Demography* 3 (1): 47–57.

Leonardi, C. 2015. "Points of Order? Local Government Meetings as Negotiation Tables in South Sudanese History." *Journal of Eastern African Studies* 9/4 (2015): 650–68.

Mach, K. J., C. M. Kraan, W. N. Adger, H. Buhaug, M. Burke, J. D. Fearon, C. B. Field, et al. 2019. "Climate as a Risk Factor for Armed Conflict." *Nature* 571 (7764): 193–97.

Magot, D. 2021. "The Drinking Trucks: In a City That Borders River Nile, Covid-19 Curbs Access to Clean Water for South Sudanese." InfoNile, December 1, 2021. https://infonile .org/en/2021/12/the-drinking-trucks-in-a-city-that-borders-river-nile-covid-19-curbs -access-to-clean-water-for-south-sudanese-photo-story/.

Mai, N. J. H. 2015. "Role of Women in Peace-Building in South Sudan." Policy Brief, Sudd Institute, Juba.

Maystadt, J. F., M. Calderone, and L. You. 2014. "Local Warming and Violent Conflict in North and South Sudan." *Journal of Economic Geography* 15 (3): 649–71.

Maystadt, J. F., and O. Ecker. 2014. "Extreme Weather and Civil War: Does Drought Fuel Conflict in Somalia through Livestock Price Shocks?" *American Journal of Agricultural Economics* 96 (4): 1157–82.

Mazurana, D., A. Marshak, and K. Spears. 2019. "Child Marriage in Armed Conflict." *International Review of the Red Cross* 101 (911): 575–601.

Mold, F. 2020. "UN Protection of Civilians Sites Begin Transitioning to Conventional Displacement Camps." United Nations Mission in South Sudan, September 4, 2020.

Nagabhatla, N., P. Pouramin, R. Brahmbhatt, C. Fioret, T. Glickman, K. B. Newbold, and V. Smakhtin. 2020. "Water and Migration: A Global Overview." UNU-INWEH Report Series 10, United Nations University Institute for Water, Environment and Health, Hamilton, Canada.

The New Humanitarian. 2018. "Water, Water Everywhere—But It's Not Fit to Drink." The New Humanitarian, November 3, 2015. https://www.thenewhumanitarian.

NUPI and SIPRI (Norwegian Institute of International Affairs and Stockholm International Peace Research Institute). 2021. "Climate, Peace and Security Fact Sheet: South Sudan." NUPI and SIPRI. https://sipri.org/sites/default/files/Fact%20Sheet%20South%20 Sudan_HR.pdf.

OCHA (United Nations Office for the Coordination of Humanitarian Affairs). 2020. "South Sudan Flooding Snapshot October 2020." OCHA. https://www.humanitarianresponse.info/sites /www.humanitarianresponse.info/files/documents/files/south_sudan_flooding_snapshot_4 .pdf?_gl=1*rt280e*_ga*MTc1OTI1MTM5MC4xNjcwNjEyMDIy*_ga _E60ZNX2F68*MTY3MDk1NDExMC40LjEuMTY3MDk1NDcwMi42MC4wLjA.

OCHA (United Nations Office for the Coordination of Humanitarian Affairs). 2021a. *Humanitarian Needs Overview: South Sudan.* New York: OCHA.

OCHA (United Nations Office for the Coordination of Humanitarian Affairs). 2021b. "South Sudan: Flooding Snapshot (as of 30 September 2021)." OCHA, New York.

OCHA (United Nations Office for the Coordination of Humanitarian Affairs). 2022a. "March 2022 Humanitarian Snapshot." OCHA, New York.

OCHA (United Nations Office for the Coordination of Humanitarian Affairs). 2022b. *South Sudan: Humanitarian Needs Overview 2022.* New York: OCHA.

Oluwasanya, G., P. Duminda, M. Qadir, and V. Smakhtin. 2022. "Water Security in Africa: A Preliminary Assessment." UNU-INWEH Report Series 13, United Nations University Institute for Water, Environment and Health, Hamilton, Canada. https://inweh.unu.edu /wp-content/uploads/2022/03/State-of-Water-Security-in-Africa-A-Preliminary -Assessment-v5-revised.pdf.

Oxfam. 2017. "South Sudan Gender Analysis: A Snapshot Situation Analysis of the Differential Impact of the Humanitarian Crisis on Women, Girls, Men and Boys in South Sudan." Oxfam House, Oxford, UK. https://reliefweb.int/sites/reliefweb.int/files/resources/rr-south -sudan-gender-analysis-060317-en.pdf.

Oxfam. 2019a. "Born to Be Married: Addressing Early and Forced Marriage in Nyal, South Sudan." Oxfam House, Juba. https://oxfamilibrary.openrepository.com/bitstream /handle/10546/620620/rr-born-to-be-married-efm-south-sudan-180219-en.pdf.

Oxfam. 2019b. "No Simple Solutions: Women, Displacement and Durable Solutions in South Sudan." Oxfam International, Oxford, UK.

Plan International. 2022. "Girls at Risk in Horn of Africa as Drought Crisis Continues." February 16, 2022, Plan International. https://plan-international.org/news/2022/02/16/girls-at -risk-in-horn-of-africa-as-drought-crisis-continues/.

Research and Evidence Facility. 2019. "Comprehensive Refugee Responses in the Horn of Africa: Regional Leadership on Education, Livelihoods and Durable Solutions: Summary of Findings." EU Trust Fund for Africa Research and Evidence Facility, London and Nairobi.

Rieckmann, A., C. C. Tamason, E. S. Gurley, N. H. Rod, and P. Jensen. 2018. "Exploring Droughts and Floods and Their Association with Cholera Outbreaks in Sub-Saharan Africa: A Register-Based Ecological Study from 1990 to 2010." *American Journal of Tropical Medicine and Hygiene* 98 (5): 1269–74. https://doi.org/10.4269/ajtmh.17-0778.

RVI (Rift Valley Institute). 2022. "Fragility and Water Security in South Sudan." Study conducted for the World Bank by the Rift Valley Institute in collaboration with the Centre for Humanitarian Change. Background paper prepared for this report. Rift Valley Institute, Juba.

Ryle, J., and M. Amoum. 2018. *Peace Is the Name of Our Cattle Camp—Local Responses to Conflict in Eastern Lakes State, South Sudan*. Juba: Rift Valley Institute.

Sadoff, C. W., E. Borgomeo, and D. De Waal. 2017. *Turbulent Waters: Pursuing Water Security in Fragile Contexts*. Washington, DC: World Bank.

Scherrer, C., R. Schweitzer, and M. A. Bünzli. 2021. "Rapid Groundwater Potential Mapping in Humanitarian Contexts: Improving Borehole Implementation in Basement Environments." *Hydrogeology Journal* 29: 2033–51.

Schots, B., and G. Smith. 2019. "Returns in Complex Environments: The Case of South Sudan." *Forced Migration Review* 62: 60–63.

Seequent. 2022. "Water to Drink: Uncovering Hidden Water for Vulnerable Communities." March 22, 2022, Seequent.

Selby, J., and C. Hoffmann. 2014. "Beyond Scarcity: Rethinking Water, Climate Change and Conflict in the Sudans." *Global Environmental Change* 29: 360–70.

Smith, J. M., L. Olosky, and J. G. Fernández. 2021. "The Climate-Gender-Conflict Nexus." Georgetown Institute for Women, Peace and Security, Washington, DC.

Sosnowski, A., E. Ghoneim, J. J. Burke, E. Hines, and J. Halls. 2016. "Remote Regions, Remote Data: A Spatial Investigation of Precipitation, Dynamic Land Covers, and Conflict in the Sudd Wetland of South Sudan." *Applied Geography* 69: 51–64.

South Sudan Ministry of Health. 2016. "South Sudan National Master Plan for Neglected Tropical Diseases 2016–2020." Ministry of Health, Juba.

SSBCSSAC and UNDP (South Sudan Bureau for Community Security and Small Arms Control and United Nations Development Programme). 2017. "National Small Arms Assessment in South Sudan." Baseline study conducted by Small Arms Survey.

Stocks, M. E., S. Ogden, D. Haddad, D. G. Addiss, C. McGuire, and M. C. Freeman. 2014. "Effect of Water, Sanitation, and Hygiene on the Prevention of Trachoma: A Systematic Review and Meta-Analysis." *PLoS Medicine* 11 (2): e1001605.

Strunz, E. C., D. G. Addiss, M. E. Stocks, S. Ogden, J. Utzinger, and M. C. Freeman. 2014. "Water, Sanitation, Hygiene, and Soil-Transmitted Helminth Infection: A Systematic Review and Meta-Analysis." *PLoS Medicine* 11 (3): e1001620.

Sullivan, D. 2018. *Displaced Nation: The Dangerous Implications of Rushed Returns in South Sudan*. Washington, DC: Refugees International.

Tantoh, H. B., T. McKay, F. Donkor, and M. Simatele. 2021. "Gender Roles, Implications for Water, Land, and Food Security in a Changing Climate: Systematic Review." *Frontiers in Sustainable Food Systems* 5: 707835. doi:10.3389/fsufs.2021.707835.

Tidman, R., B. Abela-Ridder, and R. R. de Castañeda. 2021. "The Impact of Climate Change on Neglected Tropical Diseases: A Systematic Review." *Transactions of the Royal Society of Tropical Medicine and Hygiene* 115 (2): 147–68. https://doi.org/10.1093/trstmh/traa192.

UNHCR (United Nations High Commissioner for Refugees). 2016. "The Geophysical Exploration of Groundwater for Refugees at the Kakuma Refugee Camp and the Proposed Kalobeyei Refugee Camp in Turkana County, Kenya." UNHCR, Geneva.

UNHCR (United Nations High Commissioner for Refugees). 2019. "Regional Intention Survey of South Sudanese Refugees in Central African Republic, Democratic Republic of the Congo, Ethiopia, Kenya, Sudan and Uganda." UNHCR, Geneva.

UNHCR (United Nations High Commissioner for Refugees). 2020. "Regional Refugee Response Strategy January 2020–December 2021." UNHCR Regional Bureau for East and Horn of Africa, and the Great Lakes, Nairobi.

UNHCR (United Nations High Commissioner for Refugees). 2021a. "The IDP Initiative. Quarterly Update 2021." UNHCR, Geneva.

UNHCR (United Nations High Commissioner for Refugees). 2021b. "Mid-Year Trends." UNHCR, Geneva.

UNHCR (United Nations High Commissioner for Refugees). 2022a. Overview of South Sudan Operation. Juba: UNHCR. https://data.unhcr.org/en/situations/southsudan.

UNHCR (United Nations High Commissioner for Refugees). 2022b. "South Sudan Monthly Population Statistics." February 2022. UNHCR, Juba.

UNHCR (United Nations High Commissioner for Refugees). 2022c. "UNHCR Concerned at Climate Change Impacts in South Sudan." March 15, 2022. UNHCR.

UN Human Rights Council. 2020a. "Report of the Commission on Human Rights in South Sudan." General Assembly. A/HRC/43/56. United Nations, New York.

UN Human Rights Council. 2020b. "There Is Nothing Left for Us: Starvation as a Method of Warfare in South Sudan." General Assembly. A_HRC_45_CRP.3. United Nations, New York. https://www.ohchr.org/EN/HRBodies/HRC/RegularSessions/Session45/Documents /A_HRC_45_CRP.3.docx.

UNICEF (United Nations Children's Fund). 2019. "Gender-Based Violence, December 2019." UNICEF South Sudan. https://www.unicef.org/southsudan/media/2071/file/UNICEF -South-Sudan-GBV-Briefing-Note-Aug-2019.pdf.

UNICEF (United Nations Children's Fund). 2020. *The Situation of Children and Women in South Sudan: 2018–2020*. Juba: UNICEF South Sudan. https://reliefweb.int/sites/reliefweb.int /files/resources/The%20situation%20of%20children%20and%20women%20in%20 South%20Sudan%20%282018%E2%80%932020%29.pdf.

United Nations. 2017. *How South Sudan's "Lost Boy" Brought Water to His Village*. New York: United Nations.

United Nations Secretary-General High Level Panel on Internal Displacement. 2020. "Consultations with IDPs and Host Community—South Sudan (September 2020)." United Nations Secretary-General High Level Panel on Internal Displacement. https://bit .ly/2Lvjf6p.

UN WOMEN. 2018. *Turning Promises into Action: Gender Equality in the 2030 Agenda for Sustainable Development*. New York: UN WOMEN. https://www.unwomen.org/en/digital -library/publications/2018/2/gender-equality-in-the-2030-agenda-for-sustainable -development-2018.

UN WOMEN. 2020. "A Rapid Gender Analysis on COVID-19." UN WOMEN, Juba. https:// www.humanitarianresponse.info/sites/www.humanitarianresponse.info/files /documents/files/rapid_gender_analysis_on_covid-19-south_sudan.pdf.

USAID (United States Agency for International Development). 2017. "South Sudan: Water for the World Country Plan." USAID, Washington, DC. https://www.globalwaters.org/sites /default/files/wfw_south_sudan_country_plan.pdf.

USAID (United States Agency for International Development). 2020. "Gender Equality and Female Empowerment in WASH." USAID Water and Development Technical Brief (Issue 4). USAID, Washington, DC. https://www.globalwaters.org/sites/default/files/usaid_water _gender_tech_brief_5_508_2.pdf.

USAID (United States Agency for International Development). n.d. "South Sudan Water and Development Country Plan." USAID, Washington, DC. https://pdf.usaid.gov/pdf_docs /PBAAH791.pdf.

Van Baalen, S., and M. Mobjörk. 2018. "Climate Change and Violent Conflict in East Africa: Integrating Qualitative and Quantitative Research to Probe the Mechanisms." *International Studies Review* 20 (4): 547–75.

Verhoeven, H. 2011. "Climate Change, Conflict and Development in Sudan: Global Neo-Malthusian Narratives and Local Power Struggles." *Development and Change* 42 (3): 679–707.

WASH Cluster South Sudan. 2021. "WASH Transition Strategy for Former POC/IDP Sites in South Sudan." WASH Cluster South Sudan, Juba.

WASH Cluster South Sudan. 2022. "South Sudan WASH Cluster Strategy 2022–2023." WASH Cluster South Sudan, Juba.

Water Is Basic. 2020. "Women's Well Repair Initiative." Water Is Basic.org. https://www .waterisbasic.org/womens-repair.

Wathorne, A. 2015. "Gender Mainstreaming in Water Harvesting in South Sudan." Food and Agriculture Organization, South Sudan. https://www.unep.org/resources/report /gender-mainstreaming-water-harvesting-south-sudan-technical-guidelines.

WHO (World Health Organization). 2018. "Global Health Estimates 2016: Deaths by Cause, Age, Sex, by Country, and by Region, 2000–16." WHO, Geneva.

WHO/UNICEF (World Health Organization/United Nations Children's Fund). 2021. "Joint Monitoring Programme for Water Supply, Sanitation and Hygiene (JMP) in Schools." WHO and UNICEF, Geneva. https://washdata.org/data/school#!/ssd.

Wild, H., J. M. Jok, and R. Patel. 2018. "The Militarization of Cattle Raiding in South Sudan: How a Traditional Practice Became a Tool for Political Violence." *Journal of International Humanitarian Action* 3 (1): 1–11.

World Bank. 2017. *Forcibly Displaced: Toward a Development Approach Supporting Refugees, the Internally Displaced, and Their Hosts.* Washington, DC: World Bank.

World Bank. 2021. *A Development Approach to Conflict-Induced Internal Displacement.* Washington, DC: World Bank.

World Bank. 2022. "South Sudan Qualifies for Special Funds as It Plays Exemplary Host to Refugees." World Bank, Feature Story, April 7, 2022.

World Bank Group. 2019. "Informing Durable Solutions for Internal Displacement in Nigeria, Somalia, South Sudan, and Sudan: Volume A–Overview." World Bank, Washington, DC.

World Vision. 2021a. "Child Marriage and Hunger Crisis. Case Study." World Vision, Juba https://reliefweb.int/sites/reliefweb.int/files/resources/Project%20Overview%20-%20 South%20Sudan%20case%20study%20Final%20%281%29.pdf.

World Vision. 2021b. "How Children in South Sudan's Displaced Camps Face the COVID-19 Challenge." World Vision, July 14, 2020.

World Vision. 2022. "Despite Improved Access, Millions of Women in South Sudan Still Walk for Miles to Get Clean Water." World Vision, March 21, 2022.

WWAP (UNESCO World Water Assessment Programme). 2019. *The United Nations World Water Development Report 2019: Leaving No One Behind.* Paris: UNESCO. https://en.unesco .org/themes/water-security/wwap/wwdr/2019.

4 Improving Governance: Policy, Institutions, Regulations, and Financing

GOVERNANCE AND INSTITUTIONAL STRUCTURES

Key points

- Protracted armed conflict in South Sudan stalled policy implementation and ushered in funding modalities focused on immediate humanitarian relief, hindering the development of holistic interventions and long-term, government-led planning.
- A Water Bill first drafted in 2013 continues to undergo changes and has not been ratified. Many of the proposed governance structures and regulatory bodies have yet to be established and become operational.
- Budget allocation to support recurrent and development expenditure to execute plans and policies has been scarce, especially since the conflict period.
- Sector financing is heavily dependent on donor funds and characterized by limited transparency, with an estimated 85 percent of the water sector's services provided by international nongovernmental organizations. Financial statements are not available for public utilities, nor for private or community water service providers.

Overview

Addressing water insecurity in South Sudan requires an understanding of the governance and institutional structures that can effectively spearhead policy and interventions for the sector. However, the recurrence of armed conflict has largely stalled institutional development. Amid severe capacity constraints, inefficiencies are exacerbated by overlapping institutional responsibilities between ministries, across governance levels, and among stakeholders. Compounded by human and financial resource constraints, planning, monitoring, and information management systems are significantly challenged. Furthermore, the dominance of humanitarian actors involved in the sector has effectively sidelined the government and slowed national institutional development since the outbreak of conflict (Mosello, Mason, and Aludra 2016). These governance challenges, paired with widespread poverty and inadequate infrastructure investments, play a key role in water insecurity and related negative outcomes (USAID 2021).

This chapter provides an assessment of water governance in South Sudan since its independence in 2011. The assessment outlines four major aspects of water sector governance in the country: (a) policies, (b) institutional arrangements and responsibilities, (c) legal and regulatory frameworks, and (d) the humanitarian landscape and water sector financing across water, sanitation, and hygiene (WASH), water resources management (WRM), and irrigation subsectors. The chapter unpacks the governance constraints to sector reform and service delivery and offers recommendations for taking these into consideration in the design of future sector interventions. The assessment uses secondary data, key informant discussions, and a structured questionnaire administered to the Ministry of Water Resources and Irrigation's (MWRI's) directors general in the water subsectors.

This chapter also summarizes findings from a qualitative study on informal and customary institutions for water management in South Sudan. Traditional and customary institutions play an important role in local water governance, often alongside formal state structures and informal private sector actors, but knowledge of the role of these institutions in water management, and their interaction with formal water management institutions, is limited to date. The findings are based on evidence review, expert interviews, and focus group discussions conducted in Juba county (Central Equatoria), Kapoeta county (Eastern Equatoria), and Rumbek county (Lakes).

A FLURRY OF POLICY DEVELOPMENT FOLLOWING INDEPENDENCE HAS LARGELY STALLED SINCE THE CONFLICT PERIOD

The development of water sector policy in South Sudan can be traced to the pre-independence Water Policy of 2007. Following the Comprehensive Peace Agreement (CPA) of 2005, the MWRI published the first South Sudan water policy in November 2007. The policy outlined the country's vision and established basic principles, objectives, and priorities for the water sector across WRM, rural water supply and sanitation, and urban water supply and sanitation. The role of water as a natural resource and economic and social good linked to the thriving of other sectors is key among the principles identified in the policy. Thus, access to water was considered a human right to be prioritized for effective development, management, and use. The 2007 Water Policy provided the foundation for more detailed strategies and set out the institutional, administrative, technical, and financial arrangements for implementing the policy (Government of South Sudan 2007)

After independence, the vision for development of the water sector was reiterated in the South Sudan Development Plan 2011–2013 and the 2011 Transitional Constitution, which emphasized the key role of water in the country's development. Water resources management, development, and utilization and provision of sanitation services (to improve access to safe water and improved sanitation) were high on the agenda (Government of South Sudan 2011). Also, in 2011, the Water, Sanitation and Hygiene (WASH) Sector Strategic Framework was formulated to operationalize the Water Policy of 2007; attract investment; move from ad hoc emergency relief interventions to holistic, government-led planning and implementation of well-targeted development programs; and initiate inclusive sectorwide governance and development.

The WASH Strategic Framework encompassed the full scope of the 2007 Water Policy, including WRM, urban WASH, and rural WASH, with a timeframe up to 2015 (JICA 2015). It further recommended the establishment of a Water Council as a multisectoral advisory board at the national level, along with regulatory institutions such as the Safe Water Supply and Sanitation Services Regulator for WASH and Water Resources Management Authority for WRM. The establishment of Basin Water Boards in each basin, with catchment and subcatchment committees responsible for planning and resolving conflicts, was also proposed in the framework (USAID 2021).

Another major policy instrument was a Water Bill first drafted in 2013, which sought to provide the legislative framework for the proposals in the preceding water policies. The bill continues to undergo changes and has yet to be passed by Parliament. The bill developed procedures to manage water allocation for different uses, conservation, water quality, water-related disasters, and intersectoral coordination (USAID 2021).

In 2012, the Rural Water and Sanitation Service Delivery Framework (Government of South Sudan 2012) was drafted to improve the financing and delivery of rural water and sanitation in South Sudan and outlined the institutional and financial arrangements for water and sanitation infrastructure development and service provision. Also in 2012, a National Rural Water, Sanitation, and Hygiene Sub-sector Action and Investment Plan (2012–2015) was developed to shore up rural water sector financing gaps (USAID 2013). The investment plan highlighted the need for stakeholder collaboration and participatory community-based processes; development of effective local management structures to increase community ownership, development, and involvement of the private sector; and improvement of local governance and the inclusion of women, children, and vulnerable groups in the planning and development of WASH activities in rural areas.

An Irrigation Development Master Plan was developed in 2015 with support from the Japan International Cooperation Agency. The master plan prioritized three geographic areas, Wau, Jebel Lado, and Rejaf East, based on security, accessibility, and irrigation potential (JICA 2015). In 2020, an Irrigation Policy (2020–2025) was drafted, which aims to effectively utilize the country's water resources by developing irrigation facilities, improving institutional arrangements for irrigation management, and enhancing technical human resources' knowledge, skill, and institutional working capability in the irrigation subsector.

Other relevant policy references can be drawn from the agriculture sector, environmental policies, decentralization policies, and broader development plans for South Sudan. For instance, the Local Government Act, 2009, refers to the delivery of rural water and sanitation and urban sanitation as the mandate of local government. The agriculture sector put forward the Agricultural Sector Policy Framework (2012–2017) with its vision of "food security for all." It promotes sustainable irrigation infrastructure and flood management systems to improve agricultural productivity and enhance food security. After witnessing the extent of flooding in 2020, Sudan and South Sudan signed a memorandum of understanding on water management and flood prevention (Radio Dabanga 2021) to foster cooperation between the two countries for information sharing, capacity-building, flood monitoring, and the rehabilitation of irrigation projects in the Upper Nile region. Table 4.1 provides an overview of the development of water sector policy in South Sudan.

TABLE 4.1 Timeline of water sector policy in South Sudan

YEAR	SOURCE	POLICY	FOCUS WASH	WRM	IR
2007	MWRI	**The Water Policy of 2007** addressed three main water subsector–specific issues related to water resources management, rural water supply and sanitation, and urban water supply and sanitation and outlined the vision of the country to establish basic principles, objectives, and priorities for the water sector. Irrigation was addressed in the context of WRM.	☑	☑	☑
2011	MoFP	**South Sudan Development Plan of 2011** prioritized the provision of basic services, including health, education, and water and sanitation, to the people through the expansion and improvement of infrastructure (Government of South Sudan 2011). Water resources management, development, and utilization and provision of sanitation services were high on the agenda.	☑	☑	☑
2011	MWRI	**The Water, Sanitation and Hygiene (WASH) Sector Strategic Framework** was formulated to operationalize the Water Policy of 2007. The scope of the WASH framework covered • Water resources management, • Urban water supply and sanitation (and hygiene), and • Rural water supply and sanitation (and hygiene). The framework proposed regulatory institutions under a Water Council to oversee policy enforcement and management in the water sector.	☑	☑	
2011	AfDB	**The National Infrastructure Action Plan for 2011–2013** sought to address five key water sector–related components: (a) improving basic information about water resources, (b) building sector institutions, (c) strengthening transboundary management and capacity, (d) investing in facilities for surface storage and transport of water, and (e) measures to ensure full cost recovery of water uses.	☑	☑	☑
2012	MWRI	**The Rural Water and Sanitation Service Delivery Framework, 2012,** aimed to improve the financing and delivery of rural water and sanitation by setting out appropriate institutional and financial arrangements for the provision of services in rural areas.	☑		
2012	MWRI	**The National Rural Water, Sanitation, and Hygiene Sub-sector Action and Investment Plan (2012–2015)** highlights increasing community ownership, development, and involvement of the private sector; improving local governance; and including women, children, and vulnerable groups in the planning and development of rural WASH activities.	☑		
2013	MoFP	**Draft South Sudan Development Initiative, 2013–2020.** The development initiative for the water sector captured 28 priority programs, including water resources development and management master plans and interventions and urban water supply and sanitation in the major cities as well as rural areas.	☑	☑	☑
2015	MEDIWR JICA	**Irrigation Development Master Plan 2015** details the policy and institutional framework concerning the water sector and irrigation subsector.			☑
2018	MoFP	**The National Development Strategy (2018–2021)** prioritizes the development of water sector infrastructure, focusing on developing and rehabilitating irrigation schemes and the construction and rehabilitation of urban WASH facilities (Government of South Sudan 2018).	☑		☑
Other related policies					
2009	MLG	**The Local Government Act, 2009,** mandates local governments to provide basic services, including rural water and sanitation and urban sanitation.	☑		
2012	MAFC & RD	**The Agriculture Sector Policy Framework (2012–2017),** with its vision of "food security for all," promotes sustainable irrigation infrastructure and flood management systems to contribute to improved agricultural productivity and food security enhancement.			☑
2012	MoEF	**The South Sudan National Environmental Policy** was established in 2012. The key guidance related to the water sector pertains to promoting access to quality water, protecting water resources, and ensuring the sustainable use of water.		☑	☑

continued

TABLE 4.1, *continued*

YEAR	SOURCE	POLICY	FOCUS WASH	FOCUS WRM	FOCUS IR
2020	MWRI	**The draft irrigation policy (2020–2025)** aims to effectively utilize the country's water resources by developing irrigation facilities, improving institutional arrangements for irrigation management, and enhancing technical human resources' knowledge, skill, and institutional working capability.			☑
2021	MoFP	**The Revised National Development Strategy (2021–2024),** similar to the National Development Strategy 2018–2021, prioritizes the development of water sector infrastructure, focusing on developing and rehabilitating irrigation schemes and the construction and rehabilitation of urban water and sanitation facilities.	☑		☑
2021	MWRI	**Memorandum of Understanding on water management and flood prevention.** The objective of the memorandum is to foster cooperation with regard to information sharing, capacity-building, monitoring of floods, and rehabilitation of irrigation projects in the Upper Nile region.		☑	

Source: World Bank.

Note: AfDB = African Development Bank; IR = Irrigation; JICA = Japan Intenational Cooperation Agency; MAFC & RD = Ministry of Agriculture, Forestry, Cooperatives and Rural Development; MEDIWR = Ministry of Electricity, Dams, Irrigation and Water Resources; MLG = Ministry of Local Government; MoEF = Ministry of Environment and Forestry; MoFP = Ministry of Finance and Planning; MWRI = Ministry of Water Resources and Irrigation; WASH = water, sanitation, and hygiene; WRM = water resources management.

INSTITUTIONAL ARRANGEMENTS ARE WELL DEFINED, BUT IMPLEMENTATION IS LACKING

MWRI is the umbrella ministry for the water sector; however, broader institutional development in the sector is nascent and continues to change. MWRI was established in 2006 following the CPA signed in 2005. MWRI underwent a short-lived merger with the Ministry of Dams and Electricity, but is presently the national ministry with overall leadership in the water sector and covers key water-related functions of drinking water supply, WRM, and irrigation, although irrigation development and operation of irrigation schemes also fall under the Ministry of Agriculture, Forestry, Cooperatives and Rural Development and the Ministry of Livestock and Fisheries Industry. The South Sudan Urban Water Corporation was also established by decree in 2007 to supply drinking water to urban areas. Urban sanitation falls under the mandate of the Ministry of Housing, Lands and Public Utilities.

Institutional arrangements for the water sector were outlined after South Sudan gained independence from Sudan in 2011. These arrangements are detailed in the 2011 WASH Framework, the 2012 Rural Water and Sanitation Service Delivery Framework, and a presidential order of 2011 that mandated South Sudan Urban Water Corporation as the official urban waterworks of South Sudan. The 2012 framework described the institutional structure of MWRI (see figure 4.1) and identified distinct roles and responsibilities for the five administrative levels of government.

The strategic objectives of the six line directorates of MWRI are shown in table 4.2.

The 2012 Rural Water and Sanitation Service Delivery Framework outlines the institutional and financial arrangements for water and sanitation infrastructure development and service provision across governance levels,

FIGURE 4.1

Institutional structure of South Sudan MWRI

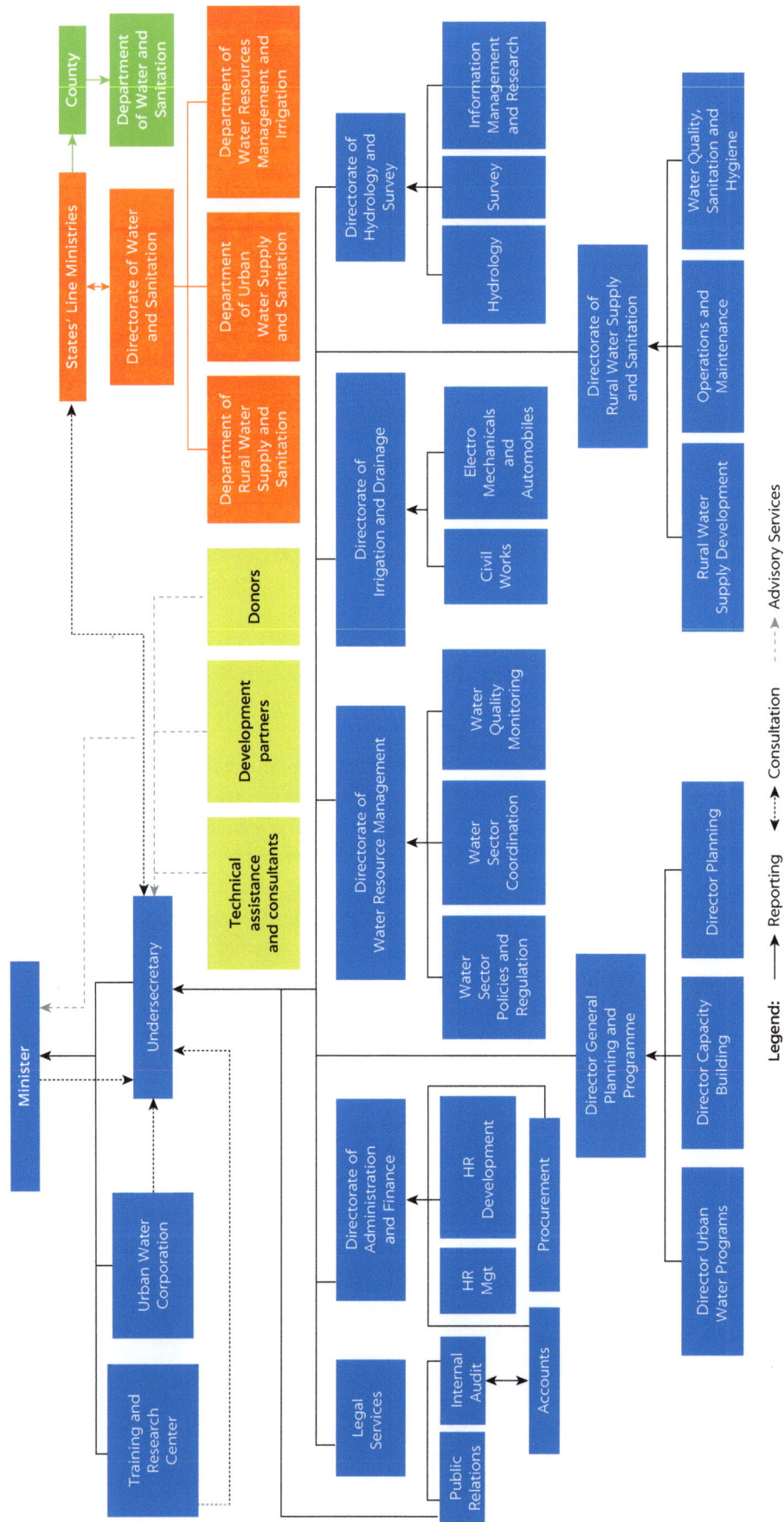

Source: Ministry of Water Resources and Irrigation (MWRI) Organogram 2012.
Note: HR = human resources; mgt = management.

TABLE 4.2 **The directorates of MWRI**

DIRECTORATE	STRATEGIC OBJECTIVE
Water Resources Management	To promote sustainable development and management of the quantity, quality, and reliability of available water resources to maximize social and economic benefits while ensuring long-term environmental sustainability
Rural Water Supply and Sanitation	To ensure availability and sustainable development and management of safe drinking water supply and safe sanitation, and safe hygiene services for all
Hydrology and Survey	To establish a data bank on water resources' potential for sustainable development, management, and utilization through research
Irrigation and Drainage	To develop, construct, and rehabilitate water storage, irrigation facilities, and water control structures for irrigation and other water development uses
Planning and Program	To coordinate staff training and planning processes, and to monitor and evaluate the implementation of programs and projects
Administration and Finance	To facilitate, support, and coordinate effective and efficient implementation of programs and projects

Source: World Bank.

Note: MWRI = Ministry of Water Resources and Irrigation.

including roles and responsibilities at national, state, county, and payam or boma levels. The responsibilities at the various levels include the following: *national* (policy development, resource mobilization, large infrastructure, for example, water control dikes and water treatment plants), *state* (resource mobilization; construction of medium infrastructure, for example, untreated piped systems; monitoring and enforcement), *county* (coordination, monitoring, regulation, and small infrastructure), *payam or boma* (coordination, water management, facility maintenance), *users* (basic maintenance), and *nongovernmental actors* (support) that operate across levels. In practice, however, many of the offices mandated to carry out water sector functions are understaffed and completely underresourced, relying on partnerships and funds from donors to be able to carry out their functions. The policy also opened the door to some functional overlaps, particularly regarding responsibility for the construction of infrastructure based on size and complexity (Government of South Sudan 2012).

Furthermore, the Water Bill, first drafted in 2013, sought to establish a Water Council with a regulatory role over both water resources management and water supply and sanitation. The Water Council was expected to function as the principal multistakeholder advisory body with representatives from the related national ministries and institutions, including managing directors of two additional proposed regulatory agencies: (a) the Water Resources Management Authority, with oversight over the management, development, and use of water resources and preparation of Integrated Water Resources Management plans based on subnational basin-level Integrated Water Resources Management plans (USAID 2021), and (b) the Safe Water Supply and Sanitation Services Regulator. The Water Council also was to include membership by the private sector and civil society. Figure 4.2 describes the water sector institutional structure proposed by the 2013 draft Water Bill.

At the state level, the MWRI's functions are discharged under the state ministry responsible for the Directorate of Water and Sanitation. However, this directorate is housed in different ministries across states (see table 4.3). Depending on the state, the mandate for water lies with the Ministry of Housing, Land and Public Utilities, the Ministry of Physical Infrastructure,

FIGURE 4.2

Proposed water sector institutional structure in the 2013 draft Water Bill

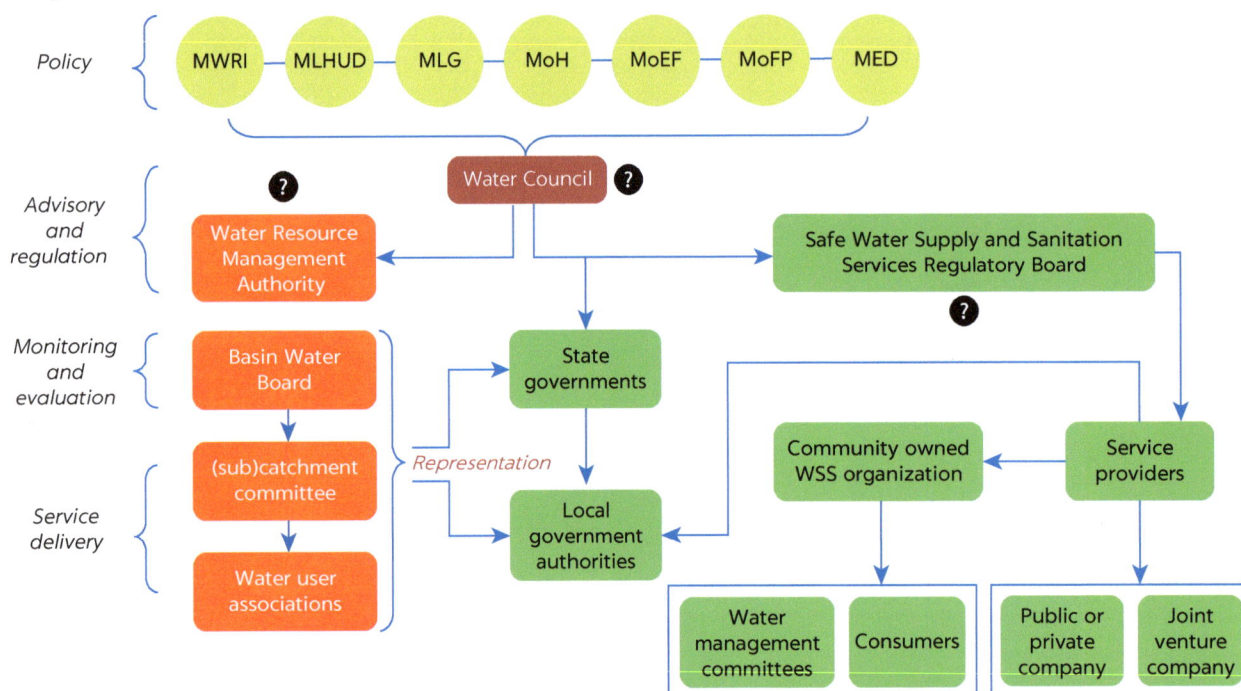

Source: World Bank based on JICA (2015).
Note: ? = not formally established; MED = Ministry of Energy and Dams; MLG = Project Coordination Office; MLHUD = Ministry of Land, Housing, and Urban Development; MoEF = Ministry of Environment and Forestry; MoFP = Ministry of Finance and Planning; MoH = Ministry of Health; MWRI = Ministry of Water Resources and Irrigation; WSS = Water Supply and Sanitation.

TABLE 4.3 List of ministries hosting water and sanitation directorates in the states

STATE OR ADMINISTRATIVE AREA	MINISTRY CONCERNED
Abyei Administrative Area	Ministry of Physical Infrastructure and Public Utilities
Central Equatoria state	Ministry of Physical Infrastructure
Eastern Equatoria state	Ministry of Housing, Land and Public Utilities
Jonglei state	Ministry of Housing, Land and Public Utilities
Lakes state	Ministry of Housing, Land and Public Utilities
Northern Bahr el Ghazal state	Ministry of Cooperatives and Rural Development
Pibor Administrative Area	Ministry of Physical Infrastructure and Agriculture
Ruweng Administrative Area	Ministry of Physical Infrastructure and Rural Development
Unity state	Ministry of Housing, Land and Public Utilities
Upper Nile state	Ministry of Physical Infrastructure
Warrap state	Ministry of Cooperatives and Rural Development
Western Bahr el Ghazal state	Ministry of Housing, Land and Public Utilities
Western Equatoria state	Ministry of Housing, Land and Public Utilities

Source: World Bank.

or the Ministry of Cooperatives and Rural Development. Within these ministries are water and sanitation directorates that have three departments (Rural Water Supply and Sanitation, Urban Sanitation, and Water Resources Management and Irrigation).

Under the Local Government Act, 2009, local governments have important mandates to provide basic services, including rural water and sanitation and urban sanitation, but lack the capacity and resources to deliver on this mandate. Local governments are inadequately staffed, and although they receive some unconditional transfer funding to support local administration and provide general local public services, this funding is rarely adequate, and is usually late and irregular. Actors at the county level include the following:

- Departments of water and sanitation are responsible for service delivery management.
- Departments of public works are responsible for managing service infrastructure.
- Basin water boards are responsible for basin management, including local monitoring and evaluation.
- Water management committees comprise local stakeholders and provide advisory services to planning and conflict resolution within the respective basin.
- Water user associations are responsible for local service delivery, maintenance, and water management.

Although there are efforts toward establishing disaster risk management policies and strategies, the institutions involved face severe capacity constraints. The government of South Sudan, through the Ministry of Humanitarian Affairs and Disaster Management, in 2021 developed a National Disaster Risk Management Policy that focuses on legal and institutional frameworks supporting disaster risk reduction efforts (MHADM 2018, 2019). Based on the policy, MWRI is tasked with acting as a lead institution with respect to disasters arising from floods, water supply, and dams. The policy was preceded by a National Disaster Risk Reduction Strategy (2018–2020) that focused on strengthening disaster preparedness and response (MHADM 2018). The institutions involved in disaster risk management include MWRI, the Ministry of Humanitarian Affairs and Disaster Management, the Ministry of Environment and Forestry, the Ministry of Agriculture and Food Security, and the South Sudan Meteorological Authority. These institutions have varying roles to play, from risk identification to mitigation, but the largest impediments to the functioning of each of them are enormous infrastructure and human resources challenges. The Ministry of Humanitarian Affairs and Disaster Management's strategic plan identifies at least five capacity constraints: limited office space, limited office equipment, insufficient office equipment, limited information and communication technology equipment and lack of training, and an austere budget (MHADM 2018).

Similar capacity challenges are highlighted in a recent Flood Forecasting and Early Warning System Assessment for South Sudan (ENTRO 2020). The report suggests that despite the Ministry of Environment and Forestry's major role in flood forecasting, it has no institutional arrangement in its administrative setup for flood forecast and early warning systems. The Ministry of Agriculture and Food Security is supposed to receive data on rainfall from both the South Sudan

Meteorological Authority and MWRI for dissemination, but there are no specialized staff employed to deal with and disseminate this type of information. In addition, there is inadequate capacity to manage early warning systems and no emergency response plans are in place.

A NASCENT LEGAL FRAMEWORK

The legal framework for water management in South Sudan is limited, with the 2013 Water Bill being the only major attempt to provide a legal basis for water sector institutions. The bill proposes building a governance and regulatory structure for the WASH subsector while handling other water subsectors through a proposed water resources management authority. Other than the concerned sector ministries, the key regulatory institutions in this proposed structure do not yet exist.

The Water Bill developed procedures to manage water allocation for different uses and for conservation, water quality, water-related disasters, and intersectoral coordination (USAID 2021). The bill also contains proposed provisions covering water sector principles and objectives, management and regulation, water resources planning and protection, permits, financial provisions for WRM, dam safety and flood management, and transboundary waters (JICA 2015)

Beyond the draft Water Bill, some sector regulations are adopted from existing laws, such as the Local Government Act, 2009, which stipulates that service delivery, including water resources management and WASH, is the local government's domain (Government of South Sudan 2009). WASH technical guidelines and manuals, as well as drinking water quality guidelines, have been developed, but there is no evident oversight of compliance with these standards and guidelines.

CUSTOMARY INSTITUTIONS PLAY A KEY ROLE IN WATER GOVERNANCE AND MANAGEMENT

South Sudan has a diverse range of customary institutions, including chiefs, informal conflict resolution mechanisms, and customary law, practices, and beliefs. Although customary institutions fulfill some of the formal functions just described, such as sharing information, creating incentives, and sanctioning behavior, they take the form of social and cultural norms rather than formal policies or laws. Customary institutions play a critical role in shaping the practices and behaviors of their respective communities. Hierarchies of chiefs, their assistants, elders, and opinion formers are all examples of customary institutions that have been recognized and have participated in public administration since the colonial period while remaining semiautonomous from the state (Idris 2017). Customary institutions in South Sudan have long played an important role in local justice and natural resource management, including water management. Although their influence has been declining over time, they will likely continue to play an important role in South Sudan, especially in the absence of strong formal institutions.

Customary institutions are involved in a range of water management functions, beginning with resolving disputes around water access. More specifically, the sociocultural influence of chiefs extends to natural resource management disputes, including water point conflicts (Liaga and Wielenga 2020). Chiefs discuss water issues at "big tree meetings" as part of their role in adjudicating sharing of natural resources (RVI 2022). In agro-pastoralist areas, determining how to share access to water for livestock is a key role for customary institutions as well as a source of conflict when perceived to be unfair, given the importance of livestock as household assets and as a source of social status and prestige (Maxwell et al. 2016).

Customary institutions also play a role in informal drinking water distribution. Informal private sector vendors of water (transported by donkeys, bicycles, or trucks), a market that has emerged to fill gaps in public service provision, are common, especially in urban areas. These vendors are largely unregulated, except in areas where customary institutions play a role in maintaining and regulating water supply to households (Matoso 2018).

Customary institutions also play a role in siting water facilities, selecting water management committee members, and disseminating information to community members. Considerations for identifying suitable locations for the construction of water facilities include avoiding contested land and potential conflict and ensuring equitable access for all community members. Customary authorities also have a key function in identifying members of the water management committee, community members to receive technical training (for example, pump mechanics) according to requirements of nongovernmental organizations, and as an overall liaison between the community and nongovernmental organizations or local government through the construction and handover of any water projects. The chiefs carry out these activities through discussions and consultations with their elders and other community members (including older women). Because chiefs select water management committee members, they appear to have an incentive to make these institutions work and take responsibility when they collapse. They are also responsible for enforcing bylaws agreed upon for improved water supply and are the last resort to raise funds to repair water infrastructure—nearly all focus group discussions reported that the chief takes responsibility for fixing the water point when it breaks (RVI 2022). Church leaders are also an important part of informal institutions because they help pass information to the people in the community and are widely respected.

Findings from the focus group discussions suggest that community members universally recognize the chief (or the chief and elders) as the most important institution in the community when it comes to water issues, followed by local government and nongovernmental organizations (RVI 2022). Older respondents, especially men, recognize the authority of "elders" in determining access to natural resources (grazing land and water); however, access to improved or developed water supplies appears not to be included in this mandate unless there is a conflict to resolve or the chief asks for some help from elders to control access in times of water shortage. Unimproved water supplies, such as traditional wells and *haffirs*, are often controlled by youths who are herding livestock. Although water experts interviewed in the preparation of this report can clearly identify a system of formal water management institutions, water users often do

BOX 4.1

Experts rate the effectiveness of formal and customary water management institutions

To elicit subject matter expertise on the effectiveness of formal and customary water management institutions, 23 experts were interviewed. The group comprised a sample of researchers, practitioners, and policy makers working on water, natural resources management, and policy in South Sudan. Their areas of expertise covered a range of disciplines (engineering, economics, political science), organizations (universities, nongovernmental organizations, donors, government), and areas of the country (Juba, Kapoeta, and Rumbek counties). The interview and data analysis protocols were developed by the World Bank in collaboration with the Rift Valley Institute and then administered by the Rift Valley Institute, as described in more detail in appendix A. Expert elicitation is a well-known and tested method for documenting expert judgment about available evidence and supporting public policy decision-making (Morgan 2014).

In the interviews, experts rated the effectiveness of formal and customary institutions for water

management. In the context of the interviews, effectiveness was defined as the degree to which institutions were able to resolve disputes around water and ensure sustainable access to drinking water supply for the population. For customary institutions, 36 percent of the experts rated them as being highly effective and 59 percent as partially effective, with only 5 percent suggesting that they are not at all effective (figure B4.1.1). Respondents who ranked the customary institutions as "partially" effective frequently qualified the response by saying that it was highly dependent on the leadership of the chief and also on the chief's relationship with local government or nongovernmental organizations. This is in stark contrast to the responses for the formal institutions, which experts largely deemed as ineffective in fulfilling functions related to ensuring access and resolving disputes. In the discussions around this topic, experts suggested that the formal structure for sustainable management of rural water supply, as described in national strategy documents and related guidelines,

FIGURE B4.1.1

Experts identify customary institutions as being more effective than formal institutions at ensuring access to water and resolving water-related disputes

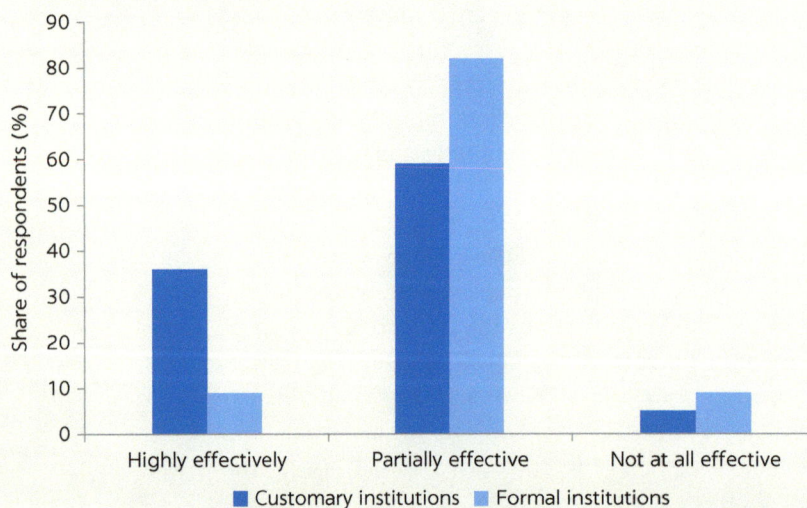

Note: One respondent preferred not to rate the effectiveness of customary institutions.

continued

Box 4.1, *continued*

has faced huge challenges in the fragile context of South Sudan.

Experts noted the lack of effectiveness of formal institutions, particularly in the context of rural water services. Many experts deemed government and non-governmental organization (NGO) provision of rural water supply services as fundamentally unsustainable. One key informant form Rumbek highlighted the scale of the challenge, citing the example of Lake state: "There are more than 2,000 boreholes and water yards across Lakes State, and not even half of these are working." Another key informant ascribed the challenges of service provision to the high levels of insecurity and mobility: "The sustainability has been a difficult question … . People keep moving, and many water points get abandoned. A big question for the government is to provide safety for the villages. Then there is a culture of shifting cultivation … . Here there is a village, two years later, it is a forest and NGOs and government have to follow that pattern."

not see a distinction. Typically for an improved water supply, the hierarchy of responsibility in the community is as follows: 1. chief (of the boma), 2. water management committee, 3. pump mechanics, 4. the group of elders working with the chief.

Humanitarian and development actors have attempted to develop local, formal water institutions parallel to customary institutions (De Simone 2015). For example, the water committees established to oversee the management of water points have engaged representatives of customary leadership (Mott MacDonald 2017). In the World Bank's Enhancing Community Resilience Project, communities have been mobilized into Payam Development Committees and Boma Development Committees (World Bank 2020). These are community institutions stipulated in the Local Government Act, 2009, and include representation from women, youth, the displaced, elders, and persons with disabilities. Although the functioning of these committees for water management has yet to be fully assessed, they offer an opportunity to overcome some of the constraints of customary institutions, such as gender inequality, and advance existing government legislation in relation to local governance.

HUMANITARIAN AND DEVELOPMENT ACTORS DOMINATE WATER SECTOR FINANCING

In the face of protracted crises, international aid has been the primary source of funding with which to address the emergency needs in South Sudan. From 2002 to 2019, all funders worldwide committed US$395 million in development finance to South Sudan for water supply and sanitation. All of this amount was in the form of official development assistance grants. The disbursement ratio for development finance to South Sudan for water supply and sanitation over this period was 75.8 percent. Development finance commitments to South Sudan for water supply and sanitation came from different funders (figure 4.3), including US$96.9 million from the Netherlands, US$74.2 million from the United States, and US$74.0 million from Japan (Atteridge et al. 2019).

FIGURE 4.3

Top donors in South Sudan, cumulative commitments for the water sector, 2002–19

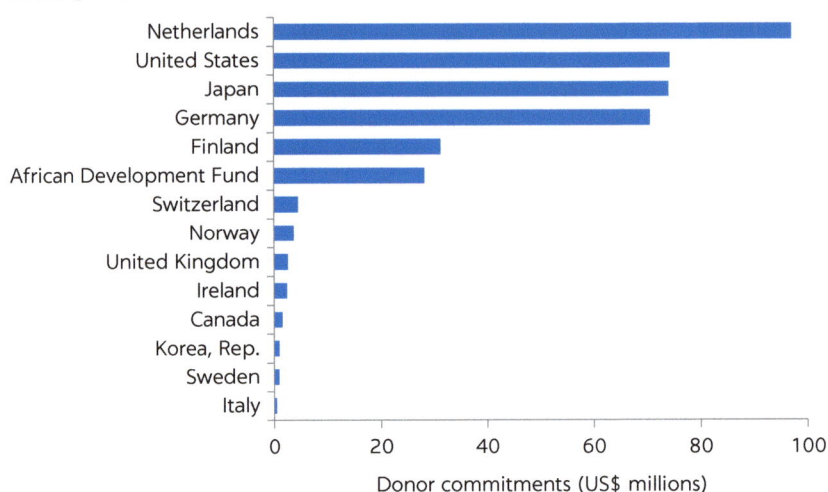

Source: Atteridge et al. 2019.

TABLE 4.4 **Water sector commitments, by subsector in South Sudan, 2002–19**

SUBSECTOR	AMOUNT (US$ MILLIONS)	SHARE (%)
Basic drinking water supply and basic sanitation	191.41	48.40
Water supply—large systems	63.96	16.20
Water supply and sanitation—large systems	63.28	16.00
Water sector policy and administrative management	45.17	11.40
Basic drinking water supply	21.36	5.40
Waste management and disposal	7.24	1.80
River basins development	1.39	0.35
Basic sanitation	0.89	0.23
Education and training in water supply and sanitation	0.49	0.12
Water resources conservation (including data collection)	0.05	< 0.001
Sanitation—large systems	0.02	< 0.001

Source: Atteridge et al. 2019.

Development finance to South Sudan for water supply and sanitation was provided to different subsectors, mostly basic drinking water supply and sanitation (see table 4.4). The largest commitments were US$191 million to basic drinking water supply and basic sanitation, US$64 million to water supply—large systems, and US$63 million to water supply and sanitation—large systems (Atteridge et al. 2019).

An overview of external funding mechanisms for South Sudan

External assistance, including humanitarian relief and development aid, was provided in South Sudan as early as 1972 after the Addis Ababa Peace Agreement. At that time, in Juba, there were six UN agencies, four bilateral development agencies, and 22 international nongovernmental organizations, all involved in postwar refugee repatriation, construction, and development activities. Further, international operations such as the 1984–86 Western Relief Operation and 1986's Operation Rainbow followed in response to drought and famine (Ryle et al. 2012). Operation Lifeline Sudan in 1989, involving more than 40 international aid organizations, was a tripartite agreement between the government of Sudan, the Sudan People's Liberation Army, and the UN to allow humanitarian relief in both government- and rebel-held territories. In 1990, a shift from a sole focus on emergency relief to more of a development plan was recognized, and

after the 2005 Comprehensive Peace Agreement, there was a very optimistic outlook to engage in a longer-term view of development planning, focusing on building central government structures and capacity rather than relief (Mosello, Mason, and Aludra 2016). To that end, a Multi-Donor Trust Fund was set up in 2008 under the mandate of the Comprehensive Peace Agreement and administered by the World Bank. In the same year, in May, donors established the South Sudan Recovery Fund under the trust fund to bridge a perceived gap between the short-term emergency and humanitarian aid and longer-term development assistance (Mosello, Mason, and Aludra 2016). Amid some progress, the widespread deterioration of security in the country led to the phasing out of the recovery fund in 2015 and a reversion of funding mechanisms to emergency and critical needs (see figure B4.2.1 for the timeline).

FIGURE B4.2.1

The humanitarian timeline in South Sudan

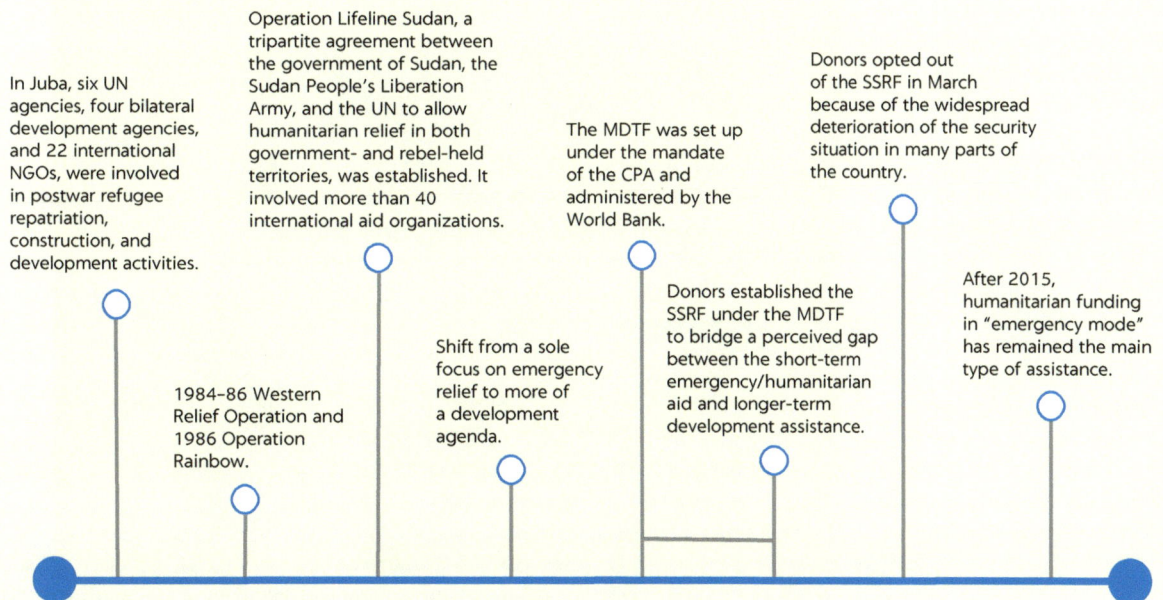

In Juba, six UN agencies, four bilateral development agencies, and 22 international NGOs, were involved in postwar refugee repatriation, construction, and development activities.

1984–86 Western Relief Operation and 1986 Operation Rainbow.

Operation Lifeline Sudan, a tripartite agreement between the government of Sudan, the Sudan People's Liberation Army, and the UN to allow humanitarian relief in both government- and rebel-held territories, was established. It involved more than 40 international aid organizations.

Shift from a sole focus on emergency relief to more of a development agenda.

The MDTF was set up under the mandate of the CPA and administered by the World Bank.

Donors established the SSRF under the MDTF to bridge a perceived gap between the short-term emergency/humanitarian aid and longer-term development assistance.

Donors opted out of the SSRF in March because of the widespread deterioration of the security situation in many parts of the country.

After 2015, humanitarian funding in "emergency mode" has remained the main type of assistance.

Source: World Bank.
Note: CPA = Comprehensive Peace Agreement; MDTF = Multi-Donor Trust Fund; NGO = nongovernmental organization; SSRF = South Sudan Recovery Fund.

TABLE 4.5 **Summary of constraints in water sector policies, institutions, regulatory framework, and financing**

POLICY CONSTRAINTS	INSTITUTIONAL CONSTRAINTS	REGULATORY CONSTRAINTS	FINANCING CONSTRAINTS
Lack of policy implementation: Intentions of the first South Sudan Water Policy of 2007 have yet to be translated into legislation, and the 2013 Water Bill has not been ratified.	**Incomplete institutional structure:** Many of the proposed governance structures and regulatory bodies have yet to be established and become operational.	**Inadequate legislative framework:** There is no coherent legislative framework to guide implementation of water sector policies.	**Inadequate budget allocations:** Budget to support recurrent and development expenditures to execute plans and policies has been scarce, especially since the conflict period.
Conflicting and duplicative policy: Lack of progress has resulted in duplication across policy instruments, as targets were not achieved and goals were derailed due to conflict.	**Weak capacity of national and state institutions:** Organization, staffing, and capacity for water services vary greatly across states and institutions, leading sector actors to play multiple roles across governance levels to fill gaps.	**Limited adoption and implementation of sector legislation:** The 2013 draft Water Bill was expected to operationalize and facilitate the creation of organizational and administrative institutions in the sector but has yet to be enacted by legislators.	**Emergency funding dominates:** Protracted conflict stalled policy implementation and ushered in funding modalities focused on immediate relief, hindering the development of holistic interventions and longer-term, government-led planning.
Ad hoc interventions are not aligned with policy and are mainly donor driven: Though sector policies have been developed, interventions in the sector remain ad hoc and driven by donors and humanitarian organizations.	**Weak capacity of local institutions:** Customary authorities have supplanted the role of local government in water management and are considered essential to water governance and ensuring access to water for all.	**Water sector lacks independent regulation and enforcement:** Although regulation and enforcement are a priority in the country's water policy, the proposed regulatory institutions for WRM and WASH have yet to be institutionalized.	**Sector financing is donor driven and characterized by limited transparency:** An estimated 85 percent of the water sector's services are provided by international nongovernmental organizations.

Source: World Bank.
Note: WASH = water, sanitation, and hygiene; WRM = water resources management.

CONCLUSIONS

In addition to analyzing the policies, institutions, regulations, and financing surrounding water sector governance in South Sudan, this chapter also presents the findings of a qualitative study on the role of traditional and customary institutions in the governance and management of water. Focusing on the trends and development of these factors from 2011 to 2020, the water sector's binding constraints are highlighted and summarized in table 4.5.

REFERENCES

Atteridge, A., G. Savvidou, S. Sadowski, F. Gortana, L. Meintrup, and A. Dzebo. 2019. "Aid Atlas" (accessed February 2, 2022), https://aid-atlas.org.

De Simone, S. 2015. "Building a Fragmented State: Land Governance and Conflict in South Sudan." *Journal of Peacebuilding and Development* 10 (3): 60–73.

ENTRO (Eastern Nile Technical Regional Office). 2020. "Final Report: Flood Forecasting and Early Warning System (FFEW) Assessment for South Sudan." ENTRO, Addis Ababa. http://ikp.nilebasin.org/en/document-repository/few-flood-forecasting-early-warning -system-enhancement-south-sudan-country.

Government of South Sudan. 2007. "Water Policy." Government of South Sudan, Juba (accessed October 10, 2021), http://extwprlegs1.fao.org/docs/pdf/ssd147091.pdf.

Government of South Sudan. 2009. "Local Government Act Section 24: Primary Responsibilities of Local Government Councils." Government of South Sudan, Juba.

Government of South Sudan. 2011. "South Sudan Development Plan 2011–2013: Realising Freedom, Equality, Justice, Peace and Prosperity for All." Government of South Sudan, Juba (accessed October 16, 2021), http://www.mofep-grss.org/wp-content/uploads/2013/08 /RSS_SSDP.pdf.

Government of South Sudan. 2012. "Rural Water and Sanitation Service Delivery Framework." Government of South Sudan, Juba.

Government of South Sudan. 2018. "Republic of South Sudan National Development Strategy: Consolidate Peace and Stabilize the Economy." Government of South Sudan, Juba. http://www.mofep-grss.org/wp-content/uploads/2018/11/NDS-4-Print-Sept-5-2018.pdf.

Idris, I. 2017. "Local Governance in South Sudan: Overview." K4D Helpdesk Report 235, Institute of Development Studies, Brighton, UK.

JICA (Japan International Cooperation Agency). 2015. "Project for Irrigation Development Master Plan (IDMP) in the Republic of South Sudan: Final Report (Main)." JICA, Tokyo (accessed December 3, 2021), https://openjicareport.jica.go.jp/pdf/12249181.pdf.

Liaga, E. A., and C. Wielenga. 2020. "Social Cohesion from the Top-Down or Bottom-Up? The Cases of South Sudan and Burundi." *Peace and Change* 45 (3): 389–425.

Matoso, M. 2018. "Supporting Sustainable Water Service Delivery in a Protracted Crisis: Professionalizing Community-Led Systems in South Sudan." Oxfam, Juba.

Maxwell, D., R. Gordon, L. Moro, M. Santschi, and P. Dau. 2016. "Livelihoods and Conflict in South Sudan." Briefing Paper 20, Secure Livelihoods Research Consortium, London.

MHADM (Ministry of Humanitarian Affairs and Disaster Management). 2018. *MHADM Strategic Plan 2018-2020*. Juba: Ministry of Humanitarian Affairs and Disaster Management. https://www.partnersforresilience.nl/downloads/files/Strategic%20Plan%20MHADM%20Final%20PfR%20S-Sudan%202018.pdf.

MHADM (Ministry of Humanitarian Affairs and Disaster Management). 2019. "Official Government Statement at the 2019 Global Platform for Disaster Risk Reduction, Geneva, Switzerland 13–17 May 2019." Ministry of Humanitarian Affairs and Disaster Management, Juba. https://www.unisdr.org/files/globalplatform/rssofficialstatement2[1].docx.

Morgan, M. G. 2014. "Use (and abuse) of Expert Elicitation in Support of Decision Making for Public Policy." *Proceedings of the National Academy of Sciences* 111 (20): 7176–84.

Mosello, B., N. Mason, and R. Aludra. 2016. "Improving WASH Service Delivery in Protracted Crises. The Case of South Sudan." Overseas Development Institute, London (accessed December 14, 2022), https://cdn.odi.org/media/documents/10817.pdf.

Mott MacDonald. 2017. "Water for Lakes: Hope for Struggling Communities in South Sudan" (accessed December 12, 2022), https://www.mottmac.com/article/59521/water-for-lakes-south-sudan.

Radio Dabanga. 2021. "Sudan and South Sudan Sign MoU on Water Management and Flood Prevention in the South Sudanese Capital Juba Yesterday," Relief Web, October 8, 2021 (accessed February 3, 2022), https://reliefweb.int/report/south-sudan/sudan-and-south-sudan-sign-mou-water-management.

RVI (Rift Valley Institute). 2022. "Fragility and Water Security in South Sudan." Study conducted for the World Bank by the Rift Valley Institute in collaboration with the Centre for Humanitarian Change. Background paper prepared for this report. Rift Valley Institute, Juba.

Ryle, J., J. Willis, S. Baldo, and J. Madut Jok, eds. 2012. *The Sudan Handbook*. London: Rift Valley Institute.

USAID (United States Agency for International Development). 2013. "Draft Water, Sanitation and Hygiene (WASH) Program 2013–2018." USAID, Washington, DC (accessed December 14, 2021), https://www.usaid.gov/sites/default/files/documents/1860/USAID%20South%20Sudan%20Draft%20Water%2C%20Sanitation%20and%20Hygiene%20Program%202013-2018.pdf.

USAID (United States Agency for International Development). 2021. "South Sudan Water Resources Profile Overview." USAID, Washington, DC (accessed December 20, 2021), https://winrock.org/wp-content/uploads/2021/08/South_Sudan_Country_Profile_Final.pdf.

World Bank. 2020. "South Sudan Enhancing Community Resilience and Local Governance Project." Project Appraisal Document. World Bank, Washington, DC.

5 The Way Ahead

PRINCIPLES FOR ADVANCING WATER SECURITY

This report depicts the multiple channels through which water influences social, political, and human development outcomes in South Sudan. Water insecurity undermines human development and economic opportunities. It also affects South Sudanese unevenly, with more vulnerable populations—forcibly displaced communities and their hosts, women, and children—bearing the brunt of its adverse impacts. The interaction of two factors exacerbates and reinforces vulnerability to these adverse impacts. First, decades of violence and marginalization have disrupted livelihoods, damaged social networks, and led to protracted cycles of displacement, further undermining the ability of South Sudanese to cope with water insecurity. Second, high dependency on variable water resources and natural assets exposes populations and livelihoods to water-related hazards, which are becoming more extreme under climate change. This climate sensitivity combines with the impacts of protracted fragility to undermine the coping capacity of populations to respond to water insecurity and climate change, so that once floods or droughts strike, damage is even greater. Figure 5.1 illustrates this vicious cycle. A broken social system and decades of conflict drive social vulnerability (1), undermining the ability of South Sudan's population and institutions to pursue water security for people, production, and protection and resulting in greater risks and impacts from insecurity (2). In turn, failure to respond to the risks and impacts arising from water insecurity further exacerbates the drivers of vulnerability (3), making it even more difficult for communities to respond, thus perpetuating the vicious cycle. Climate change brings about more frequent and extreme water-related hazards (4), leading to greater water risks and impacts and thus fueling the vicious cycle.

In this situation, the overarching priority becomes to break the vicious cycle of water insecurity and fragility. Although current humanitarian modalities of water management have provided much-needed relief and saved human lives, they are a blunt instrument for helping South Sudan break this cycle. Humanitarian and emergency responses, such as temporary embankment rehabilitation and provision of rural water points, are crucial to respond to urgent challenges and meet immediate needs. However, they are not well suited to

FIGURE 5.1
The vicious cycle of water insecurity and fragility

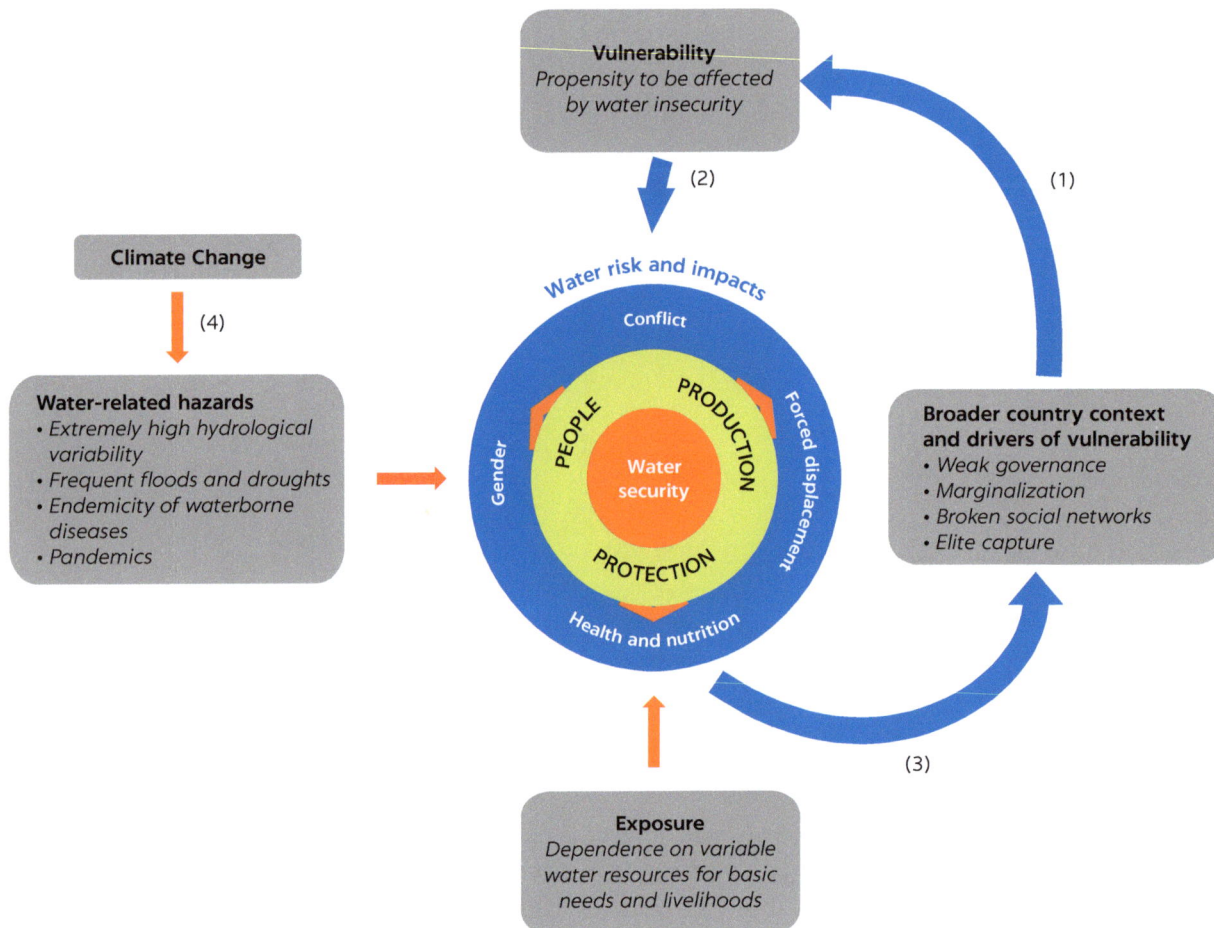

Source: World Bank.

providing long-term and cost-effective solutions to persistent water challenges, which are required if water is to become an engine for recovery and development and not a drag on people's livelihoods. A gradual transition from humanitarian modalities of water management toward a long-term and government-led development approach is needed.

What would such a transition look like? Given the complexity of South Sudan's water sector challenges, no single measure and no single actor will be able to "solve" water in the country. The long-term vision embedded in the 2013 Water Bill is an excellent starting point: it clearly emphasizes the need for a long-term approach to water management. Building upon this vision, policy makers should address the country's water issues through an iterative decision process to identify sector priorities. Figure 5.2 summarizes these priorities based on the key findings from this report.

Translating these reform and investment priorities into practice is essentially and necessarily a political task. As such, the recommendations in figure 5.2 are accompanied by a set of guiding principles presented to help policy makers not lose sight of the forest for the trees (that is, their long-term vision) as they navigate the inherently political process of water sector investment and reform.

FIGURE 5.2

Sequencing priorities for water policy and investment in South Sudan

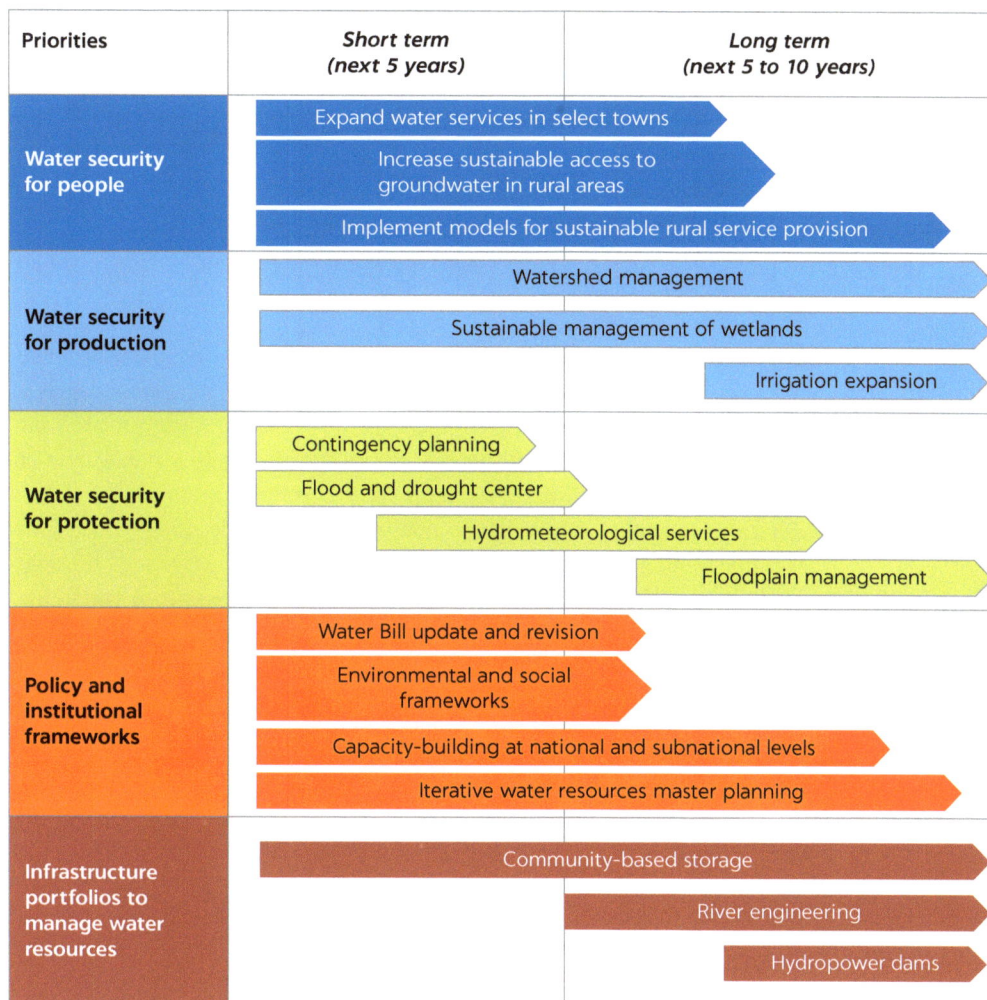

Priorities	Short term (next 5 years)	Long term (next 5 to 10 years)
Water security for people	Expand water services in select towns Increase sustainable access to groundwater in rural areas Implement models for sustainable rural service provision	
Water security for production	Watershed management Sustainable management of wetlands	Irrigation expansion
Water security for protection	Contingency planning Flood and drought center Hydrometeorological services	Floodplain management
Policy and institutional frameworks	Water Bill update and revision Environmental and social frameworks Capacity-building at national and subnational levels Iterative water resources master planning	
Infrastructure portfolios to manage water resources	Community-based storage River engineering	Hydropower dams

Source: World Bank.

The guiding principles should serve as the cornerstone of the country's approach to water sector investment and reform given that they are meant to remain permanent even if priorities, policies, and practices change.

Principle 1: Inclusion

Inclusion operates at multiple levels, from community to government. It requires involving those affected by water interventions, providing them with understandable information, and seeking their input in the design and implementation of water sector interventions. At the macro level, inclusion also requires working with a range of partners, including humanitarian and private sector actors (such as water vendors) to ensure that lessons and practices developed during emergencies can inform long-term solutions and to ensure that these actors are not disenfranchised by the transition but see it as an opportunity to gradually hand over responsibility to the government (especially humanitarian actors) and access more stable business opportunities (private actors).

Principle 2: Sequencing

Sequencing is a key principle of any investment strategy. It calls for the careful development and prioritization of a list of investments and reforms based on factors such as urgency, feasibility, and cost-effectiveness. Sequencing also requires patience, recognizing that certain enablers need to be in place before the country can pursue large-scale water sector reform and infrastructure investments. These enablers include sound governance systems, government accountability, and more stable and trained human resources.

Principle 3: Visibility

Public opinion on state legitimacy often depends on the way people collectively experience services: the visibility of services (including infrastructure such as roads, water, and electricity) and related improvements that they bring to communities can trigger public awareness and translate into positive public opinion on state legitimacy. Visibility of interventions is therefore particularly important to ensure that people (a) experience improvements in services and (b) attribute these improvements to the state, thus contributing to an improved relationship, even if marginal, between the state as a service provider and the community. Unfortunately, in South Sudan people still perceive nongovernmental organizations and humanitarian actors as the parties directly responsible for water services (Kooy and Wild 2012). Implementing this principle requires pursuing low-hanging fruit that leads to quick and visible improvements. Success breeds success; hence, these investments can be followed in the medium term by larger and more complex water infrastructure investments whose results do not materialize rapidly and whose dividend of legitimacy is therefore much less immediate.

Principle 4: Conflict sensitivity

The principle of conflict sensitivity is well-known among policy makers in South Sudan, and it is premised on the fact that in fragile, conflict, and violence-affected contexts, any external intervention (from the state or a humanitarian or development partner) can unintentionally exacerbate tensions in a community, thus paradoxically worsening the problem it is trying to solve. Hence, conflict sensitivity needs to be embedded in all water sector interventions, following existing experiences. The experiences of humanitarian partners will be particularly valuable in implementing this principle and ensuring that water sector interventions do not inadvertently trigger more violence.

Water sector investments should be carried out following the do-no-harm principle to avoid exacerbating fragilities and tensions and thereby paradoxically increasing vulnerability to climate change and water insecurity. In addition, water sector interventions should be designed to fully consider existing customary institutions to leverage their potential for inclusive decision-making (when this potential exists) or promote alternative and more inclusive modalities for decision-making and water management at the community level in accordance with relevant country legislation (Local Government Act, 2009). As this report demonstrates (chapter 4), existing localized systems of dispute resolution and resource management have proven effective in helping to manage access to water and conflicts, but they are not necessarily a panacea. Their effectiveness can be undermined by core governance challenges, including politicization, patriarchy, and corruption. Alternatives for community-level institutions include Payam Development Committees and Boma Development Committees envisaged in the Local Government Act, 2009, which typically include representation from women, youth, the displaced, elders, and people with disabilities. Specific actions to implement this principle in water sector investments include the following:

- Address community grievances in access to water resources and services, building upon the conflict-sensitive expertise of humanitarian partners
- Develop capacity at national and subnational levels for participatory water management decisions and avoid top-down mega projects
- Leverage more democratic, inclusive community groups that exist across South Sudan, such as Payam Development Committees and Boma Development Committees as set forth in the Local Government Act, 2009, to design water sector interventions and formally engage women in water management

PRIORITY AREAS AND RECOMMENDATIONS

This report identifies five key priorities and related recommendations to improve water security and gradually move toward a government-led, long-term approach to water management. Three priorities are linked to the three dimensions of water security examined in the report (people, production, and protection), while two are cross-cutting priorities, and related recommendations aim at advancing water security across multiple dimensions. Action on some of the recommendations should begin immediately (in the next five years) because of the urgency of the challenges they address and because of their low to moderate technical, social, and environmental complexity. Recommendations with greater complexity should be pursued in the next five to ten years (long term), once core water institutions and information sources have been put in place (figure 5.2).

Priority 1: Water security for people

South Sudan faces a water supply and sanitation crisis. Low coverage of water supply and sanitation services contributes to low levels of human capital attainment through its deleterious effects on nutrition, health, and educational outcomes. Access to water supply and sanitation is a daily struggle for millions of South Sudanese. Although the coverage of drinking water supply services has improved somewhat in urban areas, service levels in rural areas have declined since 2013. Overall, fewer households have access to sanitation than before the conflict period. To address the water supply and sanitation crisis in the short term, the government needs to continue working with international partners to deliver much-needed water services, including through the recommendations in table 5.1.

Priority 2: Water security for production

Although water resources encompass significant risks, they also provide benefits for people and the economy. Receding and rising floodwaters are a key enabler of livelihoods in South Sudan, and water is highly valued in pastoralist communities. Floodplains provide important ecosystem services and are a source of livelihoods for at least 6 million people living along the Nile and Sobat Rivers and in the eastern and western floodplain zones. The country's natural

TABLE 5.1 **Recommendations for water security for people**

RECOMMENDATIONS (WHAT)	RELEVANT INSTITUTIONS (WHO)	TIMELINE (WHEN)	LOCATIONS (WHERE)	IMPLEMENTATION (HOW)
R 1.1: Increase central coordination and oversight of water supply and sanitation interventions.	MWRI	Immediate	National	Bolster MWRI representation and participation in existing interagency coordination working groups and clusters and establish and implement protocols for communication and information-sharing on ongoing and planned interventions.
R 1.2: Increase access to and sustainable management of groundwater resources in small towns and rural areas.	MWRI, with support of development partners	Immediate	Rural communities across the country, in particular in the drought-prone southeast	Promote drilling of new boreholes or rehabilitation of existing ones using solar pumps where feasible paired with infrastructure and institutions for sustainable use of aquifers (for example, sand dams, afforestation, water harvesting, community-based management).
				Provide block grants to households and villages for water storage projects designed and selected by village committees (for example, Payam Development Committees and Boma Development Committees, similar to the National Solidarity Program in Afghanistan).
R 1.3: Expand coverage of water supply and sanitation services in rural areas.	MWRI, with support of development partners	Immediate	States with lowest levels of access to sanitation services	Support the operationalization of the Rural Water Supply and Sanitation Department as the centerpiece of rural-focused service delivery and promote piloting and monitoring of alternative delivery mechanisms tailored to local situations.
R 1.4: Design any urban and rural services (infrastructure design and O&M practices) around preferences and priorities of water users (in particular, women and girls) and consolidate lessons into revised WASH guidelines to include climate resilience and social inclusion considerations.	MWRI and SSUWC, with support of humanitarian and development partners	Immediate, starting from existing WASH guidelines	National	Pilot a market-based, cost-recovery O&M strategy for water services. Partner with civil society organizations to identify needs and preferences of water users.
R 1.5: Define institutional accountability and mandates for water service provision across urban and rural areas.	MWRI and SSUWC	Long term	National	Support the formalization of community water supplies (contracts with users, standards for quality of service, establishment and collection of tariffs, O&M capacity).
				Support information flow between users and providers through consumer feedback mechanisms and existing local governance structures.
R 1.6: Increase capacity, extend distribution networks, and improve service delivery performance of water and sanitation infrastructure in selected cities.	MWRI and SSUWC, with support of development partners and building upon existing feasibility studies	Immediate	Aweil Bentiu Bor Juba East Juba West Kuajok Rumbek Torit Yambio	Update existing feasibility studies to align with citywide inclusive sanitation approaches, thus promoting a diversified set of solutions. Approach international financiers for support. Ensure alignment with urban development master plans.

Source: World Bank.
Note: MWRI = Ministry of Water Resources and Irrigation; O&M = operations and maintenance; SSUWC = South Sudan Urban Water Corporation; WASH = water, sanitation, and hygiene.

TABLE 5.2 Recommendations for water security for production

RECOMMENDATIONS (WHAT)	RELEVANT INSTITUTIONS (WHO)	TIMELINE (WHEN)	LOCATIONS (WHERE)	IMPLEMENTATION (HOW)
R 2.1: Sustain flood-based livelihoods with investments supporting domestic fish production and preservation, rice production, and flood-recession agriculture.	MWRI, MoA, Ministry of Livestock, with support of development partners	Immediate	Nile and Sobat corridor, eastern and western floodplains	Introduce formal partnerships with NGOs and civil society organizations to recruit and organize labor. Leverage climate finance to support the efforts of rural communities to restore natural ecosystems and store carbon.
R 2.2: Update the irrigation master plan to include identification of areas suitable for farmer-led irrigation initiatives.	MWRI, MoA	Long term	National	Use grant resources to update the plan and build upon lessons from neighboring countries in piloting farmer-led irrigation initiatives.
R 2.3: Rehabilitate and expand irrigation infrastructure.	MWRI, MoA	Long term	Jebel Lado irrigation scheme Aweil irrigation scheme Northern Upper Nile irrigation scheme	Update existing irrigation master plans and approach international financiers.
R 2.4: Advance watershed management activities.	MWRI, with support of development partners	Immediate	Limur/Nyimur, Baro-Akobo-Sobat, and Niymur-Aswa basins	Introduce formal partnerships with NGOs and civil society organizations to support piloting of activities and recruit and organize labor with communities. Apply open-access remote sensing technology to monitor results, using positive results from pilots to leverage additional finance.

Source: World Bank.
Note: MoA = Ministry of Agriculture; MWRI = Ministry of Water Resources and Irrigation; NGO = nongovernmental organization.

capital provides a range of ecosystem services, supporting livelihoods, regulating water flows, and providing habitats for biodiversity. Furthermore, the potential for irrigation to bolster food production remains untapped. To harness water's productive potential for food and ecosystems, the report identifies the recommendations in table 5.2.

Priority 3: Water security for protection

Coping with droughts and floods presents a profound challenge to climate adaptation and development in South Sudan; however, the country's disaster risk preparedness and early warning systems remain largely inadequate. Responding to floods and droughts is not just a matter of building infrastructure, but also of preventing populations from moving into harm's way and of devising information systems and institutional arrangements to increase preparedness and early warning. Delineation of flood-prone areas and managed retreat away from areas that are frequently affected by floods is an alternative to structural protection. Moving forward, it is important for policy makers to include managed retreat as a potential option for responding to flood risks, and to identify minimum standards and principles for resettling populations living in areas at risk. Any resettlement effort would need to be based on careful conflict analysis of the groups to be resettled, their historic relations with groups in targeted resettlement areas, and how existing or potential tensions can be mitigated, and would need to be aligned with the 2021 South Sudan Durable Solutions Strategy (see chapter 3). Responding to floods and droughts is also a matter of transboundary

TABLE 5.3 Recommendations for water security for protection

RECOMMENDATIONS (WHAT)	RELEVANT INSTITUTIONS (WHO)	TIMELINE (WHEN)	LOCATIONS (WHERE)	IMPLEMENTATION (HOW)
R 3.1: Repair and upgrade existing hydrometric stations.	MWRI and MHADM, with support from development partners	Immediate	Bor Dolieb Hillet Juba Malakal Mongalla Nimule Wau	Mobilize any available resources from regional organizations and international partners. Prioritize repair in budget allocation.
R 3.2: Build national and subnational capacity to prepare and respond to floods and droughts.	MWRI and MHADM, with support from development partners	Long term	National and state level	Learn from low-cost global experiences in disaster risk preparedness (Bangladesh) and pilot a national Disaster Preparedness Program, focusing on signal distribution, disaster preparedness, capacity-building, training (including mock drills), and community awareness-building.
R 3.3: Expand hydrometric network and establish a hydro-meteorological telemetry system, including for water quality and groundwater monitoring.	MWRI and MHADM, in collaboration with development partners	Long term	Streams in the Bahr el Ghazal and Sobat subbasins and central area of the Sudd wetland	Expand and improve existing hydrometric network expansion plans and approach international funders.
R 3.4: Build knowledge base to advance flood risk management, including constructing topographic maps and defining technical standards for flood protection infrastructure.	MWRI and MHADM, in collaboration with development partners	Long term	National and state level	Use grant resources and existing open-access data sets to construct a first generation of hazard maps to be updated in an iterative manner as more information and resources become available.
R 3.5: Develop minimum standards and principles to evaluate options for a contextualized, conflict-sensitive approach when resettling populations currently living in high flood-prone areas.	MWRI and MHADM	Long term	National and state level	Partner with civil society and international organizations with experience in resettling populations at risk of flooding and document experience relevant for South Sudan. Consider piloting resettlement programs based on collected evidence and extensive consultations with involved communities.
R 3.6: Develop a hydrological assessment of the Sudd wetland.	MWRI, with support from development partners	Immediate	Jonglei Lakes Pibor AA Unity Warrap	Use grant resources from international donors and ensure compatibility with existing regional hydrological models.
R 3.7: Strengthen information exchange with Nile riparians on floods and droughts.	MWRI and Nile Basin Initiative	Immediate	All states, with a focus on Upper Nile areas downstream of Ethiopian Highlands	Use grant resources from international donors and build upon ongoing Nile Basin Initiative efforts.

Source: World Bank.
Note: AA = Administrative Area; MHADM = Ministry of Humanitarian Affairs and Disaster Management; MWRI = Ministry of Water and Irrigation.

cooperation: the regional nature of flood and drought requires coordinated efforts in forecasting and early warning and in infrastructure planning and operation.

Specific recommendations under this priority area include those in table 5.3.

Priority 4: Strengthen policy and institutional frameworks

Water governance is weak and institutional mandates are overlapping. The policy intentions of the first South Sudan Water Policy of 2007 have yet

TABLE 5.4 Recommendations to strengthen policy and institutional frameworks

RECOMMENDATIONS (WHAT)	RELEVANT INSTITUTIONS (WHO)	TIMELINE (WHEN)	LOCATIONS (WHERE)	IMPLEMENTATION (HOW)
R 4.1: Undertake technical consultations to revise and update the 2013 Water Bill and achieve its ratification.	MWRI	Immediate	Countrywide	Tap into convening power of international partners to host technical consultations with national and subnational stakeholders involved in water policy and investment and build consensus and momentum for approval.
R 4.2: Develop a capacity-building plan with targets for professionals and staff at national and subnational levels; enhance technical and professional education and training.	MWRI, with support from development partners	Long term	All levels, from institutions in Juba to boma-level institutions, where available	Use grant resources from international donors and global experiences to design and deliver capacity-building programs, ensuring MWRI keeps track of and harmonizes different activities under a single national capacity-building plan.
R 4.3: Undertake technical consultations to gather information for the development of an environmental and social framework for water sector interventions.	MWRI and MoEF	Immediate	Countrywide	Tap into convening power of international partners to host technical consultations with national and subnational stakeholders involved in water policy and investment.
R 4.4: Develop a water resources master plan, comprising (a) formulation of a nationwide investment plan to enhance water's contribution to economic growth and employment and (b) a monitoring plan to track impacts and results and adaptively update the plan.	MWRI, with support from development partners	Iterative process	Countrywide	Leverage grant resources and expertise of international partners while making the case for a central budgetary allocation to support water sector strategic planning moving forward.

Source: World Bank.
Note: MoEF = Ministry of Environment and Forestry; MWRI = Ministry of Water Resources and Irrigation.

to translate into legislation, and the 2013 Water Bill has not been ratified. Addressing these constraints is essential to begin the transition from humanitarian to government-led water management and involves the recommendations in table 5.4.

Priority 5: Use a portfolio of infrastructure options to manage water resources

In his PhD thesis, Dr. Garang de Mabior identified the economic potential of investments to manage the country's water resources and natural capital (Garang de Mabior 1981). However, he also cautioned about the potential for such large activities to lead to a range of unintended consequences, including social inequality and tensions, if not properly planned and implemented. As proposals for large river engineering works return to South Sudan, policy makers are advised to pursue more agile and easy-to-implement infrastructure options in the short term while they identify more large-scale investments needed to provide long-term responses to the country's water insecurity, as shown in table 5.5. In the long term, more significant investments in water storage are likely to be required, and should be guided by comprehensive feasibility assessments, including of their impact on social and conflict dynamics.

TABLE 5.5 Recommendations to use a portfolio of infrastructure options to manage water resources

RECOMMENDATIONS (WHAT)	RELEVANT INSTITUTIONS (WHO)	TIMELINE (WHEN)	LOCATIONS (WHERE)	IMPLEMENTATION (HOW)
R 5.1: Conduct an inventory of existing flood embankments and related status.	MWRI	Immediate	Countrywide	Consultations with partners and subnational governments, application of earth observation data.
R 5.2: Conduct an inventory of existing water storage structures (*haffirs*) and related status.	MWRI	Immediate	Countrywide	Consultations with partners and subnational governments, application of earth observation data.
R 5.3: Rehabilitate and reinforce selected existing embankments.	MWRI, with development and humanitarian partners	Immediate	Jonglei Lakes Pibor AA Unity Upper Nile Warrap	Civil works with extensive community consultation and participation in construction and O&M.
R 5.4: Rehabilitate and expand community-based water storage structures.	MWRI with development and humanitarian partners	Immediate	Countrywide, with a focus on Eastern Equatoria and Upper Nile	Civil works with extensive community consultation and participation in construction and O&M. Provision of block grants to households and villages for water storage projects designed and selected by village committees (for example, Payam Development Committees and Boma Development Committees, similar to the National Solidarity Program of Afghanistan).
R 5.5: Construct flood control and water storage structures integrating green and gray solutions.	Vice President for Infrastructure, MWRI, Ministry of Finance	Long term	Kinyeti River Multi-Purpose Development; others to be identified through master planning and feasibility	Project preparation according to international best practices for management of environmental and social impacts, consultation with international partners to identify financing options.
R 5.6: Improve the navigability and year-round safe transport of passengers and cargo along the White Nile.	MWRI, Ministry of Transport and Roads	Long term	White Nile corridor	Project preparation according to international best practices for management of environmental and social impacts; consultation with international partners to identify financing options.

Source: World Bank.
Note: MWRI = Ministry of Water Resources and Irrigation; O&M = operations and maintenance.

FINANCING

South Sudan has three general types of funding with which to meet its capital expenditure requirements in the water sector: (a) internal transfers from the government (allocations from the public budget); (b) external transfers from international donors, charities, and nongovernmental organizations; and (c) remittances from nationals living abroad. In addition, water user fees and tariffs can help keep services running and contribute to operations and maintenance; however, these sources are not sufficient to support the capital expenditures needed for building water infrastructure and related services in the country. Chapter 4 highlights that external transfers from humanitarian and donor actors dominate water sector financing.

In the short term, water sector investments should be financed by a combination of public resources from the government and transfers from international actors, including International Development Assistance grants and trust fund resources. Efforts to increase water sector financing should be accompanied by a shift from just building to also maintaining and operating infrastructure and services. Hence, attention needs to be paid to the operational expenditures linked to water investments to ensure that service delivery gains are sustained over the long term. Performance-based approaches to delivering water services provide a platform for designing sustainable funding modalities, including in rural areas (Hope et al. 2020).

In the long term, the government must leverage alternative sources of financing via reforms and innovation. Such measures, include, for example, (a) instruments for land-value capture, whereby the increase in land or property value arising from water infrastructure investments (especially in growing urban areas) is captured through property taxes or charges; (b) public-private partnerships; (c) remittances, for instance, to build resilience and respond to extreme events (remittances accounted for 30 percent of gross domestic product in 2021 [World Bank 2021]); and (d) climate finance, for instance, by accessing funds that support sustainable management of wetlands for their carbon storage and flood peak reduction services.

Finally, approaches to water sector financing need to move toward a broader understanding of the opportunities arising from the links with other sectors. Water often acts as a connector among sectors such as transport, agriculture, and energy. These links create "infrastructure systems" whose performance hinges on how these interconnections are managed and exploited to deliver positive outcomes. From a financing standpoint, this means addressing water financing gaps in connection with other sectors to capture any opportunities that might arise for reduced costs and improved construction and operation and maintenance (for example, joint investment planning to expand access to rural water supply and sanitation combined with digital and energy infrastructure access).

THE WAY AHEAD: SEQUENCING AND MONITORING WATER POLICY AND INVESTMENT

Over the long term, a more ambitious program of policies and investments is required, including strategic investments in urban water systems and water storage. The identification, design, and implementation of these investments should be guided by comprehensive feasibility assessments that include their impact on the rich biodiversity and complex social and conflict dynamics of South Sudan. Although infrastructure will be needed, it will not be enough. Water security is achieved not by trying solely to control water and diverting its flow, but by also focusing on enhancing community preparedness and delineating areas for water, leaving "room for the river," and by making productive use of the water for household consumption, livelihoods, and development. This approach is followed across the world in flood-prone areas such as Bangladesh, Japan, and the Netherlands, where planners work with—rather than against—the floodwaters and complement every investment with institutional measures to involve all levels of government: national, provincial, and local.

This ambitious water policy and investment program will involve uncertainty, making it important to commit to an iterative planning approach. Uncertainty arises from political developments, insecurity, and climate change, among other factors. Careful monitoring and evaluation are needed to detect and manage expected and unexpected negative effects arising from these uncertainties and to adjust policies over time. To successfully manage water risks, South Sudan should implement water policies, carefully monitor their impacts and results, and learn from their success and failures. A water secure future—one that harnesses the productive potential of water while managing its destructive force—can be achieved by putting in place the levers and tools needed to adapt to this complex system in a dynamically changing future.

REFERENCES

Garang de Mabior, J. 1981. "Identifying, Selecting, and Implementing Rural Development Strategies for Socio-Economic Development in the Jonglei Projects Area, Southern Region, Sudan." PhD thesis, Iowa State University, Ames, IA.

Hope, R., P. Thomson, J. Koehler, and T. Foster. 2020. "Rethinking the Economics of Rural Water in Africa." *Oxford Review of Economic Policy* 36 (1): 171–90.

Kooy, M., and L. Wild. 2012. "Tearfund WASH Service Delivery in South Sudan: Contributions to Peacebuilding and State-Building." Overseas Development Institute, London.

World Bank. 2021. Annual Remittances Data (May 2021). https://www.worldbank.org/en/topic/migrationremittancesdiasporaissues/brief/migration-remittances-data.

Data and Methods

FLOOD RISK ANALYSIS

The Fathom flood-hazard model (previously known as SSBN) is a global gridded data set of flood hazards produced at the global scale (Sampson et al. 2015). It provides flood water extent and depth for a range of pluvial and fluvial hazard scenarios, expressed as "return period," which indicates the probability of occurrence (that is, once in 5, 10, 20, 50, 75, 100, 200, 250, 500, 750, and 1,000 years). The data are at 3 arc second (approximately 90 meter) resolution and have a global coverage between 56°S and 60°N.

The data set used in this study includes the following subsets, shown for a return period of 1 in 100 years:

- Fluvial undefended: Fluvial flood hazard data, without defense estimation
- Pluvial: Flash-flood or pluvial flood hazard data

Each data set shows the simulated return period maximum water depths in meters.

To estimate the number of people exposed to intense flood risk, this study follows three main steps, similar to previous applications of the Fathom data set (Rentschler and Salhab 2020):

1. *Generate a combined flood hazard map.* For each country and each subnational administrative unit, a single flood hazard layer is created by combining fluvial undefended and pluvial data. The resulting flood map has a resolution of 90 meters, with each pixel showing estimated inundation depth in meters. For pixels where different flood types overlap, the higher inundation depth estimate is used. The flood hazard map is then resampled to ensure that pixels perfectly overlay the World Population data.

2. *Define flood risk categories.* Although the flood hazard map offers inundation depths along a continuous scale, the values are aggregated into one risk category in the maps in chapter 2: moderate or greater flood hazard, which corresponds to inundation depths greater than 0.15 meter. This flood risk threshold is defined in line with an approximation of the risk to the lives of

affected people. At up to 0.15 meter inundation depth, no significant risk to life is expected. Above this threshold, some risk to life must be expected.

3. *Assign flood risk categories to population headcounts at the pixel level and aggregate to the administrative unit.* Each population map cell is assigned a unique flood risk classification. These cells can then be aggregated to the administrative unit level (for example, state or county level). This aggregation allows calculation of population headcounts for each flood risk category and for each (sub-)national administrative unit (for example, the number of people in each administrative unit living in areas with moderate flood risk or greater). This exercise yields absolute exposure to flood risk (that is, the total number of people). To obtain relative exposure, this number is divided by the total population for the relevant administrative unit (for example, share of total people in each administrative unit living in areas with moderate flood risk or higher).

EMPIRICAL ANALYSIS OF THE LINKS BETWEEN DROUGHT AND CONFLICT

This empirical analysis builds on data compiled by Harari and Ferrara (2018) and Khan and Rodella (2021). They use gridded spatial data for the period 1997 to 2011 to present a plausibly causal effect of climate on conflict occurrence for the continent of Africa. Building on these studies, the report examines the relationship between these two variables:

- Standardized Precipitation-Evapotranspiration Index (SPEI) developed by Vicente-Serrano et al. (2010). The SPEI factors in both precipitation and potential evapotranspiration to capture the ability of soil to retain water, and thus outperforms other indexes in predicting crop yields. The SPEI is expressed in units of standard deviation from each grid-cell's historical average (and thus has a mean of zero). A negative SPEI describes dry conditions (drought), and a positive SPEI describes wet conditions (floods).
- Conflict occurrence between 1997 and 2011 from the Armed Conflict Location and Event Data Project, which records a wide range of conflict events such as protests, battles, and rebel activities derived from war zone media reports, humanitarian agencies, and research publications. As is standard in the conflict literature, Harari and Ferrara (2018) code a grid-cell as a dummy equal to 1 if the grid-cell experienced any conflict event in a given year.

The regression approach detailed in Khan and Rodella (2021) is used to assess the relationship between conflict incidence and SPEI in South Sudan. As shown in chapter 3, the analysis finds a negative relationship between the SPEI and conflict, suggesting that conflicts occur more frequently in dry conditions. The regression results in table A.1 confirm that the SPEI-conflict relationship is robust and strongly negative for South Sudan (Sudan and the Sahel are included for comparison). The base category (the first row of coefficients) refers to the rest of Africa outside of the G5 Sahel (Burkina Faso, Chad, Mali, Mauritania, and Niger), Sudan, and South Sudan. The last rows of table A.1 show controls being added progressively to make the econometric specification richer. Despite this, the coefficients remain strongly significant and stable, which is indicative of a strong slope relationship.

TABLE A.1 Conflict and SPEI

DEPENDENT VARIABLE	DUMMY = 1 IF ANY CONFLICT IN A YEAR				
	(1)	(2)	(3)	(4)	(5)
SPEI	0.0237***	0.00287	−0.00232	−0.00077	0.00977
	−0.00571	−0.0051	−0.00449	−0.00474	−0.0072
SPEI x G5 Sahel	−0.0662***	−0.0349***	−0.0219**	−0.0248***	−0.0380***
	−0.0107	−0.0101	−0.00928	−0.00941	−0.0133
SPEI x Sudan	−0.108***	−0.0809***	−0.0760***	−0.0688***	−0.0870***
	−0.0193	−0.0187	−0.0186	−0.019	−0.0243
SPEI x South Sudan	−0.0857***	−0.0835***	−0.0844***	−0.0731**	−0.0745**
	−0.0328	−0.0312	−0.0293	−0.0293	−0.0314
Number of observations	37,095	37,095	37,095	37,095	37,095
R^2	0.027	0.098	0.195	0.198	0.259
Controls	N	Y	Y	Y	Y
Country fixed effects	N	N	Y	Y	Y
Year fixed effects	N	N	N	Y	Y
Country-year fixed effects	N	N	N	N	Y

Source: World Bank.
Note: SPEI = Standardized Precipitation-Evapotranspiration Index.
**$p < .01$; ***$p < .001$.

QUALITATIVE DATA COLLECTION

Qualitative data were collected through key informant interviews and focus group discussions. The interview protocols were developed by the Rift Valley Institute (RVI) in collaboration with the World Bank. The interviews and focus group discussions were administered by RVI. All key informants and participants in the focus group discussions agreed to RVI's consent form for participation in research interviews. Anonymity and confidentiality in the aggregated findings were ensured using randomized key informant codes.

Interviews and focus group discussions were conducted in three locations, representing three very different state contexts:

- Juba county, Central Equatoria
- Kapoeta county, Eastern Equatoria
- Rumbek county, Lakes

A total of 24 expert interviews were completed, including expert elicitation on three questions to gather comparable quantitative data across the interviewees (see table A.2 for details). Experts were selected using a snowball sampling approach, with recommendations from government; water, sanitation, and hygiene cluster members; or key nongovernmental organization experts. Only four key informants were women, reflecting the significant gender gap in the

TABLE A.2 Key informants interviewed as part of this study

	NATIONAL	JUBA COUNTY	KAPOETA COUNTY	RUMBEK COUNTY	TOTAL
Government	2	1	1	3	7
Nongovernmental organization	2	5	4	2	13
United Nations and donors	2				2
Others (consultants and freelance experts)	2				2
Total	8	6	5	5	24

water sector. The full interview protocol is available in RVI (2022); only the expert elicitation questions are reproduced here:

    a. To what extent is water access a driver of conflict within and between communities?

        [On a scale of 1–5 where 1 is not a driver and 5 is a major driver]

    b. How effective are formal institutions in ensuring sustainability of water supplies?

        [(a) highly, (b) partially, (c) not at all]

    c. How effective are customary institutions in ensuring sustainability of water supplies?

        [(a) highly, (b) partially, (c) not at all]

Can you rank the barriers to women's active engagement in water management?

- Cultural disempowerment
- Gender biases of implementers
- Low economic capacity
- Education
- Workload or time poverty
- Conflict
- Disasters or shocks (flood, drought, and so on)
- Others

Focus group discussions were conducted with 14 groups. Groups were divided into men and women and, where possible, youth and older men and women. This division helped to uncover marginalized viewpoints, which may have been overshadowed in mixed-gender and mixed-age groups. The group discussions included two participatory exercises (on institutional mapping and proportional piling for spending prioritization). Although this is a nonrepresentative sample, these exercises provided some insight into perceptions and preferences across different gender, age, and tribal groups. At the end of each focus group discussion the individuals were asked four questions from the short version of the Household Water Insecurity Experience scale. An additional question on experience of safety and security while collecting water was added to reflect the South Sudan context. Clear protocols were applied in the focus group discussions around the discussions of gender-based violence but researchers found that all groups discussed the risks of gender-based violence openly without prompting.

REFERENCES

Harari, M., and E. L. Ferrara. 2018. "Conflict, Climate, and Cells: A Disaggregated Analysis." *Review of Economics and Statistics* 100 (4): 594–608.

Khan, A. M., and A.-S. Rodella. 2021. "A Hard Rain's a-Gonna Fall? New Insights on Water Security and Fragility in the Sahel." Policy Research Working Paper 9805, World Bank, Washington, DC.

Rentschler, J., and M. Salhab. 2020. "People in Harm's Way: Flood Exposure and Poverty in 189 Countries." Policy Research Working Paper 9447, World Bank, Washington, DC.

Rift Valley Institute (RVI). 2022. "Fragility and Water Security in South Sudan." Study conducted for the World Bank by the Rift Valley Institute in collaboration with the Centre for Humanitarian Change. Background paper prepared for this report. Rift Valley Institute, Juba.

Sampson, C. C., A. M. Smith, P. D. Bates, J. C. Neal, L. Alfieri, and J. E. Freer. 2015. "A High-Resolution Global Flood Hazard Model." *Water Resources Research* 51: 7358–81. doi:10.1002/2015WR016954.

Vicente-Serrano, S. M., S. Beguería, J. I. López-Moreno, M. Angulo, and A. El Kenawy. 2010. "A New Global 0.5 Gridded Dataset (1901–2006) of a Multiscalar Drought Index: Comparison with Current Drought Index Datasets Based on the Palmer Drought Severity Index." *Journal of Hydrometeorology* 11 (4): 1033–43.

State Profiles

ABYEI AA

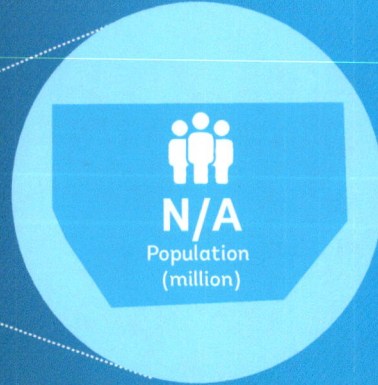

N/A
Population
(million)

WATER SECURITY FOR PEOPLE

Drinking water

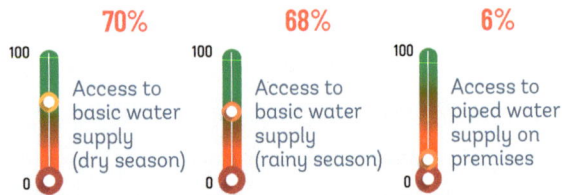

70%	68%	6%
Access to basic water supply (dry season)	Access to basic water supply (rainy season)	Access to piped water supply on premises

Sanitation and hygiene

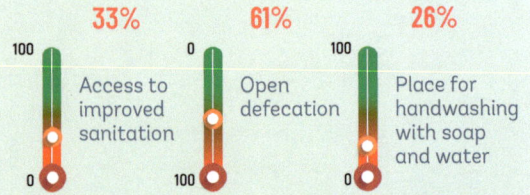

33%	61%	26%
Access to improved sanitation	Open defecation	Place for handwashing with soap and water

WATER SECURITY FOR PRODUCTION

Solar irrigation potential

N/A
with surface water

N/A
with groundwater

WATER AND HEALTH

Neglected Tropical Diseases (Number)

Diarrhea prevalence

1

N/A

WATER SECURITY FOR PROTECTION

Floods

N/A

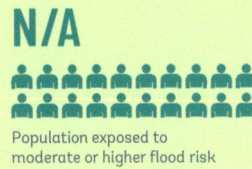

Population exposed to moderate or higher flood risk

N/A

Share of population exposed to moderate or higher flood risk

Droughts

Rank

Number of drought events (1981-2021)  N/A ⊙ 0

Drought duration (months)  N/A ⊙ 0

CENTRAL EQUATORIA

1.56
Population
(million)

WATER SECURITY FOR PEOPLE

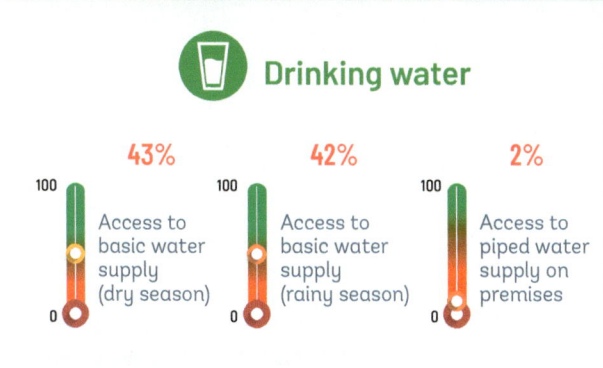

Drinking water

43%

100

0

Access to
basic water
supply
(dry season)

42%

100

0

Access to
basic water
supply
(rainy season)

2%

100

0

Access to
piped water
supply on
premises

Sanitation and hygiene

9%

100

0

Access to
improved
sanitation

73%

0

100

Open
defecation

9%

100

0

Place for
handwashing
with soap
and water

WATER SECURITY FOR PRODUCTION

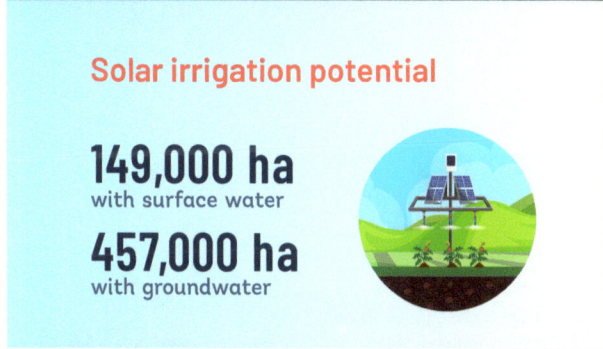

Solar irrigation potential

149,000 ha
with surface water

457,000 ha
with groundwater

WATER AND HEALTH

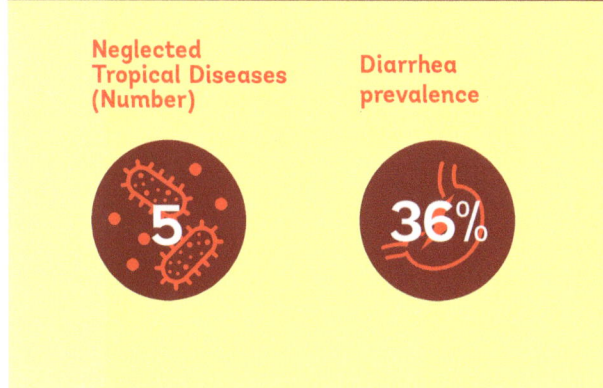

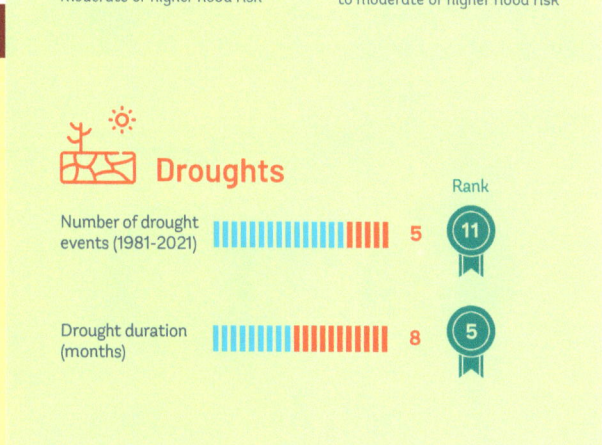

**Neglected
Tropical Diseases
(Number)**

5

**Diarrhea
prevalence**

36%

WATER SECURITY FOR PROTECTION

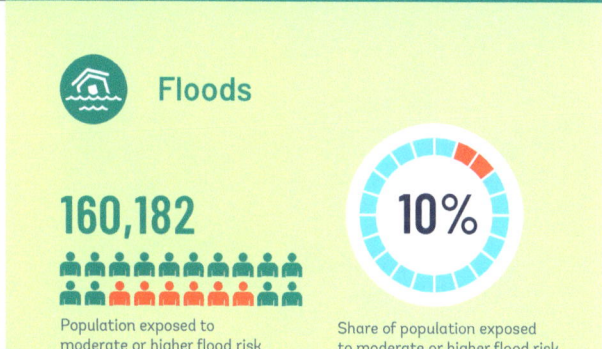

Floods

160,182

Population exposed to
moderate or higher flood risk

10%

Share of population exposed
to moderate or higher flood risk

Droughts

Rank

Number of drought
events (1981-2021)   5   **11**

Drought duration
(months)   8   **5**

EASTERN EQUATORIA

1.5
Population (million)

WATER SECURITY FOR PEOPLE

Drinking water

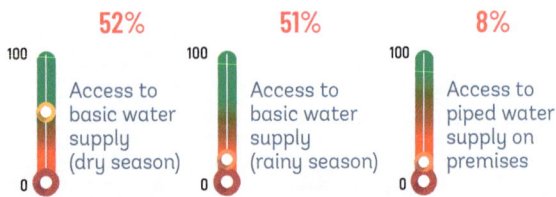

52%
100 — 0
Access to basic water supply (dry season)

51%
100 — 0
Access to basic water supply (rainy season)

8%
100 — 0
Access to piped water supply on premises

Sanitation and hygiene

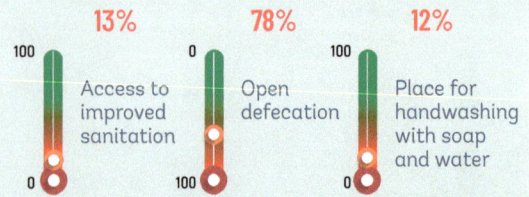

13%
100 — 0
Access to improved sanitation

78%
0 — 100
Open defecation

12%
100 — 0
Place for handwashing with soap and water

WATER SECURITY FOR PRODUCTION

Solar irrigation potential

92,000 ha
with surface water

293,000 ha
with groundwater

WATER SECURITY FOR PROTECTION

Floods

782,512
Population exposed to moderate or higher flood risk

78%
Share of population exposed to moderate or higher flood risk

Droughts

Number of drought events (1981-2021) — **12** — Rank **1**

Drought duration (months) — **3** — **10**

WATER AND HEALTH

Neglected Tropical Diseases (Number)

5

Diarrhea prevalence

29%

JONGLEI

1.5 Population (million)

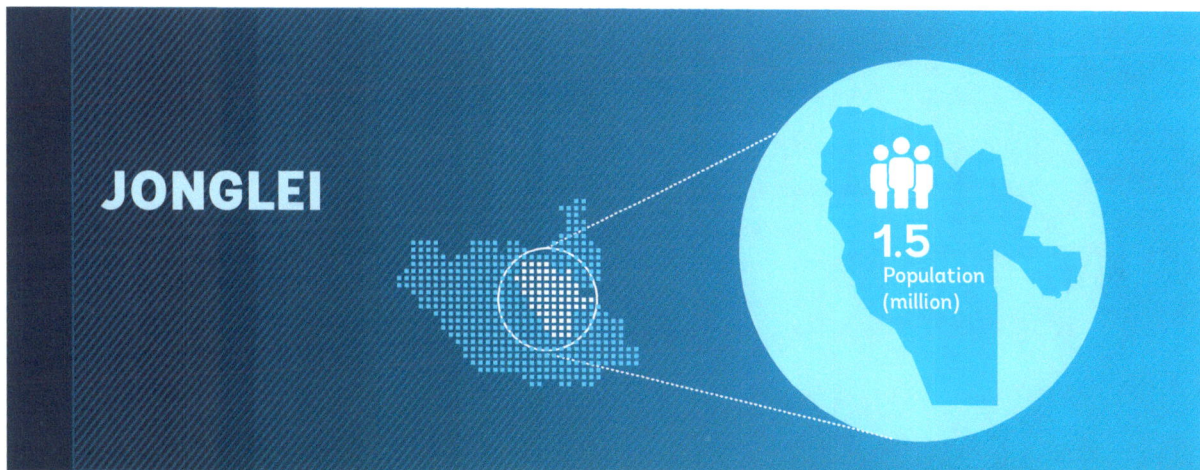

WATER SECURITY FOR PEOPLE

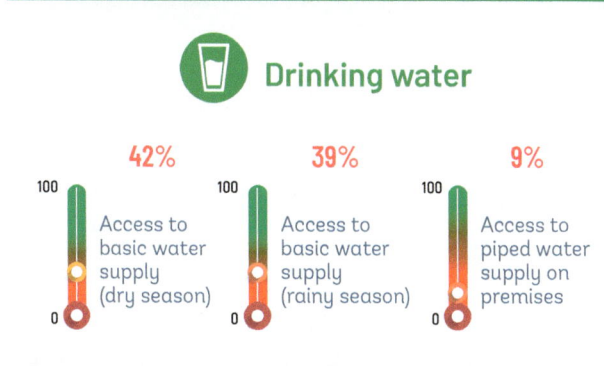

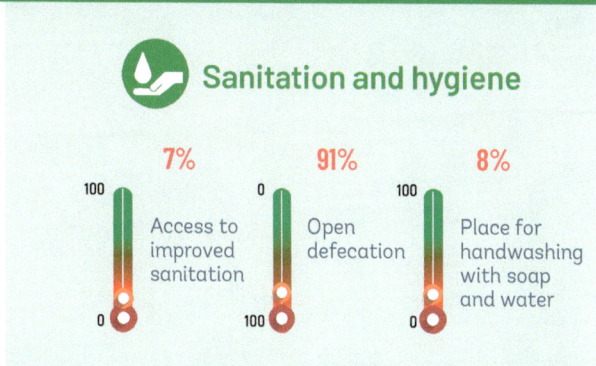

Drinking water

42%
Access to basic water supply (dry season)

39%
Access to basic water supply (rainy season)

9%
Access to piped water supply on premises

Sanitation and hygiene

7%
Access to improved sanitation

91%
Open defecation

8%
Place for handwashing with soap and water

WATER SECURITY FOR PRODUCTION

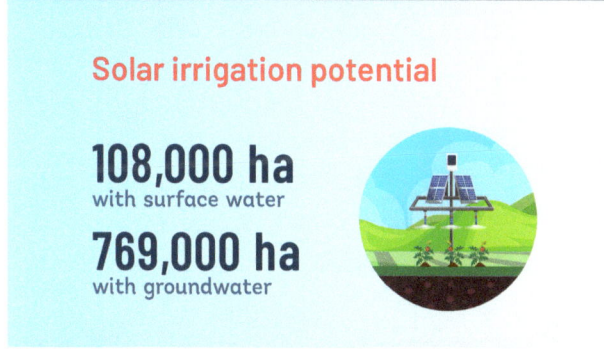

Solar irrigation potential

108,000 ha
with surface water

769,000 ha
with groundwater

WATER AND HEALTH

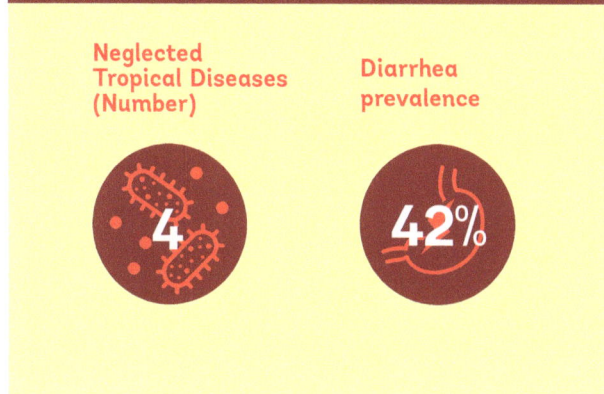

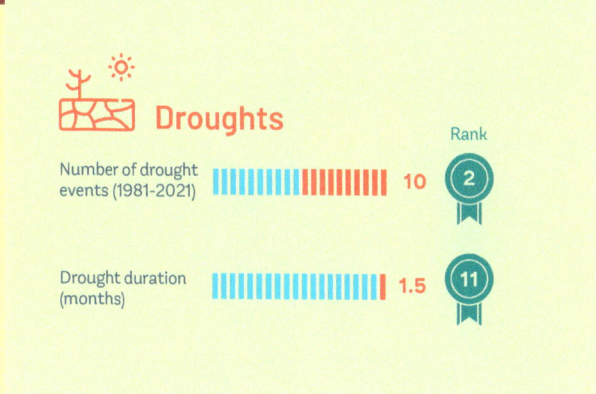

Neglected Tropical Diseases (Number)

4

Diarrhea prevalence

42%

WATER SECURITY FOR PROTECTION

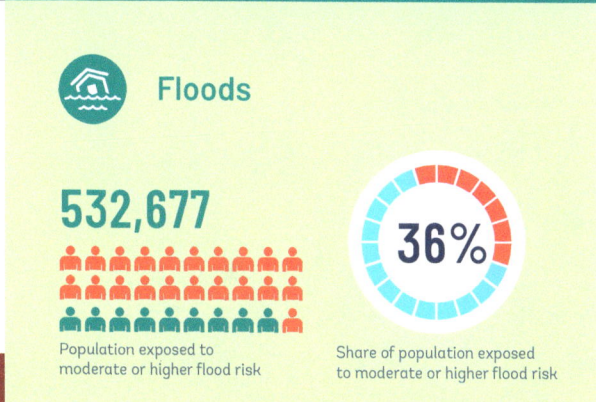

Floods

532,677
Population exposed to moderate or higher flood risk

36%
Share of population exposed to moderate or higher flood risk

Droughts

		Rank
Number of drought events (1981-2021)	10	2
Drought duration (months)	1.5	11

LAKES

1.2
Population
(million)

WATER SECURITY FOR PEOPLE

Drinking water

54%
100 — 0
Access to basic water supply (dry season)

52%
100 — 0
Access to basic water supply (rainy season)

6%
100 — 0
Access to piped water supply on premises

Sanitation and hygiene

15%
100 — 0
Access to improved sanitation

82%
0 — 100
Open defecation

18%
100 — 0
Place for handwashing with soap and water

WATER SECURITY FOR PRODUCTION

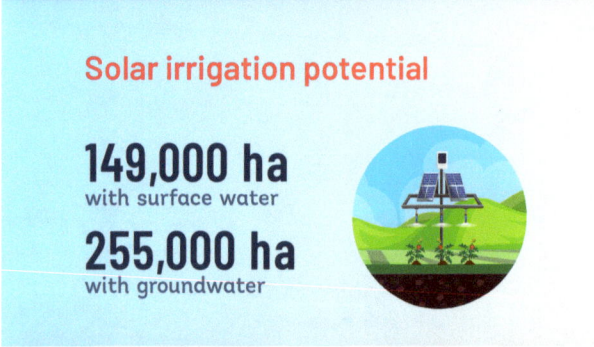

Solar irrigation potential

149,000 ha
with surface water

255,000 ha
with groundwater

WATER AND HEALTH

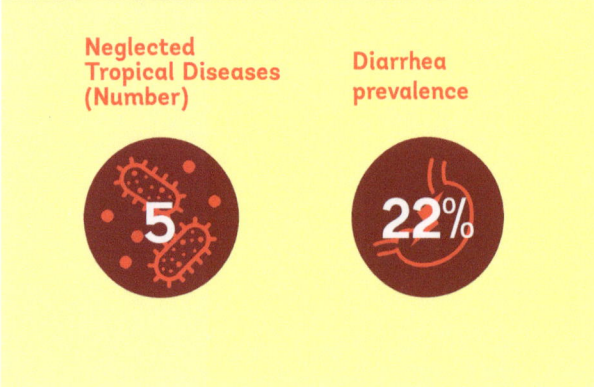

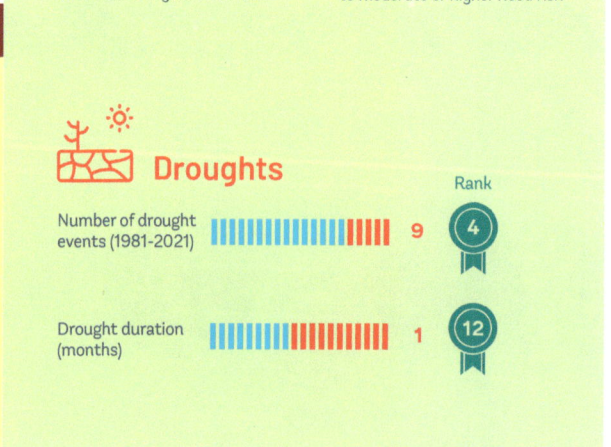

Neglected Tropical Diseases (Number)

5

Diarrhea prevalence

22%

WATER SECURITY FOR PROTECTION

Floods

181,475
Population exposed to moderate or higher flood risk

15%
Share of population exposed to moderate or higher flood risk

Droughts

		Rank
Number of drought events (1981-2021)	9	4
Drought duration (months)	1	12

NORTHERN BAHR EL GHAZAL

0.6
Population (million)

WATER SECURITY FOR PEOPLE

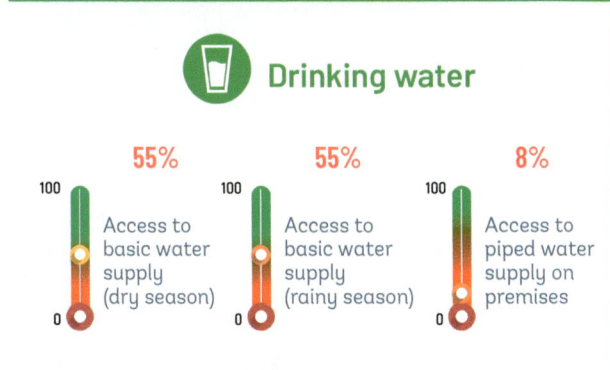

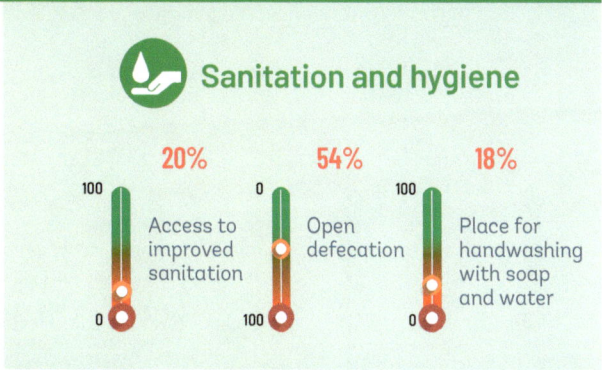

Drinking water

55%
100 — 0
Access to basic water supply (dry season)

55%
100 — 0
Access to basic water supply (rainy season)

8%
100 — 0
Access to piped water supply on premises

Sanitation and hygiene

20%
100 — 0
Access to improved sanitation

54%
0 — 100
Open defecation

18%
100 — 0
Place for handwashing with soap and water

WATER SECURITY FOR PRODUCTION

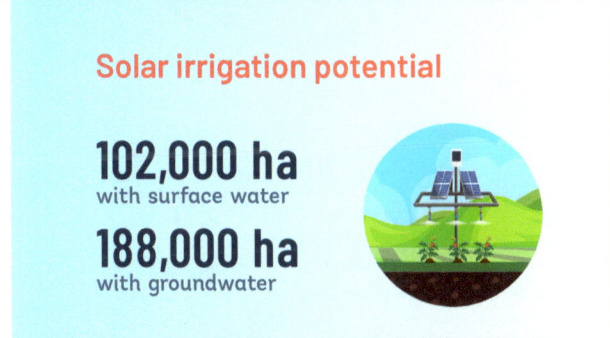

Solar irrigation potential

102,000 ha
with surface water

188,000 ha
with groundwater

WATER AND HEALTH

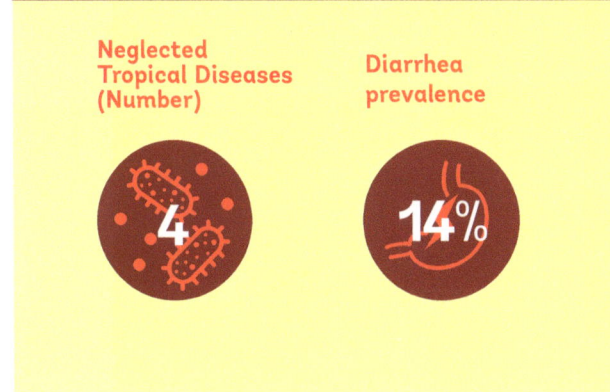

Neglected Tropical Diseases (Number)

4

Diarrhea prevalence

14%

WATER SECURITY FOR PROTECTION

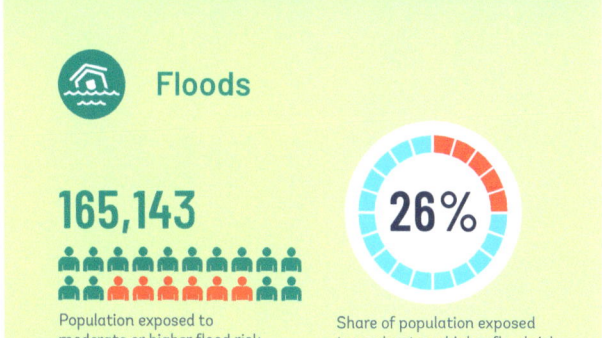

Floods

165,143
Population exposed to moderate or higher flood risk

26%
Share of population exposed to moderate or higher flood risk

Droughts

Number of drought events (1981-2021)   **5**

Rank **11**

Drought duration (months)   **13**

Rank **1**

PIBOR AA

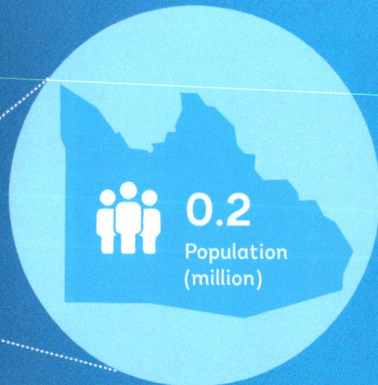

0.2 Population (million)

WATER SECURITY FOR PEOPLE

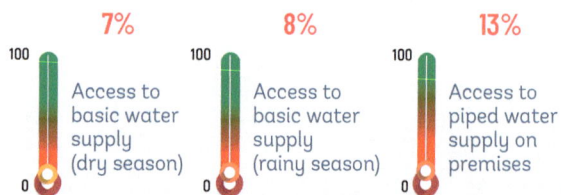 **Drinking water**

7%
Access to basic water supply (dry season)

8%
Access to basic water supply (rainy season)

13%
Access to piped water supply on premises

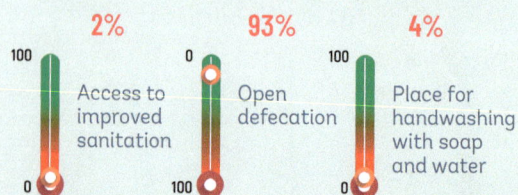 **Sanitation and hygiene**

2%
Access to improved sanitation

93%
Open defecation

4%
Place for handwashing with soap and water

WATER SECURITY FOR PRODUCTION

Solar irrigation potential

N/A with surface water

N/A with groundwater

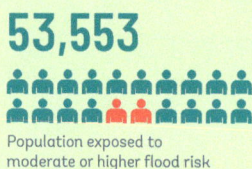

WATER SECURITY FOR PROTECTION

 **Floods**

53,553
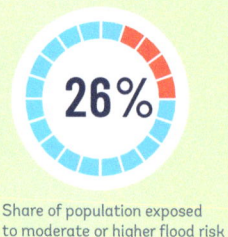
Population exposed to moderate or higher flood risk

26%
Share of population exposed to moderate or higher flood risk

WATER AND HEALTH

Neglected Tropical Diseases (Number)

3

Diarrhea prevalence

N/A

Droughts

Number of drought events (1981-2021)
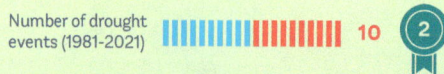 **10**
Rank **2**

Drought duration (months)
 **13**
Rank **1**

RUWENG AA

0.1
Population
(million)

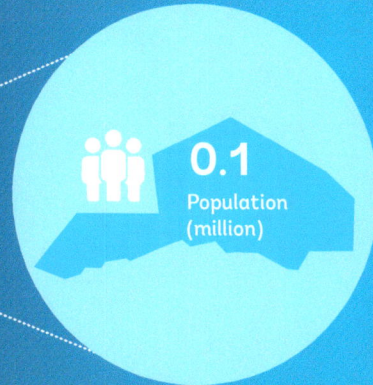

WATER SECURITY FOR PEOPLE

Drinking water

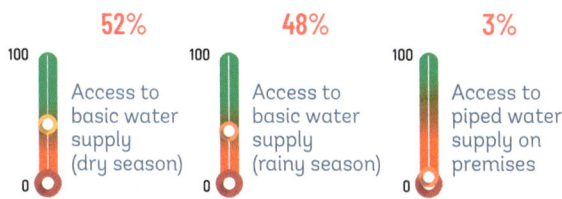

52%
100
0
Access to
basic water
supply
(dry season)

48%
100
0
Access to
basic water
supply
(rainy season)

3%
100
0
Access to
piped water
supply on
premises

Sanitation and hygiene

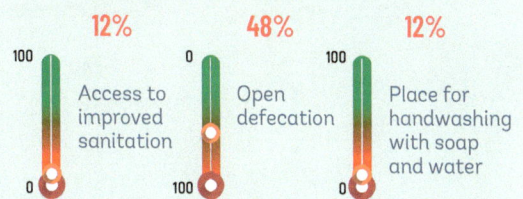

12%
100
0
Access to
improved
sanitation

48%
0
100
Open
defecation

12%
100
0
Place for
handwashing
with soap
and water

WATER SECURITY FOR PRODUCTION

Solar irrigation potential

N/A
with surface water

N/A
with groundwater

WATER SECURITY FOR PROTECTION

Floods

32,843
Population exposed to
moderate or higher flood risk

34%
Share of population exposed
to moderate or higher flood risk

WATER AND HEALTH

**Neglected
Tropical Diseases
(Number)**

N/A

**Diarrhea
prevalence**

N/A

Droughts

Number of drought
events (1981-2021) 8

Rank
7

Drought duration
(months) 6

7

UNITY

0.7 Population (million)

WATER SECURITY FOR PEOPLE

Drinking water

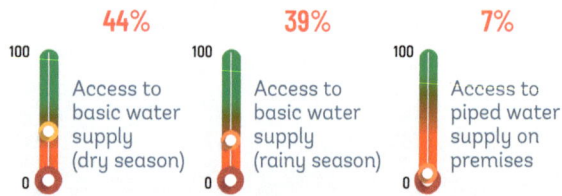

44%
100
0
Access to basic water supply (dry season)

39%
100
0
Access to basic water supply (rainy season)

7%
100
0
Access to piped water supply on premises

Sanitation and hygiene

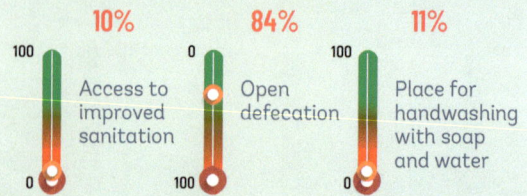

10%
100
0
Access to improved sanitation

84%
0
100
Open defecation

11%
100
0
Place for handwashing with soap and water

WATER SECURITY FOR PRODUCTION

Solar irrigation potential

125,000 ha with surface water

188,000 ha with groundwater

WATER AND HEALTH

Neglected Tropical Diseases (Number)

4

Diarrhea prevalence

30%

WATER SECURITY FOR PROTECTION

Floods

109,800
Population exposed to moderate or higher flood risk

15%
Share of population exposed to moderate or higher flood risk

Droughts

Rank

Number of drought events (1981-2021) **8** **7**

Drought duration (months) **6** **7**

UPPER NILE

1.0
Population
(million)

WATER SECURITY FOR PEOPLE

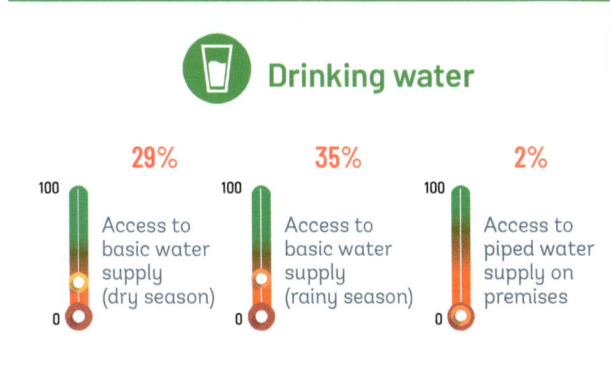

Drinking water

29%
Access to
basic water
supply
(dry season)

35%
Access to
basic water
supply
(rainy season)

2%
Access to
piped water
supply on
premises

Sanitation and hygiene

3%
Access to
improved
sanitation

95%
Open
defecation

6%
Place for
handwashing
with soap
and water

WATER SECURITY FOR PRODUCTION

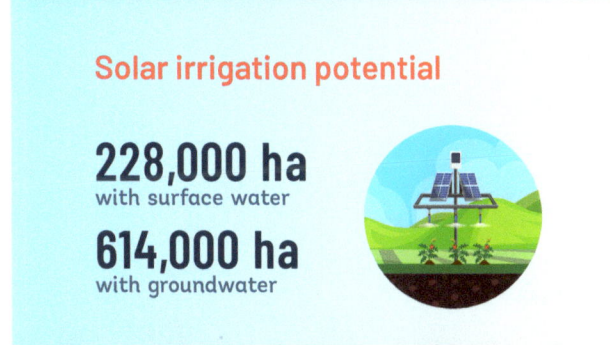

Solar irrigation potential

228,000 ha
with surface water

614,000 ha
with groundwater

WATER AND HEALTH

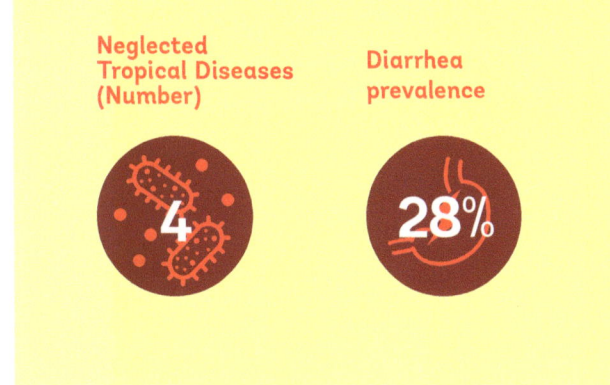

**Neglected
Tropical Diseases
(Number)**

4

**Diarrhea
prevalence**

28%

WATER SECURITY FOR PROTECTION

Floods

358,953

Population exposed to
moderate or higher flood risk

37%

Share of population exposed
to moderate or higher flood risk

Droughts

Rank

Number of drought
events (1981-2021)   7   **9**

Drought duration
(months)   10   **3**

WARRAP

1.5
Population (million)

WATER SECURITY FOR PEOPLE

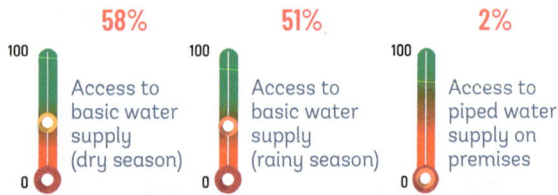

Drinking water

58%
100 — 0
Access to basic water supply (dry season)

51%
100 — 0
Access to basic water supply (rainy season)

2%
100 — 0
Access to piped water supply on premises

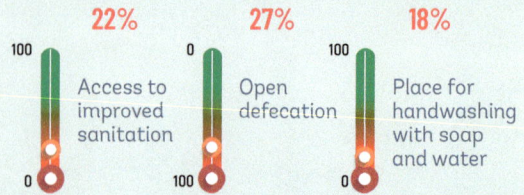

Sanitation and hygiene

22%
100 — 0
Access to improved sanitation

27%
0 — 100
Open defecation

18%
100 — 0
Place for handwashing with soap and water

WATER SECURITY FOR PRODUCTION

Solar irrigation potential

201,000 ha
with surface water

513,000 ha
with groundwater

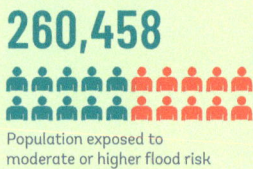

WATER SECURITY FOR PROTECTION

 **Floods**

260,458
Population exposed to moderate or higher flood risk

18%
Share of population exposed to moderate or higher flood risk

WATER AND HEALTH

Neglected Tropical Diseases (Number)

3

Diarrhea prevalence

29%

 **Droughts**

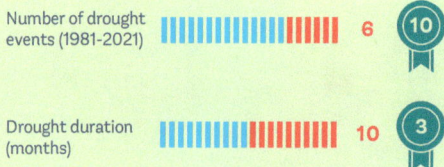

Rank

Number of drought events (1981-2021) — **6** — **10**

Drought duration (months) — **10** — **3**

WESTERN BAHR EL GHAZAL

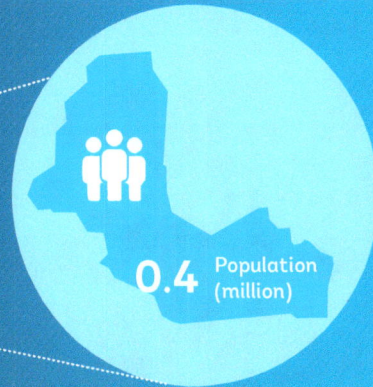

0.4 **Population (million)**

WATER SECURITY FOR PEOPLE

Drinking water

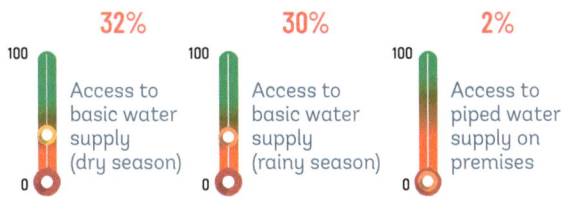

32%
Access to basic water supply (dry season)

30%
Access to basic water supply (rainy season)

2%
Access to piped water supply on premises

Sanitation and hygiene

4%
Access to improved sanitation

86%
Open defecation

7%
Place for handwashing with soap and water

WATER SECURITY FOR PRODUCTION

Solar irrigation potential

179,000 ha
with surface water

353,000 ha
with groundwater

WATER AND HEALTH

Neglected Tropical Diseases (Number)

3

Diarrhea prevalence

16%

WATER SECURITY FOR PROTECTION

Floods

37,648
Population exposed to moderate or higher flood risk

9%
Share of population exposed to moderate or higher flood risk

Droughts

Number of drought events (1981-2021) — 9 — Rank **4**

Drought duration (months) — 7 — Rank **6**

WESTERN EQUATORIA

0.7 Population (million)

WATER SECURITY FOR PEOPLE

Drinking water

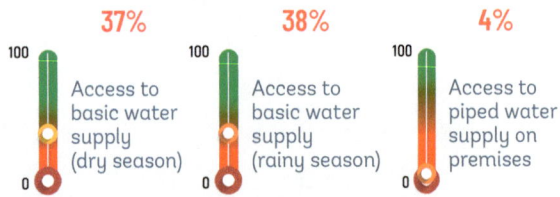

37%

Access to basic water supply (dry season)

38%

Access to basic water supply (rainy season)

4%

Access to piped water supply on premises

Sanitation and hygiene

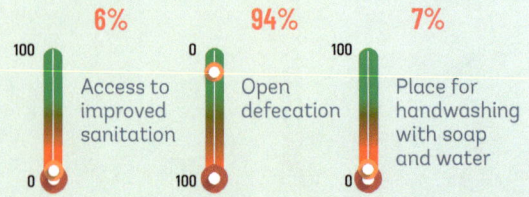

6%

Access to improved sanitation

94%

Open defecation

7%

Place for handwashing with soap and water

WATER SECURITY FOR PRODUCTION

Solar irrigation potential

113,000 ha
with surface water

172,000 ha
with groundwater

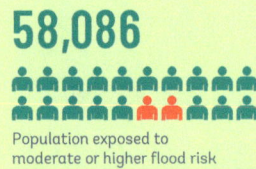

WATER AND HEALTH

Neglected Tropical Diseases (Number)

5

Diarrhea prevalence

48%

WATER SECURITY FOR PROTECTION

Floods

58,086

Population exposed to moderate or higher flood risk

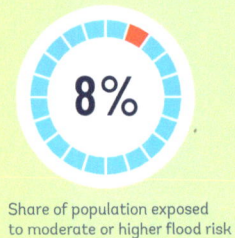

8%

Share of population exposed to moderate or higher flood risk

Droughts

Rank

Number of drought events (1981-2021)  9 **4**

Drought duration (months)  6 **7**

www.ingramcontent.com/pod-product-compliance
Lightning Source LLC
Chambersburg PA
CBHW041420290326
41932CB00042B/30